A Duke miscellany

For April and Alex

A Duke miscellany

Narrative and verse of the sixties

edited by William Blackburn

Duke University Press   Durham, North Carolina   1970

Acknowledgments

Above Ground Review: for "February" by Fred Chappell; "The Inmate Returning to the Asylum" by Burke Davis III; "The Watch" and "At the War" by George R. Wood.

Atlantic Monthly: for "Sestina for Bart" by Joan Swift.

James Brown Associates, Inc.: for "The Hundredth Centennial" by Mac Hyman.

Brown Bag: for "Darkened Light" by Fred Chappell.

Greensboro Review: for "Mr. Rudishill" by Angela Davis.

New Yorker Magazine: for "Oxygen" by Joan Swift. Permission the author; © 1962 The New Yorker Magazine, Inc.; "The Feather Behind the Rock" by Anne Tyler. Permission the author; © 1967 The New Yorker Magazine, Inc.

North American Review: for "A Grain, Perhaps of Wheat" by Kathryn Vale.

Northwest Review: for "Border Collies" and "Epithalamium for a Fisherman" by Joan Swift.

Poetry Northwest: for "Halley's" by Joan Swift.

Shenandoah: for "My Grandfather's Funeral" by James Applewhite; "A Road She Didn't Know" by Wallace Kaufman.

Sou'wester: for "Dream of Ascent" by James Applewhite.

Southern Poetry Review: for "My Grandmother's Life" by James Applewhite.

Southern Review: for "Mid-Ocean Dark" by Wallace Kaufman; "The Knowledge of My Mother's Coming Death" by Reynolds Price; "John Crowe Ransom Reads Theodore Roethke" by Joan Swift.

Stand (Newcastle-upon-Tyne): for "Stopping for Gas" by James Applewhite.

Foreword

This anthology is an attempt to bring together some of the best writing by Duke graduates and undergraduates—sketches, stories, poems—of the past seven or eight years, that is, work done since the appearance of *Under Twenty-five* in 1963. This span of time does not include everything in this volume, to be sure, the chief exception being Mac Hyman's "The Hundredth Centennial" (1953). *Under Twenty-five*, covering a period of seventeen years, was limited to the work of Duke undergraduates or of graduates who had been out of college a year or less. The composition of this present book is nearer that of *One and Twenty* (1945), in that it offers an admixture of professional and undergraduate writing. The bulk of the prose, fourteen stories or sketches out of a total of nineteen, is, however, the work of students when still in college or just out of it. On the other hand, the proportions between professional and amateur poetry are somewhat reversed. At all events I have juxtaposed things in an attempt to create as many sharp contrasts in form, style, and content as possible.

I am indebted to the Mary Duke Biddle Foundation for the generous subsidy which has made possible the publication of this volume.

I am much obliged to Ashbel Brice and his colleagues at the Duke University Press for their kindness.

Durham, North Carolina   William Blackburn
April 20, 1970

v

Contents

vii

A Duke miscellany

Josephine Humphreys

The visiting

Lura Stokes looked down the Thanksgiving Table at what was left of
her family. A thought entered her mind about this handful of people, but
then Treeny brought the vegetables, and Mrs. Stokes took off her rings,
leaving the thought for another time.

Ellie saw her take the rings off three large, pink-brown fingers. Ellie
didn't know Mrs. Stokes always took off her rings to eat. To Ellie the
action was another thing that divided her from the rest of the people at the
table; no one else seemed to notice it, or think it strange. Even her husband
Spence, sitting across from her to the left of his grandmother, kept on talking,
and Aunt Lavinia pursed her lips watching the vegetables come round, and
her husband Fred rattled his spoon and knife together as if they were
rhythm sticks.

Mrs. Stokes had taken carrots and peas in two neat piles on her plate,
and Treeny came next to Ellie. Ellie felt they were all watching her. She was
the new addition to that family, and though she had been married to Spence
a year, she was seeing his family for the first time, and being seen by it.
She limited the path of her eyes from her plate to the serving dish and back;
Treeny passed on to Fred, who took two huge helpings of both vegetables.
Mrs. Stokes thought again about these people at her table. There was
something wrong about having four children, bearing and raising them,
making all your plans on the assumption that they would marry and have
children in turn—and then ending up with only one daughter, who married
a nitwit, and one grandson, who lived three hundred miles away and married
a quiet dumb-eyed girl. The rest had died or had never been born, all those
she was counting on. And so she lost the reason she had had for counting on
them; it passed out of her mind.

"Fred, we'll wait for grace," she said. He had begun to rearrange the
carrots and peas with his fork. Ellie hoped that the dinner would go
smoothly; it was a bad beginning for Mrs. Stokes to be calling someone
down already. Lavinia looked embarrassed, not for her mother's words
or her husband's action, but because Ellie was there.

"Spence, say your grandfather's blessing."

Ellie looked at Spence, hoping he would remember the words.

"Lord, make us thankful for this thy bounteous blessing and for all thy gifts, we ask it in Christ's name, Amen."

Fred began eating. Someone had told him not to talk, and there was nothing for him to do but eat. His face was red, and wet all over; he seemed to be moving all the time, reaching for things, drinking water, wiping his forehead and his mouth.

"It's bountiful not bounteous," said Mrs. Stokes, putting her napkin in her lap, disappointed at the mistake. "I thought you would remember. It's too bad your grandfather couldn't come down for dinner, but a good thing he didn't hear you forget the blessing."

"We wanted to get here in time to see him," said Spence, and Ellie felt a twisting inside of her at the tone of his voice, the sound of someone telling the truth but afraid he will sound as if he's lying, so making it all worse. "But the traffic on the highways was more than we expected."

"And L. B. J.'s an S. O. B.," said Fred, coming to life. His face got redder, and he put his napkin on the table.

"Fred," said Lavinia in a soft tone.

"And I tell you what if I was in Washington what I'd do. I'd get that S. O. B. right out of there. Texas going to pot and cars all over the road but does he give a damn, no, and he just sits on his—"

"Fred," said Lavinia.

"I'd shoot him, that's what I'd do."

Ellie's muscles were tight everywhere in her body. Now everything will fall, she thought. Now people will leave the table and glass will be broken. But it was as if no one had heard anything. Mrs. Stokes had eaten two mouthfuls, and went on talking to Spence. Fred settled down again, and drank a whole glass of water.

"He's been better," said Mrs. Stokes, "but he still can't come down. Lavinia made me put in an automatic chair, one that goes up and down the steps. But it's not been used yet." Lavinia looked down at the table, embarrassed that the chair had to be mentioned.

"And you know his mind's not the same."

This was said to Ellie, the first thing Mrs. Stokes had said directly to her since their arrival. And Ellie found something attractive in the big face, framed by white hair, because it looked old. There were wrinkles in it, up and down, and across; but the eyes were not old. They were sharp, blue around a black, black dot in the middle. Spence had said before, "Age has not touched Grandmother's mind." When he said things like that to her, like one old woman talking to another, Ellie wanted to scream, and lose the sight of him.

"No," said Ellie, "I suppose not." She tried to think of something else to say, but what she had thought up to say, about being glad to meet the grandparents because she had no family of her own, couldn't be fitted in. Besides, she hadn't met the grandfather.

"No. It's his memory that has not returned. Everything else, buttoning things and reading and writing, but not his memory," said Mrs. Stokes.

"Tell about what happened with the nurse," said Uncle Fred. "That's the funniest thing. They had this practical nurse come in when he came back from the hospital—"

"No, don't tell that," said Lavinia. Her voice was always quiet, not gentle but worn down and smooth, and unlike her husband she was smooth when she moved, which wasn't often.

But Mrs. Stokes took up the story, and told it herself. "It was not a practical nurse, but a registered nurse," she said. She had meant to just make this correction, and then went on with the story anyway, partly to spite Lavinia and partly because she, too, thought it was a funny story. "And I was in the room, and told her name to Daniel, who then didn't understand people talking to him anyway. But I said, 'Daniel, this is Miss Greenway,' and then I left. And she told me later what he said when I left, it was the first time he said a single word to a living soul. After I left he said to the nurse, 'That is my second wife, but all my children came from my first wife, who died.' "

Uncle Fred laughed and mopped his forehead, and pushed his chair back to laugh some more. Ellie felt stifling hot.

"Of course I was his first wife," said Mrs. Stokes smiling. "And now he's so funny. If you tell him he said that, he says, 'Did I say that? Did I say that?' and he laughs. He often says things twice. It's part of not having his memory back."

Spence leaned forward, as if to exclude Lavinia and Fred, not caring about Ellie, and said to his grandmother, "What do the doctors say?" like someone in a movie. It was queer, thought Ellie; all the things she thought would make everything crash seemed to work the other way. She tightened up when Spence asked the question, but Mrs. Stokes seemed glad someone had asked it. Fred and Lavinia had heard it, and to them too it seemed a right thing to ask.

"They were surprised he did as well as he did. First they said he wouldn't be able to move or eat by himself, and he did, he got to drinking through a straw and eating mashed fruit, and watching television. I don't know if he knew what he saw but I am certain as I live the television got him on the road to recovery. And he got to talking more, first it was crazy things like that second wife—"

"And all the old times with his brothers," said Fred.

"But now," said Mrs. Stokes, "he can do almost everything. He walks around some. But I decided he shouldn't come downstairs, especially now, he'd get too excited, with your bride here, and Fred too."

There was a silent space in the talk. Fred ate, Lavinia bowed her head, Spence looked like a stranger and he hadn't talked to Ellie at all. Mrs. Stokes put on her rings, a diamond and two red ones, two on her left hand and one on her right.

"An angel's passing," said Ellie.

They looked at her, Spence far away and frowning. "Eh?" said Fred. "What about an angel? What did you say?" He was attacking her with his fork in mid-air. "What did you say about an angel?"

"Something you say when everybody's quiet," said Ellie, looking to Mrs. Stokes, hoping someone would stop Fred's fork waving at her. "You say, 'An angel's passing.' "

"Why, why?" demanded Fred, putting his napkin on the table. "Why did you say angel? What does that have to do with everyone being quiet?" Something fell between Ellie and Spence, a spoon from the gravy dish. Ellie turned to face Uncle Fred, and answered him.

"It's just something you say, Uncle Fred, like you say knock on wood or a witch has died or bowling in heaven." Ellie felt a strength in her voice and she went on. "It's just a nice thing to say sometimes and a nice idea."

"I see," he said, and the fork was back on the table. "An angel's passing." He looked around, and up at the ceiling. "An angel's passing. It's a good saying, but a lady's saying, nothing a lawyer could use." Fred was a lawyer. He had an office and some dusty old books but no business. His voice rose. "Sixty per cent of all the lawyers in this town are crooks," he said. "Crooks, cheats, bastards, every damn one of them, the whole lot, and no one does a thing about it, just lets 'em go along bribing and getting niggers off and bleeding 'em dry—"

He went on and although his voice was loud, no one listened. Ellie had looked to Spence and he had moved his eyes away. She thought about getting alone with him tonight in a room upstairs. He would be different, nervous in the way he had been since they got here, and his movements would irritate her. She knew in advance just how it would all be, how he would pretend there was nothing special that should be said now that they were alone, how he would take all the change out of his pockets and count it twice, and put it in piles on the dresser, how he would undress. In a year she had learned all his motions and gestures. There was nothing he could do to make her feel alive.

"What's that?" said Fred. There was a buzzing sound in the air; everyone looked around trying to see the sound. Mrs. Stokes called Treeny to see if it was in the kitchen. It got louder.

"The angel!" said Uncle Fred, looking around from face to face, pleased with his own words. He banged his knife on the table with a flourish of his arm.

"The chair," said Lavinia to Ellie. "Could it be the chair?" The noise stopped. They heard little sounds of slow footsteps. Then the grandfather stood in the doorway.

He was a small man, smaller than Ellie had thought of him. His hair was white and full, his face pink-white, and unwrinkled, as if the skin had tightened with age instead of loosening, giving him the Chinese look old people sometimes have. He wore a black suit, with a vest, and a gold watch chain. But it was his face that Ellie's eyes rested on. It was a handsome face, even now, with a boyish nose, and a fineness about the eyes, smiling eyes.

Fred and Spence stood up.

"Sit down, sit down," said Daniel Stokes, his voice so fast Ellie had to strain to listen and catch the words. "No one thought I'd make it but here I am. What a contraption that chair, like a ride at the carnival." He sat at the other end of the table, looking even smaller to Ellie.

"Father, are you sure you feel well enough?" said Lavinia, leaning toward him. Mrs. Stokes spoke before she could get an answer. Mrs. Stokes spoke loud.

"Daniel, have you seen your grandson Spence? He's driven all the way from Leesville to see us."

"God's sake I ain't deaf," said Mr. Stokes. "Glad to have you, Spence. I ain't deaf. My wife thinks I am deaf. Who's that?" He pointed a small thin finger at Ellie.

"It's Ellie, Spence's bride," said Uncle Fred.

Mr. Stokes looked Ellie over. "Pretty girl," he said, and his tight face spread out in a smile, folding up around his eyes. He began to hum the Wedding March, "Da dum de dum, da dum de dum." Ellie smiled back at him.

"Where's the turkey?" he said. "Where's my Thanksgiving turkey?"

"You can't eat turkey," said Mrs. Stokes, frowning at him.

"Who said it? Who says I can't? Treeny!" Mrs. Stokes' face hardened and she folded her hands in her lap. Treeny brought out a plate with some turkey, chopped up in little pieces, and two tiny heaps of vegetables. Mr. Stokes began to eat.

"Can't taste it," he mumbled. Peas rolled off his fork into the plate. He looked up, and his eyelids came together in a hard blink, with a little shake of his head, as if he were trying to clear away something that kept him from seeing things. "Who's that?" he said, more to himself than to anyone else. "Who's the pretty girl? Who is it, Lura?" He looked at his wife with a sudden pain in his eyes.

"You see what I mean," said Mrs. Stokes to Spence. "But aside from that, aside from not having his memory, not a thing in the world bothers him. You see he dressed himself even in that three-piece suit. Though I can't imagine how he figured out the workings of that chair." Mrs. Stokes' loud voice filled the room and when she finished the last word Ellie saw Mr. Stokes' mouth had been moving too, and he had been answering his own question.

"Oh, the bride," he had been saying. "That's right, the bride." It was a tiny thin sound, coming up like an echo after Mrs. Stokes' voice left off.

"Daniel, you'll regret coming downstairs," said Mrs. Stokes, not looking at him. "You know Dr. Walton said you weren't to get excited, and I told you too in case you might forget it. I told you two or three times not to come down. But it's out of my hands now."

"Maybe, father," said Lavinia, "you'd better go back up." She spoke to him as if she didn't want the others to hear.

"It's Thanksgiving," said Mr. Stokes stubbornly, meaning that gave him a thousand good reasons for staying downstairs.

"What's done is done," said Mrs. Stokes. "Just try and get him to go back now. He's just like he always was, doesn't think I know what's good for him. I told him Spence and his bride would be here and so he shouldn't come down and get all excited over them, especially over her."

"That's the bride there, Doctor," contributed Fred. He had always called Daniel Stokes "Doctor" because it seemed the best title of respect he could find for his father-in-law; Mrs. Stokes would not let him call them mother and father.

"I *know* who she is," said Mr. Stokes. "What I want to know is who is that old woman sitting down at the other end of the table from me." He laughed. Mrs. Stokes pretended not to hear, and he kept on laughing. Lavinia put a hand on his arm to stop him, and he looked at her with a sudden tenderness.

"Father," she said. "Let's go back upstairs."

"Vinny," he said, and two wrinkles formed between his eyes.

"Come on, let him stay down here," said Fred. "You can see he doesn't want to go. You can see he don't like to be told what to do any more than the next man. That's what the whole trouble is in this country, there's no more *freedom*," Fred bellowed. "There's no freedom anywhere even in this state, and nothing but S.O.B.s on the Supreme Court."

"Lavinia," said Mrs. Stokes, "I won't have that language in my house. I think it's time you and Fred went on home now."

Everyone had heard worse from Fred before. No one said anything. Mrs. Stokes got up from the table, smoothing her dress, her heavy shoes making loud thuds across the floor.

"A mistake once made binds you to it," said Mrs. Stokes to the air, as she went into the front parlor, heavy, slow, touching the backs of chairs as she went. It was something that could have been said to anyone in the room; she meant it for Lavinia. She took every chance that came up to make sure Lavinia knew she had made a mistake marrying Fred.

"Father," said Lavinia, "we must go now. Be careful," she said.

"Vinny," said Mr. Stokes. Again his eyelids closed hard in a tight blink, and his head shook.

"But we haven't had dessert," said Fred.

"We'll have it home," said Lavinia, her eyes on her father. When she looked to say goodby to Ellie and Spence, Ellie expected to see something more in her eyes than the strangely half-satisfied look they had. She had expected some sadness or some sort of frown. But there was nothing more than the calm, smooth look they had had before.

They all got up and went to the door. Spence shook hands with Fred and Fred said something to Ellie she didn't hear, she was trying to listen to what Mr. Stokes said in his quick little voice to Lavinia. Ellie thought he said, "It ain't the end of the world, is it," and he sounded lighthearted. Lavinia smiled with a face full of love, a kind of love Ellie had never known.

"Ellie," said Spence, like a command to her. How horrible he looks, she thought, with his hard face and little eyes. "You stay here," he said. "I'm going to talk to her," meaning his grandmother. Ellie tried not to look at him. She wondered how she could have touched him, only this morning, when now the sight of him, the feel of him at her elbow, and the smell of his breath made her skin shrink. She suspected that Spence was thinking somehow of money, of how much he would get when they died, but that thought was too awful to allow herself.

"Now don't you upset him," said Spence. She didn't answer. "Ellie," he said.

"Well, I won't," she said.

Spence left the room, and she could hear him going up the stairs.

Mr. Stokes stood looking out the window. When he turned around and saw her he said, "Do you know Lavinia, my daughter?"

"Yes," said Ellie.

"She was a girl, tall and thin, and she had smooth brown hair, always long. Always on Sundays she would sing and then sometimes you'd even come upon her singing when she was by herself, like a bird, singing to no one else but herself." He paused. "And you are—"

"Spence's wife."

"Yes, Spence's wife. Lavinia said she likes you. Where's that old woman, the one with the heavy shoes? I mean Spence's grandmother."

"She's upstairs," said Ellie.

"Taking a nap," said Mr. Stokes. "Needs a nap, she's so old. Takes her teeth out, too. I got all mine. Lura's always saying age ain't touched her mind. Well, maybe not, but it's gotten her teeth, every one of them." The grin came back to his face. "But she's a good old woman." He looked to Ellie's eyes.

"Yes, she is," she answered.

The sounds of Treeny and dishes in the kitchen, and a pendulum clock somewhere made Ellie's eyes close slightly and she stood still in the room.

"Not like my first wife of course." He spoke in a low quiet voice.

"What was she like?" said Ellie.

"Oh, who?"

"Your first wife."

Mr. Stokes left the window and sat on a sofa next to it. He looked at his hands. He looked at Ellie. He squinted his eyes.

"Young."

Ellie sat down in a chair facing the sofa. Afternoon light came from the window, warming her face and hair.

"She had a skin like grapes and plums. She laughed, laughing all the time, making me laugh. When people came to visit she sat by me and spoke quiet, and asked their health, and when they left she ran through the house like a child, laughing and singing. She had children, had children and loved them. Lavinia was her last. Lavinia got her singing from her mother."

Ellie didn't know what to say. Daniel Stokes leaned forward and peered at her.

"You think I'm crazy?"

"No," said Ellie.

"I ain't," he said, and laughed. "It's not hard," he said, "life ain't hard. If anyone would ever ask me I'd be able to say, sir, you're right I've had one wife only. It's just an old man's way. You see?"

"Yes," said Ellie.

"Nothing's the end of the world," said Daniel Stokes. "Lavinia knows that. One time it did, it bothered me to see her and him, knowing she could have done better, wanting the best for her. But it's no matter. And Spence, he was fifteen when his father, Wade, my son, died. It hit him, hit him hard. And . . ." Mr. Stokes' right hand jumped off the sofa into the air about seven inches, and fell back again. "But everyone's father dies," he said. "Everybody that's been born has a daddy, who is going to die sooner or later. How about yours?"

"Yes, both—mother and father died when I was a baby."

"You see. Now probably you're caught up in some other kind of worry." Ellie didn't answer.

"Aren't you?"

"Yes, I guess."

Mr. Stokes let out some breath with a little hiss. "But an old man can't tell much to a young girl," he said. He closed his eyes. The top of Ellie's head was warmed hot from the sun. She felt it with her hand. She hummed a song she remembered. She looked at the ring on her hand, just a gold circle; Spence had promised to get a diamond later. Mr. Stokes began to snore, not a loud noisy snore but a soft breathing that rattled out through his nose.

Ellie heard Spence coming down the stairs, his footsteps loud and heavy.

"Be quiet," she said, and to Spence her voice sounded frantic.

Daniel Stokes' body jumped upright and his eyes opened wide. As he woke he saw the girl standing over him, her hair falling over her shoulders, almost touching his face.

"Lura," he said, the sudden closeness of the young girl's face taking him back to times he had known before. "So pretty," he said. "You wait and let me sleep." His eyes closed and he slept again, his head falling to one side.

Ellie wanted to touch his head. She didn't. She pressed the inside of her palm to her mouth.

"Are you all right?" said her husband, now standing near her, his hand in the small of her back. "Are you all right?"

"I don't know. Yes. Yes," she said.

Mac Hyman

The Hundredth Centennial

They piled into the truck and started on the thirteen miles over the hard rutted dirt roads to the highway. The high sideboards with the straw still in between the cracks banged wildly from side to side, jerking back and forth the two girls who sat on the boxes at the end of the truck, holding to the sides with one hand and onto the skirts of their prim pink satin dresses with the other. They finally reached the highway and stopped, the steam hissing up in the top of the radiator; they waited, resting, while the clean shaven man behind the wheel craned his neck this way and that inside the clean starched collar, then shifted into first, jolted up over the hump in the highway and made the long laborious turn toward town, the tin on the hood rattling ominously, the sideboards beginning to sway rhythmically again.

The occupants in the back of the truck began shifting their weights for the new sensation over the paved roads. The two girls in their pink dresses, looking almost like twins, straightened themselves and their skirts, and Polly Ann, the younger of the two, reached back and put her hand on the top of the head of the six-year-old Maddie Claude to keep her from bouncing, giving the child a hunched squat look but not helping much otherwise as the truck still jolted and her legs still bounced up and down, the heels of her shoes clicking sharply on the bottom. Seth stood at the front of the truck his straw Panama hat sitting cockwise on his head, not holding on or balancing himself but chewing nonchalantly on a match stick, his legs in the pinstripe pants weaving back and forth almost imperceptibly, his body motionless, like a bird on a limb in a high wind. Jonny stood beside him, a small edition of himself coming up to about his shoulders, watching Seth and trying himself not to hold on but finally letting one hand steal out to the wabbling sideboards and the other to the brim of his own straw hat. The hat was too big for him; it came down over his hair and formed a line running just above the eyebrows and the top of his ears so that he seemed to be staring at you out of a deep hole, and no matter how much he tightened the muscles in his forehead, the wind kept catching under the brim so that he finally had no other choice than to reach up and shamefully hold onto it.

They headed on down the highway, the truck settling down to a steady rattle and hissing, the dirt in the bottom bouncing slightly from the small jolts in the road. Tom Hamilton gripped onto the vibrating wheel, wrapping his big knuckled fingers all the way around it, his lean gaunt face staring ahead statuesquely like an unbearded Abraham Lincoln; only the lower portion of his face moved chewing on his tobacco. He held intently to the wheel as if trying to prove to himself that he actually had control over the truck when it was moving while his wife Mamie sat huddled up next to him, her manly hands with the blunt nails resting on the baby's stomach. Her round, boneless looking face stared blankly ahead as if she were already in town pricing the food at the store. She sat silently leaving a large gap between herself and the short squat man at her side, Albert, her husband's brother, who always smelled of tobacco and whiskey and breathed in a wheezing sound and looked far more like her than he did his own brother; he sat there now wheezing and humming to himself and looking around at the fields and at the road and at the front of the truck, his small blue eyes darting from side to side. They joggled along the road and rose up slightly with the rolls in the pavement, the three of them and the baby all lifting up suddenly with the same expressions on their faces, holding the same positions, rising up into the air and down again as if they had never moved, the way a juggler can throw balls in the air and have them suspended in the same formation— they hit, rose up, came down, bounced a few more times never moving, staring straight ahead .

They had just strained up one hill and started down it, seeing Callville in the distance, when the Model A came into sight. It was about a half a mile ahead of them at the time and they could see the black heads inside of it, its high top, the right rear wheel wabbling frantically on a loose axle. They gained on it, the truck coming down the hill and getting some speed behind it. Tom Hamilton let his foot down slowly, giving the motor a different sound but with no immediate change in speed; his brogan shoe mashed it to the floorboard and his jaw moved faster, slowed up, moved faster again; his wife held the baby up and juggled her and Albert twisted in his seat, his eye on the wabbling wheel, and quit humming for a few seconds. They gained slowly, the Model A looking motionless in front of them as if it were sitting there and shaking all over like a wet dog. Seth moved his mouth, flipping the match stick over to the other side of his lips so that somehow his hat seemed to be cocked even more than before; Jonny began chewing on a straw as if it were gum, holding on to the sideboards with both hands now. Tom Hamilton pressed his foot hard against the excelerator; he then twisted the wheel with great deliberation, moving his shoulders as if it were a manly struggle, and held it there waiting for the truck to respond. Finally it jerked over and headed for the center line, the steering wheel bumping and knocking now. He turned it back and leveled out on the left hand side of the road, pulling out some fifty feet behind the Model A, settling down for the long trip around it.

None of them looked at it as they gained but Albert who leaned over staring at the wabbling wheel; they looked all around it but not at it. They came within twenty feet and then ten and then almost upon it, and then Tom Hamilton let go the wheel with his right hand and reached forward, touching the horn wire that dangled out below the dash to the charge, letting out a blare from the horn that could be heard even above the noises of the truck; then he put both hands back on the wheel again, his jaw moving rapidly. All of them kept their eyes on a point far down the road as if the car did not exist; they saw it as they went by only out of the corners of their eyes, seeing the closely huddled seven or eight Negroes' white eyeballs as the Model A pulled far over to the right. They passed it and got in front with Seth and Jonny staring straight ahead, and Polly Ann and Margaret peering intently over the top of it at something way off in the distance as it came into view behind them.

They came into Callville a few minutes later. They came over the railroad crossing on the south of town where the truck rumbled from side to side, the large sideboards banging and flapping powerfully like the wings of a huge bird. The girls and their boxes bounced around and the small girl on the floor went up and down and sideways while Polly Ann kept her hand pressed down on the top of her head; Seth's legs joggled up and down like two piston rods while his body remained motionless and Jonny's hat jumped from side to side; the three of them in the front seat moved together as if they were jointed, left and right, then rose up and came down again. The truck hissed to a stop; Tom Hamilton shoved it in first again to get it on across the railroad.

They made it on up the small incline that led into the middle of town and past the Confederate monument where the soldier on top stood poised with his rifle ready to charge North at the given signal—they were just passing around the monument when they began to notice the decorations and the difference in the uptown section. They saw strung between lamp posts entwining ribbons of red and white, going from post to post and across the streets; they saw drapes over the doors, signs in windows, red and white placards, Confederate and American flags in front of the stores and a big streamer across the street in front of the stoplight saying: "Hundredth Centennial."

They looked around the streets as they went through. The streamers went down the street toward the railroad, on the stores on either side, and up the other street. Seth took the match stem out of his mouth and looked from side to side just shifting his eyes; Jonny moved up next to him, turning his head around looking at all the decorations. "Hey, what is it?" he asked.

Seth put the match back in his mouth, clamped his teeth on it and nodded at the sign by the stoplight.

"What?" Jonny asked.

He nodded at the sign, "The hundredth centnal."

"Yeah? What's that?"

Seth flicked his eyes at him then away. He finally cleared his throat and turned his back, picking at his teeth with the match stem. Jonny looked up and down the street, then stepped back to where Polly Ann and Margaret sat and pointed to the sign. "The hundredth centnal," he said. "It looks like they done decorated up for my birthday, dont it?"

Polly Ann looked at him and said, "Huh!"

"Well, hits the same day, aint it? Today's my birthday, aint it? I'm sixteen today and they done decorated for it!"

"What's the hundredth centnal?" Margaret asked.

Nobody answered; they looked up and down the street as the truck turned at the corner, and Jonny went back to the front where Seth was and said, "The hundredth centnal is on the same day as my birthday."

"Yeah," Seth said.

"The very same day."

"Yeah."

They parked on Smoky Road in a lot in front of the feedstore where there were no parking meters, across the street from the red-corrugated-roof depot. They got out and stretched and patted their clothes right and brushed the dust off the smaller girl who stood staring at the train just coming in across the street, watching while the steam hissed and the black smoke puffed up in great explosive bursts; they fussed over her while Albert went over to the feedstore and began talking with an old man in overalls, soon arguing loudly. Tom Hamilton carefully rolled a cigarette out of the little white sack as Mamie talked at him, going over the list of groceries she had to get; he listened while he packed the cigarette with his blunt fingers and licked it moistly and put it in his mouth and lit it, the paper on the end flaming up and burning down half an inch before it reached the tobacco. He heard her out and then fumbled in his back pocket for the little greasy purse which he clicked open and counted out for her six rolled up dollar bills and a fifty cent piece while the others slowly gathered around and watched so that he finally pulled out three quarters and handed one each to Jonny, Margaret, and Polly Ann, hesitated a moment and then pulled a dime from somewhere in the bottom of it for the six-year-old Maddie Claude, then snapped it shut quickly, glancing uneasily at Seth who stood apart from the little group staring at something down the street as if he were intent on watching it.

They stood around the truck after that only so long as propriety demanded, then drifted off in different directions, Seth first, strolling off slowly, then moving faster with his steel taps clicking sharply on the pavement. Jonny hesitated; he looked first at his mother and then turned to Polly Ann who was also looking at him as if she were ready to say something. He said quickly, "I think I'll go with Seth today." They stared at each other for a second and she said, "You're not going to go with us down to . . . ?" but let it trail off as she looked away from him, and he turned his head too so that neither of them was looking at the other anymore; he then turned suddenly and started after Seth, twisting his head this way and that at the ribbons and the drapes over the doorways.

And in a few minutes, Polly Ann and Margaret left too, walking fast through the crowd, huddled over talking excitedly as if over some deep secret; and then Mamie, holding Maddie Claude by the right hand and holding the baby with the other, while Tom Hamilton went over and sat down on the steps of the feedstore and listened to Albert and old man Biggers argue; he sat there a minute or two and got up and left, going down Smoky Road to where some men sat on a bench in front of a hardware store —they moved over and made room for him.

It was about ten o'clock when they all parted at the truck; they would not meet again there until late that night. Seth, with Jonny following along, headed up past the ten cent store and the picture show to the pool room where he sat on one of the chairs on the side watching two men shoot snooker on the front table; Jonny sat next to him, blinking his eyes trying to get used to the cool remote darkness after the bright April sunlight outside. The pool room was not crowded yet; the tables in the back were racked up with the lights off. Seth lounged in the chair watching the game; he crossed his legs and lit a cigarette as Jonny watched him out of the corner of his eye. Jonny blinked his eyes again, glanced at Seth and then lounged down in his seat too and crossed his legs, watching the smoke rising up under the buzzing blue neon lights that came down across the table, the roof of his mouth drawing up in distaste as he watched the fat man with the white shirt take a cigar out of his mouth, the ends of it wet and limp, and turn up a mug of beer he had on the counter. He eyed Seth a few more times and finally leaned over and said casually and rather harshly, "Give me a cigarette, will you, Seth?"

Seth didn't answer him at first; he was dragging on his own, his eyes squenched up. Jonny turned back to watch the game again but could feel Seth shifting his eyes at him. He jumped slightly when he heard Seth say, "Give you what?" He couldn't think of anything to say.

"What?" he said.

"Give you a cigarette?"

"Yeah, come on, Seth. I want to try one."

Seth didn't say anything for a moment and he held his breath. Then Seth finally reached down into his pocket and pulled out the pack; Jonny, his eyes still toward the table, took one out and put it between his lips, holding it right in the center of his lips with them puckered out, and handed the pack back.

He took another deep breath and said, "How about a match?" and waited while Seth slowly fished it out and handed it to him. Jonny lit the cigarette and blew the smoke out without inhaling. He held it between his front two fingers, both fingers stiff, dragging on it and blowing the smoke out in great gushes, his eyes watering and stinging, staring at the red balls on the table.

Polly Ann and Margaret were at the bus station. They sat at the white counter and ordered Cokes from the fat girl in the white dress. They sipped at them, huddled over together while Polly Ann kept glancing at herself in the mirror just behind the counter. They darted their eyes this way and that at the people coming in, the country people in their clean khakis and blue jeans and overalls; they turned around to watch the bus unload, giggling together at the large colored woman with all the bundles who almost tripped off. They watched, turned and whispered to each other as Polly Ann, glancing at the mirror, pulled her shoulders back making her breasts rise a little and point more under the pink satin front, glancing at times at the fat girl and back at herself again. She then turned to Margaret who was talking to her and lowered her eyes several times, noticing the lines she was forming; she would look at her year older sister, then back at herself again—

then, seemingly satisfied, at whatever or whomever Margaret was talking about at the time. They turned their eyes from the door and concentrated on something on the counter as two boys about their own ages whom they knew came in; neither of them looked up, giving the boys a chance to speak to them without their seeming willing; they huddled and concentrated until the two boys went out the door again without speaking, and then they looked up at the same time without any kind of conscious signal and watched the people indifferently, a little irritated with each other somehow. Polly Ann turned all the way around on the stool and watched the two boys going across the street. She said, "There goes Tim and that other boy. They're the stuck-uppidist things."

"Where?"

"Over yonder," Polly Ann said.

"Oh, is that them? That aint them, is it?"

"I think so," Polly Ann said.

"Well, I'm glad they didn't see us," Margaret said. "They are the stuck-uppidest things . . ."

They were just finishing up their Cokes and ready to leave when the north bound bus came in. They each began sipping more slowly waiting to see who would get off, discussing what they were going to get Jonny for his birthday, trying to decide between the green top that Margaret wanted to buy and the cigarette lighter that Polly Ann insisted on. "What would he want with that?" Margaret said. "He dont even smoke."

"Well, he might someday. He's sixteen now, aint he?"

"Well," Margaret said, "I just dont see the sense in it when he dont even smoke, and we dont have the money for it nohow."

They argued the point, not looking at each other but at the bus outside the door, watching the blonde-headed woman who was getting off, seeing the long, red-colored fingernails and rings as she reached out taking the driver's helping hand. They talked and watched her as she walked primly on very high heels, clicking toward the door of the station, the muscles in her hips moving like a well-oiled machine under the tight fitting skirt. She came in, her eyes looking a little blank, her blonde hair seeming somehow wrong against her complexion. Polly Ann dug at a piece of ice in the bottom of her glass, turning her back as the woman sat down at the counter a seat away from her and said to the waitress who was also watching her, "Bring me a Coke, will you, honey, and put a little bit of lemon in it."

She clicked her purse open, got out a handkerchief and leaned over to look in the mirror, straightening her lipstick; then took out a cigarette and lit it. Polly Ann watched the fat girl contemptuously as she suddenly became bashful and confused when the woman asked her what all the decorations around town were for.

"They're going to have the hundredth centnal, or something like that," the fat girl said, blushing.

"What is it, honey, some kind of fair?"

"Well, something like that, I guess."

A man sitting on the other side of her, a grey-headed man with a grey suit who had been watching her, said, "I dont think nobody knows what it is, but they are going to celebrate it all right." The woman turned and looked at him and the man laughed, his voice unnatural, his laugh strained, his face turning a little red; Polly Ann could see his finger moving nervously over the sandwich he was eating. From the color of his face she could tell that he was from the country, despite the grey suit he was wearing.

"Where you from?" he asked, the smile becoming a little frozen on his face, twisting slightly on the seat.

"Jacksonville," she said, not even looking at him now.

"Where you headed?"

For a moment it seemed as if she wasn't even going to answer him. Then she said shortly, "The other direction." Some people snickered and the man turned redder in the face, looking confused and nervous, then turned back and took a large bite out of his sandwich. In a minute he left, leaving the sandwich half-eaten, going sheepishly out of the station.

They waited until she had finished her Coke and watched her walk over to the ticket window and ask about what time the other buses were going out; they got up then to leave, Margaret going for the door and Polly Ann stopping and suddenly boldly staring at the woman, up and down, as she went past. Then she followed Margaret to the door and out and on down the street, holding her shoulders back with her breasts pushing out, her hips moving slightly. "Wasnt that man disgusting, though," she said. "I'll bet he was sixty years old."

"Ugh," Margaret said. "Did you see how her hair looked?"

"She had it blondeened, I bet," Polly Ann said. "I think I'll have mine done like that."

"Oh, my goodness," Margaret said, looking at her.

"Well, she aint no bigger than I am without those high heels, is she?" Polly Ann said suddenly. But then she laughed and Margaret did too, and it suddenly seemed very funny to both of them so that they put their arms in between each other's, huddling together down the street, giggling mysteriously every time they looked at each other until they reached the corner where Polly Ann stopped giggling except when Margaret started it up again. They looked in the reflections of the windows, Margaret studying the displays, Polly Ann touching at the back of her hair as she glanced at herself.

The town gradually became more crowded as the people came in. They parked their pick-up and two-ton trucks on the street by the railroad; old cars stopped and people climbed out like midgets at a circus; there were wagons and mules and cut down Model T's, and by noon the streets were filled with Negroes and whites in overalls and khakis, women with children and bundles, men standing around in little groups on the corners talking about crops and the weather and prices and all the decorations around town. Jonny, still in the pool room, ate a hot dog for dinner sitting in the chair next to the table where Seth leaned over shooting, the cigarette smoke curling up around his eyes, holding his cue with grace and ease, chalking the end of it after each shot. Jonny watched proudly as Seth ran up thirty-three points at one time, and then he finished up his hot dog and licked the mustard off his fingers and got in a game of eight-ball with the boy who racked the balls up. He sank only two balls but learned to powder and chalk the cue without all the awkwardness that he had noted somewhat contemptuously in the other beginners.

Albert ate dinner by himself at a little restaurant near the railway station and kidded the waitress who giggled at him; he drank three beers and left with a man to go to the ball park where they were going to have some ceremonies and speeches. He rode out with the man and was disappointed in the fact that no more than thirty people were there, and the speakers on the platforms became self-conscious and ended up by kidding each other over the loud speakers, making private jokes so that nobody else laughed much. Albert finally got tired of it and walked back to town and back to the restaurant to drink some more beer and talk with the waitress some more; he was just starting on his second one when the woman came in.

She came in behind him so that he could not see her at first, but from the perfume he almost knew what she was like without looking. He sucked in his breath sharply, his nostrils contracting, and turned to see her short, well-formed, small body and the blonde hair and the red fingernails as she slid herself onto the stool right down from him, the sharp line of the indentation of her bloomers making a little ridge in the silkish dress just below her buttocks. He breathed shortly for a few moments, shifting his eyes at her. He grinned broadly suddenly and moved down next to her, saying, "You're a stranger here, I bet. What's the chances of buying a stranger a good cold brew." He held a good-natured smile on his face, his eyes twinkling, as she looked him over. He stood there grinning; she stared at him coldly then angrily, then contemptuously, and finally, when he did not wilt, cordially, and said, "Well, I might at that, being as you offered."

"Sho," Albert said. "Besides, we're having our hundredth centnal today. And besides that my nephew's having a birthday—going to have to do something for that boy. Good boy, sixteen today."

"Well, I'll have one to your nephew then," she said smiling. "I remember when I was sixteen."

"Well, sir, I wish to God I could," Albert said. "Honey, bring the lady here a good cool brew . . ."

At about four o'clock that afternoon, the man from the radio station came uptown. He parked his truck with the man inside who controlled the output down near the picture show, then got out and started stringing out the wires leading from it, testing it for the program that was supposed to begin at four-thirty. He worked busily getting everything set up, moving among the silently forming bunch of staring faces, with an apologetic smile frozen on his face. He begged pardons and excused himself, smiling from one to the other, the short bow tie bobbing up and down on his Adam's apple as he tested saying, "One, two, three, four . . . Do you hear it, Charlie?"

The people formed a little half circle around the busy man in the middle, staring at him. Old man Biggers stood watching, chewing violently on a wad of tobacco, asking every once in awhile, "What's that fer, there?" Tom Hamilton came up from the bench where he was sitting and stood next to him and they watched the goings-on. In a little while Mamie came out of the grocery store holding the baby and the groceries in her arms with Maddie Claude tagging along; she came and watched a minute, then took the groceries back to the truck before coming to see the movie that she always went to on Saturday. She came back just as the man was beginning the program, standing by her husband and blankly watching the tangle of wires around the truck. "I wonder where Jonny went off to," she said. "I thought I'd take him to the show being as it's his birthday and all, you know."

"He's off with Seth somewheres," Tom Hamilton said not looking at her.

"And usually he's deviling me to death to go," she said.

Tom Hamilton nodded his head, not answering her but watching the man in the middle. Mamie looked around vaguely for Jonny, finally said again, "Well, I wonder where they went?"

Tom Hamilton looked at her; he leaned over and spat and wiped his mouth off on the sleeve of his shirt. "Well, there aint no sense in waiting around here on him," he said. "Maybe he dont want to go nohow."

After that, he didn't say anything else to her. He got interested in the announcer's answer when he began clicking the microphone and Mr. Biggers asked, "What's that fer, there?" Mamie finally turned and headed for the box office and paid her money, looking back over her shoulder for Jonny before disappearing into the darkness where already the horses thundered and the shots were ringing out.

At four-thirty, just as Mamie went into the movie, the announcer got a nod from the man in the truck. His face became suddenly animated with a wide grin; his voice rang out loudly and enthusiastically, his little bow tie jumping up and down on his throat. He talked, nodded, smiled and bobbed around, waving his arms exclaiming on the crowd that had gathered on this, the Hundredth Centennial of Callville. He described the decorations and the crowds and told about the street dance they were going to have that night with Roy Bolton and his boys playing right here in the middle of town. Then he began his interviewing, looking around mischievously, and tried to get a large woman with a bundle of groceries in her arms to say just a few words, only she tightened her lips and moved back and started on up the street, as he described her departure with a great many forced chuckles in his voice.

Seth and Jonny came out of the pool room and stood around the edge of the group, Seth's head coming up above the others, Jonny secretly standing on his toes. Tom Hamilton took out the little sack and began to roll a cigarette and Mr. Biggers stared at the tangle of wires around the truck, his jaw moving rapidly. The announcer had cornered a lanky boy who looked at him stupidly, grinning, shaking his head from side to side. The announcer said, "Won't you just tell us your name?" The boy smiled broadly at the announcer, showing an ungodly amount of teeth. "Just your name. Won't you just tell us your *name?*" He was leaned over holding the microphone in front of the boy's lips and the boy still looked at him grinning, both of them staring at each other as the boy's lips started to move and stopped, as the announcer leaned over bobbing his head up and down like a mother with a daughter who had forgotten her nursery rhyme, trying to force the words out of the grinning face. Then he jerked back the microphone and began talking into it, his face assuming a hideous smile that barely exposed his teeth. "Well," he said, "that young man didn't seem to care to talk over the radio. But there are lots of other folks around today. Yessir, you folks at home by your radios . . . You, sir, how about telling us your name . . ." This to a tall, hard-looking man in overalls. "Won't you even tell us your name? . . . Well, maybe this gentleman . . . ha! ha! ha! . . . Well, I guess he was in pretty much of a hurry; he just kept right on going. Yessir, you folks at home . . ."

The crowd watched him impassively as he went on like this for some fifteen minutes without getting anybody to say a word, his laugh by this time becoming a forced gurgle that he seemed to push up out of his stomach, his face knotted into a smile so tightly that sometimes his lips would begin jerking involuntarily. They stood and watched as he cornered one man who for some reason kept grunting at him, and one other who didn't say anything but did at least start to, only to get strangled at the time and begin coughing and keep coughing until the announcer had to pull back the microphone to say a few words himself to keep the program going; he waited, moving from one foot to the other while the man gasped and strangled and hacked, holding the microphone over when he thought he had stopped, then having to jerk it back again, saying once or twice, "Well, he really did get strangled, didn't he?" He waited another minute while the man heaved and choked, said again, "Well, he really did get strangled, didn't he?" and tried to laugh again. He managed to wait this one out hopefully though until the man finally stopped, then held the microphone over his lips only to get the sounds of the man hacking, clearing his throat, spitting, and then blowing his nose loudly, after which he went on down the street like the others.

Albert and the woman whose name he had learned was Clarene came out of the restaurant and saw the crowd and started for it, Albert walking bouncily, smiling and talking and pointing to things along the way as she walked beside him in her short steps, the heels of her shoes clicking loudly and the muscles in her body moving rhythmically. They stopped and stood on the edge of the crowd, smelling like a mixture of perfume and beer, as the people moved back slightly to look at them. She looked vaguely at the truck and the announcer and said brightly, "Oh, they're having a radio progum," slurring over her words and ending them with a slight hiccup, after which she raised one hand to her mouth daintily.

The announcer was trying to use up the rest of his time now, seriously describing with dead-pan face the different decorations around the stores, and trying to get eloquent once or twice, saying, "It's too bad that some of our fathers and grandfathers and great-grandfathers are not here today to witness this tribute to the hundredth anniversary of our town. Yes, we miss them and wish they were here, but we know that they are out yonder somewhere watching us today—and we wish you folks at home listening in were here too . . ."

They stood listening, Albert looking around smiling from one to the other, his hand straight down by his side so that when Clarene moved it brushed up against the silky smoothness of her bottom. Clarene listened to the announcer's eloquence and reached in her purse and got out a handkerchief and dabbed at her eyes which were beginning to smart, mumbling, "Yes, they are off somewheres, seeing us. I remember when I was sixteen."

Seth saw her over the crowd of heads and his eyes stopped suddenly and he clamped his teeth down on the match, staring at her, then turned to Flip who had come out of the pool room with them and who had just seen her too, and they nodded their heads at each other. Flip shook his head sideways unbelievingly and a light hissing came out of his teeth.

"Aint that your uncle with her?"

Seth nodded, staring at them. "Je-sus!"

"Man," Flip said. "Lordy, lawd!"

"Je-sus!" Seth hissed.

"What is it?" Jonny asked standing on his toes. "What is it?"

The crowd was just breaking up when Polly Ann and Margaret came out of the ten cent store. The announcer had wound up the broadcast five minutes before time actually so that they had to fill in the rest of it with music; he was now helping to load up the truck, moving listlessly, his eyes rather blank, taking deep heaving breaths every once in a while·as some of the crowd still stood there and watched him silently, jaws moving up and down on wads of tobacco and chewing gum. Polly Ann and Margaret saw the crowd and wondered about it but neither of them mentioned it as they were arguing at the time; neither one looked at the other. "You go on and get what you want," Polly Ann said. "But I aint going to put nothing in it. He dont care nothing about a green top no more."

"Well, he sho dont care anything about a cigarette lighter."

"Well, that's what I'm going to get. I dont care what you say. He's sixteen now and dont want no green top."

"Do you know how much those things cost. I think you are losing your mind or something. The cheapest one you found yet was that one at the drugstore and that cost a dollar and a half! And you got fifty cents and I got thirty . . . I dont see how you expect to get it and I dont see what he would want with one anyhow. Honest to goodness Polly Ann sometimes you act like you crazy. I dont see why Jonny would even want one anyhow. I . . ."

"There's lots of things you dont see," Polly Ann replied bitterly, and headed on up the street, not even looking back to see if she were following.

Seth and Flip and Jonny had followed along behind Albert and Clarene, getting glimpses of her from time to time through the crowd of Negroes and whites that now crowded the streets, seeing her small body twitching below the curvature of her back they had followed them down to Red's Place on Smoky Road where they had gone inside out of sight, and Seth and Flip stood outside talking about it and hesitating, Flip saying, "Hell, let's go on in."

But Seth hesitated while Jonny leaned up against the wall waiting, his hands in his pockets. Seth bit the match stick and thought, saying, "I kind of hate to cut in," and Flip said, "Hell, you dont cut in on one like that. You take turns. He's your uncle, aint he?" They finally decided and went into the place that had a wood cracked floor and little blue lights and a gaudy juke organ that changed colors from pink to green as the music blared out; they went back to the booth where they saw Albert who not only invited them but seemed very happy to see them, moving over so that Jonny could sit next to Clarene, saying, "You slide in here, Jonny boy. We're going to celebrate your birthday."

"Oh, is this him?" asked Clarene. She smiled and put her hand on his arm. "I remember when I was sixteen," she said and lifted the bottle with one finger stuck out, taking a great gulp of it.

They stayed in Red's Place until nearly eight o'clock and when they came out, the festivities were blaring. It had developed in a very peculiar way. At first, it seemed as if the whole thing was going to be a flop. Roy Bolton and his boys had not shown up and the juke organ that they had put on the platform of the decorated truck did not work over the loud speaker, and when they did get it to working, the records wabbled so that it didn't even sound like music. Then while they were trying to repair that, one of the men from the Chamber of Commerce tried to entertain the crowd with a long joke, only the microphone went dead in the middle of it, and finally when he did get to tell the joke, he was so angry that nobody laughed much. They had sprinkled sawdust along the street but this did not work too well either as it only filled up the holes in the pavement. People moved around in little groups talking and looking on; high school students standing around became rather contemptuous; the country people talked of the same things they usually talked about, the Negroes hung about on the corners greeting one another in their elaborately polite manners. It wasn't until Roy Bolton and his boys showed up that things started moving at all, and this was not because of the band but because of a man who fell off the truck trying to manage a keg of beer and broke his leg. The screaming siren of the ambulance did something to the crowd, and then somebody set off a string of firecrackers and Roy Bolton and his boys started playing, and within about fifteen minutes, what seemed at first a dismal evening developed into a melee that was worthy of this, the hundredth anniversary of Callville.

So that when Seth and Albert and Jonny and Clarene left Red's Place, it was like leaving a comfortable, cozy place into a mass of confusion. Somebody was setting off another string of firecrackers which exploded rapidly and loudly, the smoke and the smell of burnt powder drifting down the street. Mr. Biggers gave a whoop and began dancing with a woman next to the truck and then somebody set off the first skyrocket; it went screaming into the air with the fire out behind it along with moans from the crowd and then exploded with a noise that made everybody gasp. Albert laughed and pointed and gave a whoop himself, and Clarene grabbed onto Jonny's arm. The band swung out on "Rocky Bottom on Saturday Night" and the street became more crowded with people as they started to dance—men in overalls dancing stiffbacked with their wives, younger people bouncing around self-consciously, and one high-school boy who held his head up high and his buttocks poked out, doing intricate steps with a good many twists and turns and dips; Mr. Biggers finally got up on the truck and did a buck dance all by himself, his brogan shoes banging up and down; they crowded in the street in an incongruous mass of farmers and storekeepers and clerks and women in country gingham with hard-knuckled hands and town women in prim dresses with soft diamonded hands; Roy Bolton sang, his voice cracking and yodeling, and the base fiddle player straddled his instrument as if riding a horse, beating on the side of it, while children screamed and swarmed around the truck. The storekeepers that were still open came to the doors and watched, and the Negroes pointed and clapped each other on the back and finally got up a little dance of their own down on the corner; somebody else set off some firecrackers and the women squealed; the smoke floated down the street and another bunch went off. Mr. Travis, the bank president, donated two more kegs of beer, and watched, smiling to himself as he sat fat-stomached behind the wheel of his Buick as they opened it; Albert danced with Clarene, springing lightly and laughing, and then Seth broke in and danced with her, his hat still sitting cockwise on his head—she broke away from him finally and went over to get Jonny, taking him by the arm saying, "We're just about the same size, aint we?"

Jonny followed her out, trying to swagger but only succeeding in looking stiff all over as he started to dance. She showed him how to hold her, saying, "I couldnt dance neither when I was sixteen. No, honey, like this. What's the matter, you never held a girl before? That's right. That's right. Oh, honey, you do learn fast!"

He moved around in circles with her while she led him, pushing up against him as if somebody were tickling her in the back. Jonny tried to follow, stumbling, glancing around while Albert and Flip and Seth yelled at him. Albert waved his arms around in the air and shouted, "Yessir, that's my present! That's what I'm going to get for you. By God, I remember my first time!" He cupped his hands around his mouth and called, "Go to it, Jonny boy. You the best they is!" He kept yelling and taking on until Flip finally looked sourly at him and made a remark about him trying to hog everything.

Albert made so much noise that people began looking at Jonny, and then Polly Ann, who was up near the truck saw him. She and Margaret were standing there with two boys, and Polly Ann's eyes lighted up and she punched Margaret viciously in the side, saying, "Look at Jonny. What did I tell you? What did I tell you?" Margaret looked at him, her lips coming together, and said lamely, "Oh, well, you aint got the money nohow," then turned back to her partner; Polly Ann stared another minute, then walked off by herself, leaving the group of them alone.

Jonny kept dancing until Flip got disgusted with it and went out and broke in on them, taking Clarene in his arms tightly and whispering in her ear until she shoved away from him, saying loudly, "You keep away from me, you bastard!" and left him standing there. Albert laughed and Flip turned red. She went back and got Jonny again, and Flip turned, cursing her, and headed up the street away from the group. He started for the drugstore when he saw the pink satin dress of Polly Ann going through the door alone; he hurried along, went in and sat on a stool watching her and running his eyes up and down her as she fingered the cigarette lighter and asked the girl behind the counter how much it was. She looked a little angry when the girl said, "Aint it marked on the side?"

She turned it over. "Oh, yeah, I just didnt think it would be that much."

Flip edged over to her, glancing at it, saying, "How much?"

She looked at him coolly, but he was looking at the lighter and not at her. She said, "A dollar and a half."

"That's a right nice one all right. I think I'll get me one." He smiled at her. "You're too young to be smoking anyhow."

"Huh!"

"You are, I bet. I bet you dont even know how."

"That's how much you know."

They both looked at the box; he reached over to hold it, touching her hand so that at first she gave a jump; then, her eyes shifting, left her finger next to his as he wrapped it around hers. He said, "Yessir, if I didn't think you was too young, I would just buy it for you myself."

"I dont even know you," she said, still looking at the box.

"If we dance some, you'll get to know me. That is, if you aint too young."

"I aint too young," she said.

She stood in the door and waited for him, looking uneasily up and down the street; he came out in a minute sticking the package in his pocket. He led her toward the crowd, saying, "We dont have to dance long, do we? There are other things to do, aint there?" giving her arm a squeeze, as she walked along, glancing up and down the street excitedly.

Jonny felt that he must be drunk. In his hand now he held the paper cup that had beer from the keg in it and whiskey that Clarene had poured into it; his head whirled and his face felt numb and he decided that now he was actually for the first time really and truly drunk. He would be dancing and then without knowing it, they would have stopped dancing and he would be standing with Albert on one side and Clarene on the other, talking and laughing, with Albert clapping him on the back. Everything in front of him was confused; firecrackers kept exploding and he looked up once to see another skyrocket just above his head; he never heard the sound of it—it seemed that it had just floated up there silently by itself. They were standing there and then he was going across the street again and he and Clarene were standing next to the truck with a paper cup in her hand pulling a bottle out of her purse again; then they were dancing and he could feel her body jerking convulsively every once in a while from the hiccups. He was drinking again with it going down smoother than before, and then he was dancing, floating, doing steps that he had never thought possible before. Then they were back at the truck and somebody had put a cigarette between his lips but it wouldn't stay in because his lips were so numb; it fell out to the ground and then she was holding it in his mouth for him saying, "I'll light it for you, baby. Here you go, baby."

And after that they were on another street which he didn't recognize even though he knew every street in town, and Seth was sitting on the curbing. Nobody was around, and he couldn't figure out what Seth was doing just sitting there, and then he remembered Albert.

"No, you just wait a minute." It was Clarene standing close to him, holding his arms. They were up against a wall and she was kissing him. "Albert will be back in a minute. He had to go see the man." She was leaning up against him; he felt something stirring in him; then she was saying, "Wait, honey. Wait. Albert will be back in a minute. You're a little devil, aren't you? Oh, wait, wait just a minute."

Then Albert appeared from somewhere and they went up the long dark steps that creaked under his feet. Somebody was holding him saying, "No, on down the hall," and then the next thing he knew he was sitting in a chair asleep, and Albert was rubbing a wet rag over his face, saying, "Is that the way a man should act? Boys sho have changed since I was a boy."

Then all of a sudden, except for being dizzy, he was sober. He knew he was sober even though he didn't know how he got over to the door, but he knew immediately what was behind the door. He gave a quick shove against Albert and fell against a chair trying to get around it, going for the hall. But then he was back at the other door again and Albert was laughing and Seth was holding him by the arm grinning at him, and then the door opened and Clarene's head stuck out; she said, "Come on now, honey. Now." And as he went into the darkened room, he felt her bare arms around his neck, her small bare body grinding painfully against him. He never knew how it was they got to the bed.

It was all over about two o'clock that morning, and the Hamiltons headed back for the truck from the different sections of town. The town was quiet now; the big truck with the platform on it had moved off and the ropes had been taken down; the crowds had gone home leaving the scattered mess, the beer soaked sawdust in the middle of the street, many paper cups, pieces of fireworks. Candy and bottles and pieces of ice cream cones littered the gutters and the sidewalks; the breeze came along from somewhere and picked up a newspaper and skidded it along the pavement like a small white dog running across the street. The lights burned dimly on the corners and from somewhere came the sound of a car shifting into second. Seth's iron taps clicked loudly on the sidewalk as they headed back

for the truck which sat by itself now. Tom Hamilton was in the front
seat, his hands on the wheel, looking around as if he were driving; Mamie
sat next to him still holding the baby in her arms, her head falling down
sideways and jerking back up again; in the back of the truck Margaret
sat on one of the boxes with her head leaned up against the boards, her
neck looking out of place and uncomfortable, her legs stretched out before
her as she slept. Polly Ann sat-hunched over on the box on the other side,
her eyes wide open and knees together, staring at the corner light as she
waited, holding the small package in her hands with her fingers clasped
around it. She leaned forward listening, her lips tight together. She and
Tom Hamilton both turned their heads hearing the steps coming closer,
clicking on the pavement like somebody hitting a nail with a hammer; the
noise echoed up and down the windblown and beer soaked streets like small
sharp cracks from a rifle. Tom Hamilton quit chewing a second and twisted
his head around while the steps got louder, watching the corner as the sound
reached a peak and the three forms turned the corner, looming up black
and shadowy against the light. Seth was in front and Jonny followed
along behind, his shoulders hunched over, his hands in his pockets, having
to stretch to keep up with the pace that Seth was setting. Albert rolled
along something like a bear, his hair messed up, looking at the sidewalk,
walking like a man who has long since given up all attempt to move of his
own accord but just keeps going by habit.

They got to the truck and Seth reached up and put his hands on the
boards and slung himself in and took his stand at the head of it; Albert went
around to the side of the front door and opened it, causing Mamie to jerk
up awake suddenly, and move over next to her husband, saying, "My lands,
we been waiting . . ." but not bother to finish, only blinking her eyes again
and letting her head nod back over. Albert got in, first having to pick up
the lifeless form of Maddie Claude and drop her in his lap like a sack;
he gave a deep sigh and then reached out and put his hand on the door
and with what seemed like the absolutely final act that he could perform,
hesitating a second to muster all his strength, slammed it shut with a
loud clanging sound. Tom Hamilton hit the starter saying, "We don bout
give yall out . . ." but Albert said nothing; he leaned back breathing heavily,
resting, as if he did not yet have strength enough to close his eyes and sleep.

They drove off then up the main street where only two cars were left;
they turned and went down the sawdust covered street moving aside to avoid
one bottle broken in the middle of it; they went past the place where the
platform truck had been, its tire marks now showing in the sawdust; they

turned and headed out of town again under the ripped banner hanging down at the stoplight so that it read: "HUNDR-" with the rest of the sign hanging down so that it couldn't be seen. They passed the monument where a man was sleeping and bumped over the railroad, going down the dark highway as the breeze, fresh and clean and cool, blew in whirls around the truck, the stars overhead bright and motionless. They settled down then for the ride back in the quietness, the motor sounding quiet somehow, the frogs and crickets setting up a chatter in the woods along the way. They drove past branchy places where the mist settled ghostily, Seth standing at the head of the truck letting the wind beat him in the face, Albert sitting in dry-eyed exhaustion; the wind whirled in the back blowing up some of the trash on the floor, getting some in Polly Ann's eye so that she gave a little cry and put her finger in it. Jonny looked at her and moved back beside her. He said roughly, "Well, dont rub it then."

She snatched her head around at him angrily, almost crying. "Well, who asked you about it anyhow? Who asked you about it?"

"Well I dont care then. Who cares anyway?" Jonny answered, turning his head aside from her. They didn't say anything else to each other until they had reached the place were they turned off; at that time Polly Ann abruptly and rudely shoved the little package at him and said, "Here!"

He stared at her, not making any move to take it. "What's that?"

"It's your present."

"What is it?"

"Open it and see," she said angrily. "You can open it as good as I can."

He opened it sullenly, begrudgingly. When he took it out and looked at it, his face flushed somehow and he said quietly, "What makes you think I smoke?"

"If you dont want it, just throw it away then," she said to him. "Just throw it away."

"What would I want with a cigarette lighter?" he accused angrily. "Just because you run around smoking dont mean everybody . . ." Then he looked at her face and said, "Well, I didnt ask you to get it, did I? I didnt ask you to get it!"

Then she yelled, almost hysterically, her small hands clasped in her lap, leaning forward and staring at him with her eyes wild looking. "I dont care whether you want it or not! Throw it away! Throw it away then!"

"Well, you neednt yell at me," he shouted furiously, getting on his knees in the bottom of the truck. "I didnt ask you to get it, did I?"

"Throw it away! Throw it away!"

32

"What do I want . . ."

"Throw it away!"

She grabbed for it then and both of them tussled over it trying to hold on to it; her voice broke out in a high wailing furious sob as she snatched it toward her, throwing her body from side to side. Jonny held on too, jerking at it, his voice cracking almost effeminately as he cried out in anger and tried to hold onto the package and jab his elbow in her stomach all at the same time. They snatched and jerked and screamed, their voices rising up in unreal chatter like squirrels; then they both at the same time began cursing each other, using words that neither had used before. She fell off the box then to the bottom of the truck and Jonny got his elbow in her breast and bored it in until she gave a stifled, pitiful cry. He pulled at the package and she jerked herself to her knees and snatched it and threw it so that it sailed over the side of the truck and into the bushes along the edge of the road; then she sat on the box, sobbing, staring at him and saying wildly, "There! There!" and he kept drawing back his fist at her as if to hit her, saying through clenched teeth, "You shut up now, goddamn you. Goddamn your soul!"

It was all over then. Seth had turned and looked at them with his eyes blank, showing neither approval or disapproval; Margaret woke up and opened her eyes and stared as if she couldn't move, her feet still spread out before her; she watched them on the floor beside her, watched them get back up and Jonny go up to the front of the truck again, saying nothing as if she were looking at a dream. Her eyes focused dully on Polly Ann's back for a moment after it was over; then she went back to sleep again.

They finally got to the house and got out, one by one, creaking, the truck sitting there making clicking noises in the motor as if it had not stopped yet. They passed into the house in stunned exhaustion; lights were turned on, then off again. The car settled down and quit clicking and the hounds stretched back out on the porch again to sleep. There was only the sound of the wind in the top of the pine trees, rustling lightly, mysteriously, god-like, like far off faint voices. Down in the woods somewhere a kill-dee began to cry, clear and lovely, piercing and deadly.

Michael Brondoli

A correspondence

march 10, 1969

dear KAREN (baby) my true LOVE,

mucho thanks for your epistle. it was really you know profound. but i
have some like wisdom for your also: dont worry about me so much. i mean
i can take care of myself—okay? and quit waiting around for me to freak
out completely; im not gonna so quit worrying. i can be this very sort of
straight cat when i have to, like when i go for law school interviews, so
just quit sweating it—okay? like i'm a man of a million roles but im always
in control of what's really me.

by the way are you for positive that Marcie is like PREG? i just cant
feature that you know? shes not gonna marry that little wimp is she? what
a WIMP that guy is! i hope also she quit that freaky job selling those rug
shampooers or whatever. wow its just so crazy you know for i could scarce
get a hand on her and then that weenie comes along and WHAMO!! well
anyway jesus dont let her hurt herself. you can really mess yourself up bad
so dont let her. those 10-in-1 rug shampooers blew her mind. well also drop
me Jess's phone no. him and me have got to have a good rapp like mucho
quicko or he'll flip out again—and Richmonds only like 50 miles from here so
we could get together really easy. please dont let marcie like go to pieces.

in addition ive got also some other wisdom. (a) dont let college gook
up your mind too much. (b) this wisdom has to be a like story, like jesus
teaching in parables. and i dont know what the wisdom is yet but im for
positive it's there. im just gonna work it out as i go along for i need to find it
myself also.

all right heres the like scene:

i was over at sylvie's place for she was having this like continuous three
day and three night blowout and she invited me and some mutual friends
and about 82,000 freaks id never seen before—for her parents were in miami
at this sort of tire dealers convention. i really used to like Sylvie you know
and we had GOOD TIMES and FUN and a really good relationship til
she went so freaky i couldnt even EXIST she was so freaky. i mean i think i

34

told you about the night she sort of climbed out of the window in the john and got up on the roof of BIF BURGERS and stripped down to her like coordinated panties and bra. that just switched me off you know—i mean uninhibited is one thing but . . . wow that was too much. anyway she invited me to this blast so i figured what the hell (dont ask me how my polly sigh courses are coming altho im really gonna get back to work soon) especially since melvin and lanny and rog were gonna be there. so friday night i just sort of wandered over to her house which is this really sort of standard executive suburban house made of bricks at the top of this curvy road which curls along the golf course of the Balihai country club where we used to go sleigh riding. so im just kind of moseying up and the house looks fairly quiet but you pop open the front door and all this sort of Hendrix and iron butterfly music just about blasts you into the 17th hole. but there was like nobody upstairs so i went through the kitchen—the refrigerator which is the same yellow as the walls, its door was hanging open and also it looked like somebody had been breaking dishes and grinding them up in the garbage disposal but everything else looked pretty straight. but i opened the basement door and the whole place was a real madhouse. i mean a real horror show, wow there were all those 82,000 freaks plus sammy's $13,000,000 stereo system that just about lacerates your eardrums. i mean jesus id never seen anything like it. anyway i went down the steps and the Sanders have this standard basement with her mother's washing machine and dryer at one end and a ping pong table, the whole scene: but all the furniture and the ping pong table was stacked up against the walls and there was just a like sea of bodies bobbing up and down.

Then wow like the weirdest thing happened. it was like ZONK rite out of the blue: epiphany. (remember epiphany?) im standing there at the bottom of these graypainted wood steps and i see this girl—only i really dont see the girl, just her hair long black hanging all down over her body which is curled up into a little cone in the corner. it just really zapped me you know and all i wanted to do was go over and rapp with her or something she looked so alone and crying. it was just so amazing—because like it was really dark down there but this girl seemed to have a spotlight on her that only i could see. i mean nobody else even knew she was there. i was starting to go over to her when crazy sylvie came running up to me with this joint hanging out of her mouth trying to plant a big smackie on me. like she was all over me saying how she'd thought i'd never come and why hadn't we seen each other since sophomore year—and she spent last semester in London (yea the same old sylvie we knew and loved) taking

this course in contemporary british theater. wow she was so high i couldnt
believe it. i mean i thought she was gonna swallow me or something she was
so giddy. she still has that same hair like the glass wool you use for xmas
trees but like it was down to her ankles. and shes got these really psychedelic
eyes with sequins and like neon lights and all. wow so she grabs my hand
and just plomps into this ocean and we come out on the other side and lanny
and melvin are leaning against the pingpong table toking up. so i start like
huffing and puffing too and got feeling a lot better. and i just like start
rapping with these two guys and they tell me how theyve been heads all
year. lanny's hair is maybe two feet long and really kinky like he's just
plugged himself into an electric outlet in one of those sort of walter lance
cartoons. but he's still got those really brown eyes and really white whites
of his eyes that kind of zap you right away when you see him. he's playing
like fuzz bass in this group called ***The Joint Enterprise***. they're making
150 bills a job now. melvin still has the like U S MARINE flattop but his
eyes just dont look at you anymore. i think his brain's really scrambled.
anyway i got feeling really fine, not flying or anything, but just kind of
floaty around—you know transcendental sort of. wow you remember how
depressed id get sometimes at things wed go to—like id be either really
really depressed or else id be brachiating from the rafters, either upsie or
downsie all the way. well at this point i didnt know which way id go.
    well then jesus things started happenning that you wouldnt like beLIEVE.
like there was crazy sylvie chucking her clothes off again. and like 80%
of everybody there was tripping their minds out. and sammy went over and
zapped up the vol on his stereo til it was just really you know GRONKING
out all these sounds and there was sylvie dancing on top of her sort of
Maytag dryer going out of her head. and she has these real dangly boobs
which we discussed once for they are much to her chagrin but they looked
hilarious and you know how you get sometimes when youre a little stoned—
well jesus i just started laughing til i thought i was gonna herniate and i
just couldnt stop. everybody was like standing around looking at sylvie
and somebody gave her this spangly necklace which flopped around with
her boobs and i was laughing myself to death; but also at the same time i
start feeling really down and bluesy like i didnt have the energy to shut my
jaws and there were all these tears spewing down my face. lanny had
zoomed over to put the kabachee on poor alice macintosh or whatever her
name. but melvin was still standing there like he was asleep, but with his
eyes popped open like my black mollies the ones that died with all those white
fungus spots that made them wriggle to death—well, jesus this syntax is

something for a lawyer huh?—anyway like my black mollies Gordon and
sarah used to sleep, that was the way his eyes were. there was lanny
exploding himself all over alice (tiny little blond girl, like she should be the
sort of Sunbeam bread girl you know) but there she was squinching around
with lanny matching him taking off pieces of clothing. melvin hands me
another joint and i start wheezing like crazy but i just keep getting sicker
and sicker—like seasick you know: i mean its really dark down there in the
Sanders wreck room and there were just all these black bods glumbing
and oozing up and down and this like blue haze floating over everything. i
was choking on the joint and on the incense. jesus my lungs were being
scorched all to hell. and i was getting so drowsy i thought id rack out right
there, except suddenly i remembered i had to find that girl with the hair in
the corner and i looked around for her.

but as luck would have it however sylvie dropped by to see me—i mean
she like really dropped: everybody passed her over their heads and plonked
her at my feet laughing like a hyena. then i really got uptight for i knew i
had to utter something really witty but all i could think of was the girl with
the hair. and the freaky thing was, i kept getting this like religious feeling
about that girl, like maybe she used to be in my SUNDAY SCHOOL class
or something when we met at the VISULITE theater and i was in love with
becky birnley but her father got transferred—well like i was six at the time
so i got over it. and it was really really stuffy where i was so i just plunged
into the fangy faces all mobbing around and kept saying,—pardon me
sir,—all the way thru to the maytag and i scrambled up on top it (it was
pale blue enamel) and started screaming,

   —THE DEVIL IS A LIE AND ALL HIS WORKS ARE LIES!!**
   **at this auspicious point Sammy canned his machine.
   —i just wont believe in lies. i dont believe in satan and lucifer and powers
and principalities! like GOD IS LOVE!—i declaimed in this like Billy Gra-
ham accent looking out over the freaks.—my children be seated,—said i and
they sat at my feet with their little upturned leering faces. somebody handed
me this joint.—im telling it like it is brethren and cistern: unless ye be like
little children then youll be hungup for all eternity. like i mean here's the
fundamental problem with you people (i heard crazy sylvie whooping and
shrieking in the back somewhere), here's where you freaks are going wrong:
you're not freaked OUT; youre freaked IN,—said i, puffing on the joint,
eyeing the sick faces ad nauseum,—but me i'm freaked OUT, and anybody
else who thinks he's freaked OUT i want you to stand up rite now, stand
rite up on your own 2 feet, and make your personal commitment to the lord

37

jesus christ our freaker. for this is the hour of INCISION!—spake i.

—tell it brother, sammy zonked in.

continued i, —like your HEART is where it's at. and weird saint paul like he's the main man babies. he says you got to have circumcision of the HEART. well you cant do that in your present condition because youve got to be under anastasia,—spake i, pointing my bony digit at Anastasia,— when your like cardio-circumcision is being incisioned. and you cant do it alone: somebody else has got to do it babies for you wont be conscious when it happens, at least no more conscious than a child laughing as he races in a windy wheat field: for a child laughing is like well GOD. so git up and quick come here and touch me babies touch me babies touch me babies—, and i was crying and just like crumpling down into these arms.

then what happened was i looked up and there were like these 82,000 creatures bent over me and their bodies and faces were warping up and down the way heat waves from a radiator make something look. i was really you know kabacheed—wow like jesus i thought i was at the bottom of the Dead Sea and this sort of loch ness monster was flumping toward me like the squid in 20,000 leagues. i mean my mind was like BLOWN. it wasnt like the smoking or anything but my mind just blew itself. and i felt this seaweed kind of drifting over my body and feeling real silky on my face and i just reached out for it, and what it turned out to be was her hair, the hair of the girl in the corner. i couldnt believe it i was so happy. i started laughing and laughing, and she had this tiny narrow face with really big orbs and a very thin long nose and exceedingly high teeth—and these terrific shimmering braces. i mean it was the like palisades amusement park when she smiled. but you know she was really really beautiful. and she had these like parenthesis marks when she smiled that came around her mouth. she was laughing too. my head was lying on her knees which were really knobby because she was skinny as a stick figure you used to draw. and then i realized that she didnt FEEL like she was laughing and there was no sound coming from her.

—are you okay?—she queried me.

—yea hes always like this,—i heard melvins voice saying.

—well im fine,—i said trying to regain my composure somewhat. —something just hit me like kablammee.— i managed to prop myself on my elbows and everything started swimming again. and then you know how you get sometimes when youre a little stoned: you get ravenous as a ***30 ft. GILA MONSTER*** or something; i mean i just started going out

of my mind with these hunger pangs. wow ive never been so hungry in my
life. maybe just looking at her made me hungry she was so skinny. anyway i
hobbled up to my feet: and sammy had started his stereo again playing this
real zingy zangy and staticky noise that panged my eardrums like needles.
so there we were like standing by the maytags. she was about up to my chest.
and then she started woozing like she was about to keel over also.—lets go up
to the kitchen and scrounge up some grunts,—i suggested in a friendly
manner.

—that would be good,—she returned.

nobody much was like dancing anymore so we just walked over to the
steps and went up to the kitchen that had these like black and white squares
on the floor you know the whole scene. and then some really groovy things
started happening. she started going around the kitchen opening and
shutting all the cupboard doors one after another til she found a jar of
JIF PEANUT BUTTER: and it was so great just to watch her going around
like that, like a magician, then pulling out this peanut butter like
abracadabra. wow it was great. so i just sat down at the Sanders very
formica table of imitation wood and started looking at the flies that got
zapped in the bottom of the light fixture above the table. and she kept
shuffling all around and reaching into the refrig.

—is orange marmalade okay?—she asked.

—yea its super,—i responded.

so she got a little white plate from the dish rack where all the dishes
were drying and set it in front of me. i heard her rattling around in some
silverware, and also she got some slices of whole wheat bread from the
aluminum breadbox on the counter. and then she put this very carefully
constructed sandwich on my plate and then the greatest part was she set
this very sedate glass of milk beside the plate. i mean i just couldnt believe it.
the glass of milk started getting all this terrific condensation on the outside.
i started eating like a piranha.

—would you care for another?—she questioned.

—three more,—i enthusiastically replied.

wow it was just so great. there i was zonking 4 PB&J sandwiches into me:
and i dont even LIKE peanut butter and jelly, especially orange marmalade.
all of a sudden she sat down also at the table and put her head down on
her arms. her hair spilled almost over to me. —do you feel bad?—i asked.

i heard her like sighing and then she said,—well ive been on speed for
three days and im just coming down,—in this very reedy voice like when

you blow on a blade of grass between your thumbs, a really weird voice.

—wow no wonder youre so withered. like why did you do it? like that's just crazy you know?

—i guess i just wanted to explode myself,—she said pushing her head even harder into her arms.

—why.

—well melvin.

—oh jesus whatd he do.

—well nothing really, just told me why he wanted me around. and it wasnt like i didnt know that already but telling me just popped everything i guess.

—zap: no more illusions,—i said wondering how her small body had taken it, being burned out by melvin first then the speed.

—no thats whats so ridiculous because there werent any left anyway.

then my mind started like floating around the kitchen. the sanders have this you know pineapple clock. its this plastic 3-D pineapple with green spears stabbing out of the top and a clock sort of splatted smack dab in the middle of this bloated yellow pineapple thing. and my mind like got caught on the second hand the way they always have in the movies when somebody sort of latches onto a windmill: and the 2nd hand kept going round and round and round, and the minute hand and hr. hand kept slicing by like sabers, and i was seeing like the floor 1st then the sink then the splotchy ceiling then the refrig then the floor, you know just going around and around. wow it was really freaky. and i could see her still lying down there on the table and she wasnt doing anything. so i said really very innocently,—would you like to go to bed? and she just sort of looked up at me with these very blank eyes. she had this narrow little face.

i went down and took her by the shoulders. i wasnt any like pillar of strength myself but i led her out of the kitchen and down the hall past the lavender john and into the bedroom. well you know how a party is: theres always one room where everybody dumps their coats and stuff that mrs salvage always called a Cloakroom in the 3rd grade. well this was it, her parents sort of baroque bedroom: like there was everybody's coat in a heap on the bed. i started shoving them onto the floor. then wow when i looked up she was taking off her blouse which was this real thin blue silk with pointy collars. i just stood there watching her til she was all undressed and her head bent down so i couldnt see it for her back was to me. like she stood there in this little pile of clothes and she had this really bony structure, really fragile looking. i mean her hips didnt balloon out like yours or somebody's. they were just kind of gentle curves and had a dimple on each side. i went over and turned the lock in the door and flicked the lights off. i stood there til shed rustled all the way into bed and lay there looking at the ceiling her fingers playing on the satin border of the blanket. so then i just walked over and sat on the bedside. then I like pulled the blanket up and stuffed it around her neck you know really softly and watched her top eyelashes til they met the bottom ones.

love,

Mike

Sean Devereux

Day work

Alone, because the rest of the family was gone from the house, quiet, because she did not wish to disturb the sun-heavy stillness, Ruth Ann, sixteen years old in this June summertime, was sitting on the porch of her house, reading, when the man came to the door. She had been there, in the wicker chair for a long time, since early in the day, even before the maids had come down the street, hours ago, in the morning. The arrival of the Negro women had been the only break in the flow of the hot, cloudless morning and Ruth Ann had looked up to watch them trooping down the street from the bus stop, moving together, as they did, in force (like a herd of something, she had thought), until they reached her block, where, cross-ing the street, the group fragmented, as each maid straggled off and dis-appeared, for the day, into the house where she worked. Watching the thick, black figures moving together, then separately, Ruth Ann could tell no difference between them: all heavy bodies in dark dresses which had passed at nine o'clock and whose passing had broken the rhythm of the sun's slow swing up the sky. But the sun had gone on overhead and it was after two when the man came to the door. Ruth Ann thought that he was the mailman and did not look up until he spoke.

"Ma'am," he said, and that was strange to her, because being called "ma'am" by adults, except at laughing times, had not come to her yet. Maybe he could not see very well through the screen and could not tell how old she was.

"Ma'am," he said. "There is a colored woman up the street." The man motioned with his hand. The centers of his eyes were probably tight and small in the sunlight, so that he could not see in where it was dark and cool on the porch of her house.

"She says she's ya'll's maid. Says she's sick. I'd say somebody better go on up there and get her. She looks pretty bad off."

"Where is she?"

"Up at the head of the street by the highway, where the bus stops," he said. "She was sitting down by the ditch there. Sounded like she was crying or somethin' when I walked by, so I went'n stopped. She quit her moanin' soon as she seen me and she wouldn't say what was wrong with her. I'da carried her on down here, but I didn't know she was ya'all's girl or nothing." The man smiled pleasantly. "You see 'em like that all the time," he explained. "They'll go and drink cooking sherry or sterno 'til they cain't even move."

It's Mercita, Ruth Ann thought. Crying, he said. On the ground beside the ditch.

"Thank you," she said and looked directly at the man who had seen Mercita at the side of the road and did not feel as though she must say "sir" to him, because she was older now and felt a certain new power (to decide and act) with her age.

"I never seen her before or I'da given her a hand, ya understand." The man shrugged and turned to go back down the steps.

Ruth Ann put her magazine on the glass-topped table beside her chair.

"All right," she said. "I'll go and see what is the matter with her."

The man walked across the lawn and onto the street. Half-expecting him to be transformed, vaporized in the shimmers which rose up lambent from the street or the asphalt itself to melt and begin to flow, lava-like, around his ankles, Ruth Ann watched the man move on down the street, slowly, as if stunned and held to a listless shuffle by the glare.

"Alibis. And alibis. A waste of time," she said, looking around this porch, her house, her domain, feeling herself there in it. "I think I will go out to the pool. After I see what is wrong with Mercita."

The man was almost out of sight, down the street, where it dipped. She had never seen him before, but he had called her "ma'am." She was glad for that, secured in a certain way by that recognition of what she herself knew, that she was every day older and growing into a certain solid rightness.

She stretched in the chair like a cat, in a long yawning protest at having to leave the cool of the porch where she wanted to remain, slowly turning the pages of the magazine, looking at the pictures, which were in color. The stretching felt good. She tucked her legs under her, closing her eyes, curling back into the chair. When will mother be back? she was thinking. What could be wrong with Mercita? John will call while I am gone and no one will be here. And Mercita is crying by the ditch.

"That's fine," she said to the silence. "Really great. She eats too much greasy bacon for breakfast and I have to go hold her hand."

She got up, put on her shoes, because the street and even the sand beside it would be hot, and opened the door. As she went down the steps, out from under the porch, the sunlight was very bright in her eyes and the heat was all around, like a solid mass which received her and closed in behind her.

Ruth Ann decided to take the car, which was there in the driveway, because it would be quicker that way and not so hot. Mercita might need to be brought back to the house.

She lowered the top, letting the sunlight pour in and fill the car until Ruth Ann was sodden with warm light, because right now was summer which had been so long in coming but which was here now and which was very hot, but it would pass and be over too quickly for her and she could always stay in her house where it was cool, when the sun made her anxious with its heat.

With her foot light on the accelerator, driving up the street, looking at the houses on both sides, the stucco houses, which were pastel bright in the sunlight now, Ruth Ann was wondering if John would call while she was gone and wondering then what was wrong with Mercita who never got sick like the rest of them.

"Mercita wasn't with the others at nine," she said to the radio. "I didn't think of that. But Mercita never gets sick."

She was healthy, so big and always laughing, quietly, to herself, then suddenly out loud, with a strong laugh when you said something to her.

"Cain't keep a stick a furniture in the house for that boy a mine. He goes and ramshackles everything I got." She was always speaking of her children and laughing.

Mercita was so big. Ruth Ann slowed in front of a friend's house, but saw no car in the drive, so she went on. Big. Not fat. Not fat like white women are fat, anyway, with fleshy, wattled arms. Mercita's arms were heavy and thick, not wrinkled, flabby. She never missed work. Thinking of her dependability, thinking how well she knew Mercita and how much she liked the big Negro woman, Ruth Ann smiled and then these thoughts blurred and were gone because the houses were good to look at in the sunlight.

Ruth Ann did not see Mercita until she had driven almost to the highway. The colored woman had crawled back under the trees on the far side of the ditch and, with her back against the base of a pine tree, she lay on a plastic raincoat, which she had spread on the ground under her. Ruth Ann parked the car on a narrow shoulder between the street and the ditch. She had never seen a Negro lying down before. When Ruth Ann stepped from the car, Mercita leaned forward and tried to stand, but she rocked back

44

limply against the tree and was watching Ruth Ann with a look which was blear and sad and something more.

Ruth Ann walked toward Mercita who did not say anything and who was holding onto the pine tree.

"Are you all right, Mercita?" she said, stopping at the edge of the ditch, staring back at the woman who was very dark and whose eyes white and big that way did look comical almost. And I will have to get her into the car and take her back quickly, Ruth Ann was thinking, because John is probably trying to call me now and mother is not back yet.

"How long have you been here?" Ruth Ann said, looking down at the mud in the ditch at her feet. "How long have you been waiting here?"

"Most all day." Mercita spoke as if she were tightened up inside.

"What is wrong?" Ruth Ann smiled to ease her and dispel the fear of the woman whose eyes were wide from that fear, she knew, because Negroes always looked that way when they were afraid. "Today's the hottest it's been so far. Everybody's feeling it. Get in the car and I'll take you on down to the house."

Ruth Ann spoke to her and stayed beside the ditch.

"Where'd you figure I was at?" Mercita said. "What'd you think when I didn't come this morning?"

"I forgot it was Tuesday. I didn't notice."

"Your mama home?"

"No she went into town."

"You go on back to the house," Mercita said. "Go on back and leave me be."

"Mercita," Ruth Ann said. (What is wrong with her? Anything so wrong that she can't get into the car and come to our house, where she can sit on the porch and drink ice tea from the Mason jar which she always keeps in the refrigerator?)

"Go on away from here."

"Mercita, you'll be all right, if you come sit in the shade and cool off. It's just the heat."

"Let me be, Ruth Ann. Take your car back to the house. I found me a cool place under these trees and I kin wait all right now."

"Mercita, are you sick or what?"

Mercita looked at her for a time.

"This ain't no place for you."

"What do you mean?"

"You know and you can go on now."

Ruth Ann started across the ditch.

"Go on," Mercita said. "If your mama asks, tell her that I felt bad, I was dizzy and sick on my stomach when I got up this mornin'."

"You better come out of the sun then."

Mercita was looking away.

"I had me the first feelin' before I even got to the bus. I was draggin' an' had to ride the late bus, so the rest of them come on without me. I been waitin' right on since then." Mercita was tearing long strips of plastic from the sleeve of her raincoat.

"We have . . ."

"It was real bad for a while and I asked a man who came by . . . I asked some man to bring your mama . . . I don't guess I shoulda done that. There wasn't any need to do that." She began to shred a corner of the sleeve with her teeth now.

"But, Mercita, we have . . ."

"You go on back to the house."

"Why?" said Ruth Ann, now on the edge of knowing why the woman did not want and why she would have to stay.

"Mercita, don't be crazy like that. Its too soon," Ruth Ann said (We knew; the whole family knew. We have laughed with her and teased her about not being sure, because she was so big, always, anyway.)

Mercita was shaking her head slowly. Ruth Ann reached under her arm to help her up.

"Come on," Ruth Ann said. "You just feel faint from the heat. I am waiting for a phone call, so if you keep on being this way, I'll have to drag you down there."

Ruth Ann laughed thinking of that, of taking her by the two hands and dragging the heavy, black body along, bouncing through the ditch and scraping over asphalt and gravel.

Ruth Ann looked at her and was laughing, when, with suddenness, Mercita was heaving forward and pressing her hands, one over the other, low on her stomach, and was saying,

"Oh, sweet Jesus. No."

Ruth Ann felt a searing contraction across her stomach at that moment when she knew all up and down her own body what was happening, at that moment when she was wrenched out of fascination into something else which became the abstract, bookpage quality "fear" given substance and texture by the look and by the sound and by the smell and by the touch of a writhing, sweating, clutching black woman. Ruth Ann pulled her hand

back and looked away, seeing stucco houses, pink and yellow and green
and white in the sunlight, but none of the men and women, whom she knew,
nor their children, whom she knew, none of them came out of the houses.

Ruth Ann stepped back from Mercita.

"You can't let this happen here . . . There are cars going by on the high-
way, Mercita. You can't . . ."

Ruth Ann wanted to take her by the shoulders and shake her to make
her stop. (I would be right to leave here; this thing is in no way connected
with any act of mine, past, present or future.)

The cars—some of them bright and new—were blurring past them and
because they were easiest to watch now, Ruth Ann held her face toward
the road and let the metal shapes, shining with the sun on them, she let
these solid, certain shapes advance toward her and, as they grew larger,
fill her mind, pushing out any thought which began to form there.

She was keeping her eyes away long enough so that when she looked at
Mercita again, the colored woman would be smiling and would talk about
her children who were small and shy. When Ruth Ann turned, slowly brush-
ing her gaze across pine trunks and over sandy ground, she saw Mercita
doubled over, hugging herself with her arms crossed, but the moaning sound,
which throbbed from low in her body and was involuntary as the whole
happening was involuntary and beyond anyone's control, this moaning had
stopped. Mercita spat in the sand.

"Ain't the first time," she said, staring.

When Mercita coughed and spat again, Ruth Ann turned her head and
was looking away, far down to where the mailman was climbing up a sloping
green lawn, where a sprinkler played in circles over the wet grass and shot
silver arcs into the hot, dense air. The grass was greener there than here
where Mercita lay on a raincoat in the dry, pine straw littered sand and
the figure of the mailman was far away from them and small, but becoming
bigger now and then bigger and moving up and down because Ruth Ann was
running to him, falling now in the thick grass on the slope of the ditch, but
up again and running, running.

She heard Mercita shout something behind her but did not stop because
she was building in her mind what she would say to him, running to him to
ask—this first, because she did not wish to shock him—if he had any mail
for her family, saying this which he expected to be said to him. Yes, 5118,
the red-brick house on the corner. Ruth Ann was running over the asphalt
with the heat coming up through her shoes and she was planning to tell him
(saying it out loud, practicing so that he would not laugh) tell him slowly,

because he would be inclined to laugh at her, that Mercita, who was their maid, who ironed for them and cleaned and stayed late to cook dinner on Thursdays when her mother had the meeting, that their black Mercita was having a child born of her at the edge of the woods, by the highway, where the cars were going past. On his route, on his daily rounds, the mailman probably had little opportunity to see anyone do this and he would be surprised by this birthing beside the ditch.

Then she stopped by a yellow sign with words written on it in black: "SLOW, Children at Play." Ruth Ann held onto the sign, breathing with hard, abrasive gulps, and looking for the mailman down among the green lawns. She saw him moving down the street, away from her, steadily, with an efficient walk as if he had many more letters to deliver before his day was finished and he could go home. He walked as though he did not have time to listen and believe her, as if his mechanical movement could not be stopped until his rounds were completed and the winding had run down.

Still, she reflected, he would be surprised. This was the last thought she had before some apparatus in her brain locked gears and clamped tight, leaving her conscious only of the sun, certain that above her someone held a huge magnifying glass and concentrated all the rays of the sun on the top of her skull (the center spot, where a baby's head hardens last; where a man's head grows bald first). A red, gaseous, explosive sun was burning a hole there in the top of her head, where the hair parted. She held onto the sign with both hands. The yellow of the sign was crusted over and dulled by a layer of road dust and she rocked the sign back and forth, strangling it, but the dust would not shake off, so she reached up and ran her hand over the face of the sign and wiped a swath through the dust. She was pushing her hand against the sign so hard that it bent backwards and her hand was rubbing in wide circles, faster and then faster to keep the thoughts away. The dirt felt gritty against the metal as she rubbed and this angered her, so she took her hand away and looked at it. Seeing it dirty and cut meant nothing to her because she did not know what to do now and she slammed the base of her fist against the sign.

A woodpecker thrummed on a pine trunk above her. With wonder and a warm grateful feeling, she looked up at the bird: the constrictions on her brain loosened, fell away and thought was drawn out of her by the drumming. Listening to the loud, distinct staccato of the red-headed bird, which was the only sound in the times between the passing cars, Ruth Ann was distant from what was happening up the road behind her back. Her feeling for the bird was easy and right, but finally after a long time, she took her hands away from the sign and began walking back toward Mercita. With her eyes above, then below the dark tunnel of Mercita's gaze, Ruth Ann came up the street and crossed the ditch at the place where the grass was trampled down.

"I went to get some help," she said. "But there isn't anyone."

Mercita did not answer her.

"Hear the woodpecker?"

The bird telegraphed some secret, coded message against the wood, and then was gone, leaving her.

"Shall I try to call a doctor or something?" (What would I say to him? How would I explain? People do not have babies in places where there are no doctors.)

She was thinking again, with intermittent visions, like the quickly gone, upsidedown numbers flicking on the screen at the end of a movie. Then her mind fixed on the thought of clean sheets and hot water. (How and for what do they use the sheets and use the water?)

Mercita was unmoving, expressionless, silent.

"I don't have to stay here. If you just stay there, feeling sorry for yourself, I am going to leave. If you won't even help yourself, I have every right to do that," Ruth Ann said, speaking to no one, really, because the light-headedness made her uncertain that she spoke at all. Hard, so that her jaw clicked, she dropped to her knees on solid ground near Mercita and, feeling the blood flow back into her brain, giving it ballast, she was wondering with something of fear still, what she, Ruth Ann, who was no more and no less than the-girl-next-door to the people who lived in the house beside hers, what she was doing here.

It was quiet now and a dog barked on the next block and everything was as it had been before, but Ruth Ann saw a dark stain in the middle of Mercita's dress. The dress was black and had white flowers on it. A first breeze stirred the tops of the pine trees, giving Ruth Ann a coolness under her arms where it was damp, and the coolness spread into a chill over her.

"Come on, Mercita. I can take you to a doctor." Ruth Ann reached under Mercita's arm to help her to her feet. Mercita bent forward, resisting, withdrawing.

"Ain't no doctor gonna . . ." Mercita began to speak but stopped, shook her head and let it go limply back against the tree. Ruth Ann saw that she had bitten through her lower lip and was drooling a thread of blood onto her chin. The blood did not look the same to Ruth Ann, was not like blood that she had seen before, but was a strange color and different against black skin. Mercita was crying, with tiredness, and Ruth Ann, closer to her now, saw that her eyes were not so white but were yellow and netted with small blood vessels. Red lightning against a discolored sky. Whenever a tear came, the brown center of her eye was magnified, the yellow and red ran together and were blurred and when the tear dropped away on down her face, the angry red lines were there still, distinct against the sickly yellow, like scratches on smooth skin.

Ruth Ann, sixteen years old, who was the child of her parents, who lived down the street in the house which was now in the sun, who was there as a witness, and whom no one of all the people she knew, whom no one, least of all herself, would ever have expected to be anything more than a witness, she because of all these things (and more, of course) saw pain and weariness and humility and some shame, wet on rough brown skin, and Ruth Ann bent over to offer her pity and her understanding and the touch of her white hand.

"Come with me now, Mercita," she said softly, conscious of the softness. (This, her vision then: crowds, watching and weeping, writhing in violined catharsis.)

Mercita pushed the hand away from her shoulder, and offered Ruth Ann only the mask, the stare, direct and unmoving, as if Mercita no longer looked upon her—Ruth Ann, a person—but upon a decision now formed which she regarded with tightlipped finality.

Then Mercita grunted and stared differently, stared the way Ruth Ann did when the wind was knocked out of her and she could not say anything or even move. Mercita was taking in air with tight, quick breaths and her hands, wrinkled on the back, Ruth Ann saw, were up the side of the pine tree, gripping it and clawing at the loose bark. Mercita was flexing her left leg and her heel tore through the raincoat and was digging a furrow in the ground underneath. Then, she breathed a deeper easier breath and her leg stretched out with a jerk and lay flat on the ground. She leaned back against the tree. As she took her hands away from the bark, one hand was sticky with pine sap so that the sand stuck to it when she let her hand fall to the ground. Mercita ran one bare arm across her face where the crying ran down.

Ruth Ann reached out to the solidity of the pine trunk; she never wanted to hear that gasping sound again.

Ruth Ann looked over her shoulder, down the street, but saw no one. She looked back to the highway. It was a short time after three and the first wave of homecoming traffic had begun; husbands and fathers, on the way to their homes, were driving by fast. Ruth Ann closed her eyes and the sound of the cars going by went on and on and did not stop.

"Can you get in the car, Mercita? If you can, please, somehow, get into the car, I will take you to the hospital. Please."

The sibilance of cars going past her through the air was soothing.

"Where at?"

"Baptist Hospital," said Ruth Ann. "I can take you to Baptist Hospital. It's not that far. They have everything and its clean there."

Ruth Ann waited, looking at the ground. A swarm of ants was portaging a large beetle toward a sand volcano which poured a stream of many more ants.

"Shit," said Mercita. "That place cost me more'n I kin make in two years."

"Mercita, what . . ."

Ruth Ann looked up quickly and saw the sweat-drop trails down the side of Mercita's face and the patches of black hair, which were stuck, wet and flat against her temple.

"Ain't nobody livin' on day work pay, goin' to no Babdist Hospidal," she said.

"You have to do something."

"Last time and time before I went to the Medical Center."

"That's where they take people who've been stabbed and shot. You can't go there. I'm not allowed to drive down there."

"I ain't goin' to no Babdist Hospidal."

Ruth Ann was certain that it was at least three-fifteen now. The sun was down lower; the edge was gone from the heat, but the afternoon was still a vat of warm, soupy liquid, from which she was unable to climb. Mercita had said nothing for a long time. She was no longer leaning back against the tree but was sitting up now.

"Why did you ever come to work today?" Ruth Ann said, because she had to talk now, to batter back the silence with any words. "Mother wouldn't have minded, if you had stayed at home."

More ants had joined the task force; the dead beetle was on his back moving forward on a hundred little legs.

Because the afternoon sun hesitated and hung red there before it dropped into evening, the air was hot yet and the heat rose up from the highway, as the sun, at that angle, glared off the asphalt.

"It's still hot," Ruth Ann said, wanting to scrape away the layer of

51

sweat on her own body, seeing the dress wet and darker against Mercita's back. She could barely smell the earlier, flimsy-sweet smell of department store cologne which had been washed away in the heavy sweat of a long day's labor in the sun. After two cars went by and then a school bus, Ruth Ann could see the dust hang thick in the air.

"Mercita, can't you tell when this is going to happen? Why didn't you stay home today?"

Mercita did not look up.

"You were stupid to come today."

Mercita was rubbing her hands together, wiping them on her dress, but the sand was stuck to the pine sap and would not come off.

"It's your own fault for coming. You can't expect . . ."

Mercita turned around, embraced the tree and started to pull herself to her feet.

"Mercita, don't. Stay there. I'll get someone."

Ruth Ann stood up and took Mercita's arm, but she, standing now, shook off Ruth Ann's grasp.

"I have to help you. I have to do something. Please get into the car and let me take you to the Medical Center."

Then, Ruth Ann saw that, down where Mercita was watching, the maids were leaving the houses and coming together in the street. Like a net, she thought quickly. Thrown out at nine in the morning and pulled back in at three. With the constancy of fishermen and their tides. Standing there, with their paper shopping bags, milling around in the street, they always waited until they were together like that in a body, before they advanced.

Behind Ruth Ann, Mercita began a staggering movement toward the road. Then, she was falling, surprisingly silent as she fell, lurching forward down the bank of the ditch, down into the high grass which grew out of the mud. Then, she lay there in the grass.

Ruth Ann was kneeling beside her, trying to lift her face out of the mud.

"Mercita. Mercita. Why did you do that? I was going to help you."

Mercita pulled her arm out from under her and pushed Ruth Ann away. She lifted her head from the mud, like a huge, ageless turtle; Ruth Ann almost laughed, was horrified by her own impulse. When Mercita looked at her, she saw a smear of oily slime on one side of her face, over one eye.

"Where you been all day, white girl?" she said. "The sun's been hot."

Crawling forward, pulling at the grass stalks, Mercita kept watching down the street, seeing the formation gather strength, as the Negro women came out of the houses and fell in with it. They were less than a block away, when the maids saw Mercita crawling out to the side of the road. They stopped laughing and talking. Coalescing in a new silence, they moved faster.

Ruth Ann watched the approaching phalanx of heavy, dark bodies. She saw that one woman in front had an arrangement of artificial flowers pinned to her hat. Ruth Ann kept her eyes on the flowers. They looked like a Christmas ornament and were colorful and wrong there with the dark print dresses.

Then, they were coming closer up along the ditch. The woman with the flowers was running toward them with her feet tearing through the high grass and splashing, sinking into the mud. Ruth Ann stepped back as the woman came up beside them and stopped, looking down at Mercita, who lay on her side now.

"Mercita, your time come, honey?" the woman said. There was mud splattered on her bare leg and on the bottom of her dress.

"Yes," Mercita answered and the other women were in a circle around her now, some of them kneeling and talking softly to her. She was crying again. Then the woman with the flowers and green leaves in her hat was kneeling on the bed of bent grass, fanning Mercita's face with a piece of cardboard.

"You're gonna be all right, 'cause we're here now," she said.

Ruth Ann saw that the harsh strained look was gone from Mercita's face, which was wet with the now released tears. The colored women did not speak to Ruth Ann, who had risen and backed into the shadows under the trees.

They helped Mercita to her feet. One of them wiped her face with a large handkerchief. Looking straight ahead, with the tears following the furrows down her face, held upright by other arms, black and thick like her own, Mercita stumbled across the street, toward the bus stop, without looking back.

"Wait. I have a car," Ruth Ann said, but it was too late for Mercita to hear her, because she was sobbing out loud now and the other women did not stop to listen. They moved ahead toward the road.

"Let me go with you. I won't know what happened. Please. I did help you, Mercita. I tried to take . . ."

The colored women waited for two cars to pass and then led Mercita across the highway.

"Please," Ruth Ann cried, watching them from behind.

She wanted to look on down the street and see the good late-afternoon things, of children playing and of fathers coming home, but she was seeing at this end of the street now: these women, these people, were moving away from her like one silent beast which had awakened now after a long sleep and which groped forward in mole-like blindness, with gathering strength, on many dark thick legs.

Ruth Ann was standing at the edge of the woods when the bus came. All of the maids got on and Mercita was with them. They all climbed onto the bus, because their day of work was finished.

Not until the bus was gone did Ruth Ann think of the child. Now, her mind fixed on this, which was—should have been—the central fact of this happening; she wondered about his, or her, life which would begin today and which would continue simultaneous with her own for a time. But she tired of these thoughts, because they went nowhere, only into confusion. With the car behind her, top-down, forgotten, she began walking down the street toward her house.

Then, she saw a brown whiskey bottle ahead of her in the ditch beside the road. The bottle was embedded in the mud and the label, fuzzy, white, was nearly worn away. Ruth Ann picked up the bottle and threw it down hard against the asphalt. With her foot, she crushed the large pieces of broken glass, grinding them against the surface of the road.

"If she was dumb enough to come to work, then . . . What was I supposed to . . .?"

Still talking, unaware of what she was saying, Ruth Ann looked for another bottle in the mud, but there were none. The thought that now she would have to call John became important and annoying somewhere in her mind. She walked on down the street toward her house where she would sit on the porch until her mother called her to wash her hands for dinner.

Joan Swift

Six poems

Halley's

Whether my grandmother's large red hand
shook their shoulders awake
or the coil of her braid shooting sparks
in the kerosene lamplight was touch enough,
they've forgotten.

Sleep was a syrup in their thighs,
the cool linoleum slipping beneath their feet.
Was there a window dark as a river?
They cannot remember
odor of pulled sheep sorrel,
the scrubbed smell of her flannel nightgown,
not even the waiting sky itself,
nor that it was May in nineteen-ten.

When the brilliant bow was drawn against the dark
at the top of their heads,
the comet springing from one horizon to the other
like a fox with its tail on fire,
they may have held breath or exclaimed
for the streak, the extraordinary,

but remember only
that she woke them into the blaze of her caring,
stirred the bottom of the night
with her scintillant eyes
which keep returning.

Oxygen

Bearer of finches and clouds, pale atmosphere
Holds it, a rose in a bouquet of daisies,
Although odorless, the one-fifth of each breath
That keeps flesh firm on the bone, the old blood warm,

Thought bright as young fish in the brain. Botanists
Say that plants exhale this element, push it
Out through olive skin. But who can say whether
It is this calm expiration or merely

Twilight and the first dew when, bending above
Vinca, hovering viburnum leaves,
Underneath wide maples, we fill our nostrils
With a cool abundance of what gives us life?

Epithalamium for a fisherman

May those ruddy auguries, rainbows,
sunlight and waterflash,
blaze in their streams,
steelhead beat on anvils
of riverrock, joy.
May the acrobat salmon
illumine this day.

Where your two boats turn
in their moorage,
lilies on stems
gliding the still lagoon,
may gulls cross canopies
over you,
candlefish light your bows.

May the pole star bait your journey
north, north
to ice-green halibut fields
with porpoises weaving you
garlands of foam.
May you dream on a level deck.
May the moon fill your net.

Border collies

They might be angels
Guiding the ark to its peak,
The way they gallop through snow,
Two black border collies
With our sleigh.

No horses draw us
Under the star-hazed night,
But a tractor,
And the steer shuffle and low
Behind gates.

When the sled runners buck in drifts,
One nips the tires
Or barks *take care, take care,*
The night is a sea of twigs.
When we jostle in the rough hay,

Their herd,
They leave the headlights
Spilling yellow pool
To bound in the shadows
At our feet.

Collies, the hills roll on like waves,
Yet we are safe.
Here is a level pasture,
Aspen-hedged, a bridge,
The windows of a farmhouse.

They wag their tails
And the air is plumed.
Giving us ground and light,
They poke wet noses
Into heaven, our hands.

Sestina for Bart

He sits stiff as a stalk
In that forest of metal bars
Surrounding his hospital bed.
He avoids my eyes time
After time, prefers the straw
Rooted in soup, the watch

A grandmother gave. I watch
Him grope for it, a stalk
Of fingers scratching his straw-
Colored shirt. Numbers, bars—
The watch is a toy, its time
Without motion like his bed.

He finds it on his bed,
That huge moon of a watch,
Caresses its rigid time,
Listens for the stalk
Of minutes, shrugs. Behind bars
He fingers the orange straw.

His grandmother's put a straw
Of hope beside his bed
In water: petals, bright bars
Of color for him to watch.
He is four. He has a stalk
Of cancer telling time

Inside his stomach. Time,
Time is an orange straw
Every four hours, a stalk
Of paper brought to his bed,
Or nurses changing watch,
The slip of the moon's bars

Down walls, the cinnabars
Of dusk, dawn. Sometimes
Time is T.V. I watch,
A stranger blown like straw
To sit between bed and bed.
Like wolves the minutes stalk

The still bars of his bed.
One straw of time, one straw:
Each day is a watched green stalk.

John Crowe Ransom reads Theodore Roethke
May 25, 1964

Cheeks the dead man bent to,
kissed (o spring!)
sway forward on dark heads.
We are still with listening.

John Whiteside's daughter's bells
toll for Jane.
Pinewoods of Tennessee
sough on the ear like rain.

A southern tongue. Suddenly
in the mind
that other voice unfurls
its shadow on the sand.

Caroline Krause

Dinesen

None of us had ever given much attention to Drummont until he disappeared. As his assistant, everyone expected me to know where he had gone, but more than that—why. He and I, however, had never worked together closely, for he rarely came to his official laboratory. We had been assigned chromatographic analyses of a larger experiment involving two of the other men at Dinesen. It was this work that occupied my own time as I had soon found myself working alone. During the hours away from the laboratory I read in the library for further research. The only other event of my day consisted of the walk from my cabin to the laboratory.

The estate of Dinesen had been set in an old pine forest about twenty miles from the nearest town. None of the men who worked here ever went into town for living necessities, they were always somehow available for us. We were, rather, left to work alone and each man had his own three-room cabin removed by sight and sound from all other cabins. The only buildings in intimate proximity were the two laboratories and the main lodge. Each man was assigned one portion of the largest laboratory, Pinewood. At the time of Drummont's disappearance only nine of us worked at the laboratory, so the kennel of dogs had been moved from the smaller building into the second floor of Pinewood. It did afford more room for work with the animals, but the noise was often unbearable and I had thought that it was this irritation that had kept Drummont from the laboratory. His disappearance was discovered rather slowly. I had not seen him in the kennels for several weeks, but it was not until we had all gathered in the lodge for the monthly reports that it was evident he had disappeared. These gatherings were never compulsory, but it had become a tradition for all of us to meet once a month. Clark had been at Dinesen longer than the rest of us and when I had arrived, five years ago, it was he who had informed me of the custom. Drummont had told me after one of these meetings that Clark had begun this tradition as he felt that too much isolation was unhealthy.

I was glad for these meetings and for the reason that Clark had set forth. Drummont had explained to me, in his usual patient manner, that it was because I had been here only a few years and, after I had been here a while, would find these meetings far too frequent. That was over two years ago, when I had first become his assistant, and I still cherished the gatherings in the lodge.

The one clock at Dinesen, placed in the main hall of Pinewood, was only used for experimental timing. It had become almost superfluous to our existence, for the men in the labs knew their materials so well that no timing was necessary and the remainder of our lives was centered on the sun. Each cabin had been so constructed that the morning sun would serve as a single alarm clock. By the time we had washed and dressed, breakfast would be in a basket outside the cabin. Pinewood followed breakfast and for most of us was the whole of each day. I had always been amazed that, in all my years at Dinesen, there had been only three times that I had walked up the hill to Pinewood with another man. Lunch was usually served in the laboratory but we rarely stopped working long enough to sit down to eat. I had taken my cue early from Drummont, marvelling at his quiet sense of dedication. Nothing could keep him from his work. He seemed to receive more sustenance from the laboratory than from any meal he ever ate. Every-day at noon he would go to the dumbwaiter and take out our food. He would give me my allotted portion and then return with his own to his working table to continue whatever he had begun. He always ate all that he had been given but it was rather an unconscious effort, well-learned from years of habit.

None of us was compelled to remain at Dinesen. We could come and go as we pleased and leave whenever we so decided. However, it was like the unspoken custom of the monthly meetings and no man had ever left Dinesen once he had arrived. Drummont was the first.

Clark had been sitting by the fire when I finally arrived at the lodge. Sisemont and Hannon were still upstairs in the library. When the other five arrived, the meeting would begin.

"Sit down, Emile."

I would always be the child of Dinesen to these men. Even Clark called me by my given name while everyone else was addressed by his surname. I always felt less offended by Clark than the others. His age had given him a warmth and softness unlike anything else at the estate. Drummont was the only other man in whom I sensed this gentle quality; but he was so much the loner that we rarely shared our lives. I always felt, that in spite of him-self, Drummont would have liked to share whatever mysteries he felt with me, above all the others. Clark seemed to realize our latent kinship and it was for this reason that he had expected me to know about Drummont's unprecedented departure. It was Clark, too, who knew how much I disliked the continual isolation at Dinesen.

"And how is your work progressing, Emile?"

"So much is routine, Clark, I often feel superfluous. Someday I think I shall begin something on my own."

"Now don't underrate your training, Emile. To do something on your own—all that we know now must be second nature."

"You mean like Drummont running Pelt's analysis?"

"Pelt's analysis?! I thought you both were running tests for Forestier and Kedgewick."

I immediately regretted my allusion to Drummont. No one had ever been officially in charge of us, but Clark had silently become our leader.

"Drummont has been here longer than any of us, Emile. I am sure that he is very much aware of what he is doing. I was surprised only because Pelt's analysis involves a relatively new field of science and there are few men who understand its implications."

I could not help feeling free with Clark and, as I had been puzzled by Drummont's actions of late, I continued.

"I've been doing Forestier's analyses myself. Why for the past year Drummont has been coming less and less frequently to the labs, until . . . well, for the past several months I have seen him perhaps two or three times."

"For an old man he has too many secrets in his head. I think I shall have a little talk with him tonight. He works too much alone."

"He has my curiosity up, too, Clark. I don't dare question him when he does come to the lab, for he always looks so tired and ever so busy."

"He's not like anyone else that you will find here, Emile. He arrived just before I did and no one ever knew exactly where he came from. As you well know, he never speaks unless questioned and . . ."

"Well, good-evening, Clark et petit Emile."

It was Forestier. I didn't have to turn in my chair to know—no one else addressed me as he did. He had come from France eleven years ago and, unlike the rest of us, had never lost his identity to Dinesen. I had walked to Pinewood with him one morning and it was our conversation that had led me to work with Drummont on Forestier's experiment. That had been over two years ago and, since then, I had only seen him at the monthly meetings.

"Please be seated, Forestier. Ah, we are almost ready to begin— Kedgewick, London and Plummet have just arrived."

"Isn't Drummont in the library? When I came by his cabin, all the lights were shut off and the place seemed deserted."

"He probably left early to walk a while, only Sisemont and Hannon are upstairs."

"We shall wait a few moments for him, he knows all too well when we begin here."

The few moments turned into many, and I watched Forestier put new logs to the fire, letting each burn well before he added another. The room was quiet, and it was not unusual that we never had any extended conversations. Each man had his own work to do and it was by gracious consent that many of them shared that much with us. I sat, slightly hypnotized by the fire, beside Clark. Every now and then my thoughts would turn to Drummont in a futile attempt to understand why he seemed so different from the rest.

It was Kedgewick who first became impatient.

"We have certainly waited a sufficient time for Drummont. He has obviously subordinated custom to some independent folly."

"Now, we all know that that is quite unlike Drummont. He may not like the frequency of these meetings, but he still comes. Emile, go to his cabin and see if perhaps something has delayed him."

I complied with Clark's suggestion and left the lodge for the forest. My lamp was low so I borrowed Forestier's to make sure of my way, although I could have easily gone through the darkness. The light from the lamp cast heavy shadows within its circle of illumination, and I walked slowly from the lodge enjoying this unscientific observation. I was greatly surprised to find Drummont's cabin so completely deserted; but the others were incredulous. We all hurried back to his cabin and found proof of his departure in the empty rooms. Only his bed and chair remained. He had left, but he had not left in haste.

Sisemont was the most unreasonable in his reaction. He even felt it a good riddance and suggested that we not admit him should Drummont ever return to Dinesen. Forestier, however, suggested that I try to find some reason for this unprecedented departure.

We had no meeting that night; I was to call one when I could account for this disturbing event. I understood their reasons for choosing me, but as I returned to my cabin, I felt so very unqualified. We had had little conversation and only meager efforts at speculation. I had eagerly agreed to meet with Clark after I had done some searching, and then we two would present the matter to the rest. I found it quite difficult, however, even to impose a method on my task and soon found it impossible to sleep. Drummont and I had been closest friends; at least we had shared a closer understanding than anyone else at Dinesen, but that, too, was meager.

It was still dark when I finally decided that sleep was futile. I dressed hurriedly and lit my lamp in the darkness. I had never been about at this hour, and it was impossible for me to tell the time. Drummont's cabin was farthest of all from Pinewood, and I worked my way slowly through the darkness. I discovered no hint—nothing that would help me to understand his sudden disappearance. He had very carefully emptied the entire cabin. Only those things—the bed and chair—which had been issued us, remained. It even appeared that he had carefully cleaned everything so that not even a vestige of his own dust would be found.

It was still quite dark when I went outside to look around. Not knowing what to look for, I made several careful circles about the cabin easily. I had last visited Drummont a year and a half ago and still remembered how important it was for him to keep his entry clear. At that time it was in better condition than my own, but now the forest growth formed an even tighter circle around his cabin. The juniper at the back of the cabin hugged the sides and had begun to reach into the front. It seemed that he had not even lived here at all. The lamp flickered and cast confusing shadows over the ground. I walked to the back of the cabin and sat down to wait for the sun to rise. The lamp did not yield enough light to give the area any real search. The ground was slightly moist and the hewn logs of the cabin did not afford a comfortable back rest; but I was reluctant to go inside as I might miss something that only the morning sun could reveal.

In spite of my awkward position I managed to fall asleep and it was only by well-learned habit that I finally awoke to find the woods well-lighted and the day very much begun. The lamp was still burning so I snuffed it out and placed it inside the cabin—I had little use for it now. The day was crisp and quiet and I marvelled at the beauty of the forest so far removed from the activities of the laboratory. Drummont must have loved it here, for his cabin was on the border of the estate with nothing but woods all around him. The tall pines provided formidable shelter and the brilliant sun was diffused gently here. At the base of one of these pines I noticed a slightly worn trail into the woods. The path had not been travelled often for there was a great deal of juniper obscuring its direction. It must have been a walk for Drummont and, following it, I found myself going deeper and deeper into seemingly interminable forest. The path came to an end quite suddenly, and it occurred to me that perhaps this wasn't a mere walking-way, after all. I began to search the area for something. I wasn't quite sure what I expected to find, but I knew that one does not build a path into nowhere . . . and just stop. But I could find nothing and no other trail lay before me. I had put too much faith in Drummont . . . it *was* a path into nowhere.

I sat beside an old cedar and lit a cigarette, quite fed up with the whole business of the search. Drummont had clearly left and taken all his meager belongings with him. The ground was cold and hard here in the depths of the forest and I took off my coat to lay it on the ground. When I stood up I realized that I had not been sitting on the ground at all, but rather a wooden door. Eagerly I grabbed the latch to pull it open, but it would not move. I broke off a sturdy branch and worked it under the edge of the trap. After a few tries, I succeeded and the door sprang open. Below was a dark tunnel into the earth. I cleared some of the fallen debris from the entry and found a handmade ladder fastened to one side.

The descent into the earth was rather long. The ladder had, at one time, been a sturdy pine, but now lay hewn and quartered—a link, perhaps, between Drummont and the rest of the world. The ladder led me into a long narrow corridor skillfully cut through a maze of great roots. I regretted not having brought my lamp but, by extending my arms at each side, I could feel my way through the tunnel by pulling myself from one root to the next. I attempted to pace the length of the hall and had marked twenty-one when I reached a dead end. This time, however, the wall ahead was made of wood, not soil and root, so I felt its surface for a latch.

The door opened into what seemed to be comfortable living quarters furnished with several chairs, a desk and a bed, and all appeared to have been made by hand. The room itself was approximately twenty feet square and was well lighted by five hanging oil lamps. Most curious of all features of the room, however, was its general appearance. If this were Drummont's underground home, he had not disappeared at all, but rather moved all his belongings here. The bookcases were full, papers and notebooks were scattered on the desk and the bed was unmade. Drummont was obviously living here now, and I had chanced upon his secret while he had been out.

I sat in the chair beside the desk and decided to wait for his return. The room had been well-kept, and, although the ground at the surface of the forest was moist and cold, the walls and floor here seemed to generate warmth. A cigarette, obviously laid down and forgotten, lay on the corner of the desk. Fortunately, it had burned itself out without setting fire to all the papers strewn over the desk. Drummont's handwriting was rather illegible, but I could determine that most of the papers were letters he was intending to mail. Three or four notebooks were piled carefully on one corner of the desk. All of them were of the standard set issued us at Pinewood. They were slightly dusty from apparent neglect and were capped by a paper-weight reading: "Esse quam videri."

Lighting a cigarette, I decided that Drummont wouldn't object to my browsing about the room. The bookcases delighted me. Everything had been placed on the shelves according to subject and the subjects were profuse. He had more variety in material here than in the massive library in Pinewood: Huxley, Aquinas, Locke, Reich, Goethe—even several copies of the Bible paired with the Koran and the Upanishads. The walls, too, were more than soil and roots, for numerous prints, carefully matted and hung, gave great vitality to the dark space. The majority of the prints were works of da Vinci, but Drummont had obviously collected from all periods of art. Wouldn't the others be surprised to see a place like this? Here was enough to satisfy a man for his entire life.

The whole room overwhelmed me, but more than my amazement at Drummont's collection was his ingenuity in building the underground home and furnishing it so magnificently. His cabin had been alone on the outskirts of the estate and moving quietly by night would have been easy for him, but he was not young and such evacuation of the earth must have been a tedious chore indeed. If he had only asked me, I would have gladly kept his secret and carved each nook with my own hands. I had only been to his cabin three times since I had known him and had never seen all the books and paintings he had stored there. Had he gone beyond the bounds of the estate? It was possible, but surely Clark at least would have been alerted.

The more I searched, the more I discovered. One of the bookcases contained several shelves of musical scores—even a small piano fitted neatly into the wall! The bookcase afforded the most attraction for me, so I knelt beside the shelves and began scanning all I could. Time passed all too quickly and I was soon quite hungry, in spite of this great discovery. Drummont would not have overlooked this biochemical facet of man in his grand conception, and I scanned the room for some hint of food.

It was in this search that I noticed the second door, overlooked in the excitement of my first find. It, too, had been constructed of cedar, and, like everything else in this underworld, had been made by hand. Eagerly I made my way to the door and swung it open. I found myself in the entrance to a laboratory. Shelves and shelves of chemicals, long rows of working tables displayed numerous experiments—all in progress. In the center of the room was a large sink and ground pump, well placed to insure efficiency. At the farthest end of the room a partition had set off still another area, and I could see that the wall beyond was lined with more books.

Here I expected to find Drummont, so I stood in the doorway a few moments, scanning the room desperately for some sign of the man. I now began to feel quite uneasy, for I had chanced upon the closely guarded sanctity of another. I could see no sign of Drummont, however, so I closed the door quietly behind me and stepped into the laboratory. Some of the experiments in progress were familiar, but most were not. The burner heating one of the liter flasks had burned out and there was a slight odor of gas about the room. I turned the jet off as I did not know what he was doing and was afraid to destroy anything. As I inspected the lab, I turned back in the direction of the door. The wall adjacent to the entrance consisted of cage upon cage and each contained a different animal. There were even several aquariums, well lighted and aerated. This menagerie, however, was not like the kennels at Pinewood, for there was no sound, no movement from any of the cages—only an ominous silence.

A sense of terrible incomprehension swelled within me and I longed for Drummont to return, if only to chase me out. I stood in the center of the room, not daring to move, and scanned the laboratory several times. The only sounds emitted by the room were the impersonal bubblings from the heated flasks and the occasional drippings of the titrations. No other doors remained to be opened and only that small enclosure behind the partition remained to be inspected. I proceeded to the partition with an almost dread caution, regretting that I had ever started this search. Everything appeared to be alive, but there were no live sounds—only the awful stillness.

The partition appeared to have been set up temporarily and was, in truth, no more than a hastily built screen. I stepped inside the enclosure. The wall facing me was an extension of the larger library in his living quarters and the far left was punctuated with a second desk; it, too, scattered with papers.

Drummont! I could barely whisper his name. He was lying on a small cot at the other end of the enclosure, apparently sleeping. I knocked gently on the wall of the partition. He made no response. In desperation I shook him gently. Still silence. His chest heaved ever so slightly with each long slow breath. I placed my ear against his heart and heard the quiet prolonged throbs of a system just barely functioning. His body was relaxed and his face expressionless. It seemed that he was in a coma and had been so for quite a while, as he appeared slightly emaciated. He lay calmly on the cot and produced no movement in excess of merely remaining alive.

I remained kneeling at his side, trying to decide on some right action. I knew that before I could notify the others I would need something more than Drummont's sleeping form to show them. I walked to the desk and sat behind it. Papers, graphs, charts, drawings. The desk was an organized pile of research. The drawings first attracted my attention, for the ten or fifteen carefully drawn sketches were of the brain—not only that of man, but apparently of all phylogenetic levels. The center of interest was obvious by the extreme detail given the cerebrum. Although I could see something different between these studies and the ones with which I was familiar, the difference was too subtle for me to grasp at the moment, so I placed the drawings on one side of the desk and decided to search elsewhere for an explanation. The mass of hand-written papers seemed highly unrelated, however; and I was puzzled to find numerous problems in topology, several pages written in some type of hieroglyphics and scatterings of poetry illustrated with pen and ink sketches.

I sorted all the papers into a fairly comprehensible order and added them to the pile for later consideration. The desk was now cleared of everything but a rather small notebook. I pulled it toward me and was stunned to find scrawled upon it: "Emile—this is what you need." I quickly pushed the book away and backed off from the desk as if everything were alive and deadly to the touch. I called across the room once more to Drummont—one last effort to wake him.

Returning to the desk, I pulled the notebook toward me and opened it. Carefully printed across the first page was "Philipe H. Drummont, Daily Log," and recently added in an almost illegible hand: "for Emile Boureaux."

The diary had been dated eight years ago. The first six years had been infrequently recorded and it was only the past year and a half that had been given careful notation. I turned to the beginning and started to read:

April 26:   Today Clark gave me Quandro's book. I have spent all afternoon with it and am thoroughly convinced that it is possible to manipulate the power of the mind by scientific means. But I think there is a better way.

At the bottom of the page he had quoted:

All men's gains are the fruit of venturing.
                            —Herodotus

The following entry in which he decided to attempt the experiment was not made until eight months later:

> ... I believe that by this increase in the cerebral convolutions, man can attain a greater consciousness of his inner being—his very being—and a subsequent greater understanding of all things.

The log continued with weekly recordings of sedative dosages for his cerebellum in an attempt to subordinate his awareness of physical being. It was not until two years later that he finally entered:

> I have finally succeeded in anesthetizing my biological functions. For the past month my metabolic rate is minimal and functioning. There is no exertion on the part of any other organ of my body. I am in a state of perpetual biochemical somnambulism and now begin to act on my mind.

He had then begun an extended series of similar functional experiments on animals of all types. I was astonished to realize that he had begun tampering with his own body before testing his method. These records seemed proportionately analogous to the progress he himself had made. Once he had achieved a similar state in many of the animals he began various attempts at increasing the cerebral convolutions of a select few. The first results were recorded a year later:

> The Siamese cats responded most quickly to the imposed convulsions and have excelled at all the tests given them.

The listings of tests which followed were valid manifestations for abstract thought. I was amazed at the apparent increase of the conscious intelligence of these animals. The tests proceeded for several months until:

> March 10:   I came to the lab today to find two of the cats dead. During the completion of Moore's tests the third cat went into convulsions and also died.

The entries for the following year duplicated the progress and subsequent death of the cats with several other animals of lower cerebral levels. The year of my arrival was marked by Drummont's entry:

March 6:   I have decided that the failure to maintain the lives of these animals is due to their incomplete cerebral development. I shall continue experimenting with other animals but I believe that only the mind of man is developed sufficiently to withstand the increase in conscious awareness. So today I shall begin with myself.

The subsequent records were now more frequent and regular, and, little by little, Drummont abandoned all other work and continued to experiment on himself only. He had followed the procedure of chemically induced convulsions first applied to the animals and it was less than three months later that he had written:

I sense that I am becoming continually more alert, as though I were an addict to some stimulant. I am aware of my surroundings not through sensual perception, but rather through what seems to be an acute awareness of my inner self. Thoughts that once came to me only while asleep are now part of my daily thought process.

Progress now appeared to occur quite rapidly and two weeks later he had entered:

I am unchanged physically still, except for an increase in pupil dilation, but I find it difficult to contain myself within these meager records. I feel as though my conscious and subconscious are no longer divorced. I have become a single whole of extreme sensitivity and acute awareness. I can not sleep. My body has long been forgotten—it functions automatically and I am totally unaware of its presence. I am now continuing the experiment with extensive reading—perhaps my last human effort to develop my awareness through knowledge. I have been walking often as well, as each view of the world outside appears as it must for one who sees it for the first time.

I laid the notebook on the desk and lit a cigarette. Drummont had not moved. He still lay on the cot in that slow sleep. What had happened? Only a few pages remained to be read, but I felt saturated by something too overwhelming to grasp. I returned to the laboratory and listened to the bubblings and watched the titrations. What must it have been like for Drummont to stand here as I did now? His eyes and ears no longer served him as mine did me. I could not begin to conceive of such a state of awareness. Complete receptivity. It must have been a terrible joy for him. The faintly pungent odor of gas still lingered and, eager for the remainder of the secret, I returned to the desk.

Remaining were four entries. He had decided to move from his cabin when I had become his assistant, knowing that he would not be missed with me there to run the analyses:

> ... moreover, I am no longer satiated in their lab. There is so little meaning in all those little discoveries.

It was the following entry, however, that proved the success of his experiment:

> April 12:   How feeble is the human verbalism. We are too much contained in a catalogued existence. I can not convey my feelings and yet they must be written here. Perhaps I shall be understood.
>
> I walked out of the estate today to a large pond which I have visited often. I felt at one with all about me. Not merely the trees and brilliant morning, but everything. I was able to grasp with immediate facility all that which to other men seems beyond the realm of human thought and understanding. I am able to feel, simultaneously, evil and good, love and hate—all mankind's listed moral standards—to such a degree that all right action is immediately clear to me. Who would have believed that such power lay within this feeble frame? And it is this feeble frame that contains—no—captivates me now. I feel as though I were wont to explode—to free me from me.
>
> I know too well that I must control this great comprehension and so today I have decided to redirect my thoughts and, in doing so, perhaps gain some command over myself.

The following passage was a series of efforts on his part to restrain his awareness and thought patterns. He began chemically to induce sleep, he ceased his reading and daily walking and attempted only simple thought. It was not until six months later that he recorded his success:

> September 23:   At last I feel that I am safely housed again. That terrible sensation of inner captivity has passed. The self-imposed limitations have enabled me to enjoy this acute perception.

It was probably about this point that Drummont had written those poems and made the pen and ink sketches, for the quality and symbolism were on an extremely high level—as though he were seeing the world all too clearly. Eagerly I turned to the subsequent entry:

> December 18:   It is gone!

Gone? Stunned and confused, I turned to the last entry. It was barely scribbled across the page, a very difficult task to read:

> December 20: The experiment has failed. All I had is gone. I can not make it come back. I have tried all the ways I used in the beginning. But it is gone. My body is still living as it always has. I can not write, I have not been able to speak for a long time. I must lie down . . .

The entry had not been finished and the last few words had obviously been a great effort to form. I picked up the notebook and walked to his cot. He still lay there, his chest rising only slightly at long intervals. His body would probably continue to survive until it starved, for he was clearly incapable of any movement. I removed the blanket from the foot of his bed and covered him.

The others would learn that he had disappeared and left no trace. He had simply tired of Dinesen. I carried the notebook out of the laboratory, intending to take it with me, as he had meant for me to know. Someday, however, the notebook might be discovered. Sadly I placed the diary on his desk and made my way up the ladder and out, into the forest. I pulled the ladder loose and let it fall to the floor before shutting the trap door.

I returned only once to that spot in the woods and removed the door, filling the entrance-way with dirt. I thought it fitting that he should have a private grave.

Clifford Johnson

The way they really are

I hadn't made a sale all week, and it looked like it was going to be another bad day. I sell photo albums for the Family Album Company, and Durham is my territory. And pretty lousy territory, too, let me tell you that. For instance, now, the first place I went to this morning, this pretty cute little broad answered the door with a kid on her arm, and before I could get through my door-opener, she said, "If you're selling anything, I might as well tell you, my husband is dead." What could I do? I just said "Thank you," and went away. That's the first time I ever hit that rebuttal, and what can you say to something like that? Not that I believed her. The little bitch had just discovered a good way to get rid of salesmen.

I had a lead to a place down the street. It was a pretty cheap-looking block, with sand in the yards instead of grass, but the houses had been there long enough to have some trees growing around them. There were a lot of junky kid's toys made of plastic out in front of the houses. The guys that live on streets like that, they put out a dollar ninety-eight for some piece of crap for their kid, and then they feel generous as hell. I like to work that kind of neighborhood because you find a lot of mullets living there, and if you make them believe they're getting a bargain, they'll buy the Empire State Building. Also, you find the kind of people that buy a family Bible with a picture of Jesus on the front cover. If I ever see one of those Bibles lying on a table, I say to myself, "Nick, baby, you got yourself a sale."

My lead took me to a white house that looked like it was dumped out of a sack instead of built. Out front was a '53 Ford with no front bumper and a flat tire, and which probably didn't have an engine, either. As I walked up to the door, I saw a sign tacked onto a tree which said, "Building Permit. Edgeton Realty is hereby entitled to enlarge house located 1012 Oak Street from a three-family dwelling to a four-family dwelling. Building code, section 495, paragraph D." I checked the address. My lead was to a family that had just had a baby. There were two front doors, and I picked the one on my left. Through the screen I saw a girl ironing shirts. I couldn't see her face until she came to the door. She would have been pretty if she had worn some makeup, and if it weren't for the receding chin. I gave her a grin. A big grin is the best door opener in the world. "Hey, there," I said. "You're the folks that have the new baby, aren't you?"

She said, "Yes," but she wouldn't smile.

"Fine," I said, grinning hard. "I've got a real nice surprise for you, sent out by the company. Have you got a few minutes?"

"Well, what's the surprise?" she said.

"If I told you that, it wouldn't be a surprise," I said. (You never tell 'em what it is at the door.)

"Well, ordinarily I don't let people in, but my husband's at home today, so I guess it's okay." She opened the screen about an inch and I helped myself in. I figured her husband weighed three hundred pounds and drove a garbage truck. He would either be a complete bastard, or he'd be real sentimental. They had a living room suite from Sears, and I sat down on the couch. The coffee table was too low, as usual. I looked around for a Bible or a set of encyclopedias. The only books in sight were a battered dictionary and a still more battered Bible on the coffee table and a pile of magazines called *The True Word*. "Uh, oh," I figured. "I've got a couple of religious nuts on my hands." The girl looked uneasy, and she wasn't saying anything, but only sitting and looking at me, with her bare right foot laid on top of the other one. I looked at her legs and decided she needed a shave.

"I see they're going to move another family in here with you all," I said. I usually gab a little to make them more curious about why I'm there, and to put them at their ease.

"Yes," she said. "They're going to fix up the basement and put someone else down there."

"That'll make it pretty crowded, won't it?"

"Yeah." She still had that lifeless expression she was wearing when I saw her at the door. The curtains were drawn, the room was dark, and her face looked gray like a photographic negative.

"How old is yer all's baby?"

"Two weeks."

"Gee, you're up and around pretty soon. Most gals are still in bed two weeks after they've had a baby. Doesn't ironing tire you out?"

"I do all right." I paused to see if she would go on, but she wouldn't. People like that intrigue me because I always want to see if I can make them talk, get them interested in something. I decided to mention my wife's pregnancy. That always gets 'em.

"We're expecting a baby here before too long," I said. "Twentieth of October."

"Oh." That's all she said. Just, "Oh." That teed me off. Most everyone asks if its our first one.

I don't know how I could have sat in that room so long and not noticed the pictures on the walls. I guess I hadn't noticed them because they were so big. It looked like the walls were made of pictures, all of Bible characters. "Hey, those pictures are real nice," I said. "Where did you get them?"

"Oh, those are Jim's. He paints," she said. Her voice showed about as much pride as if she were describing her hernia operation.

"Gee, those are good. Does he take courses in painting?"

"No, he never had a lesson in his life. He taught himself."

"You must be real proud," I said, still trying. "I guess I've got Michelangelo on my hands," I said to myself. There must have been a dozen large paintings and drawings on the walls, and there was a stack of them in the corner. There were a couple of crucifixes, in bright color. The crucifixes looked like he had copied them out of an illustrated Bible story book. There were some madonnas, too, and they all had the traditional golden glow behind Mary's head, and Jesus lying there with his eyes open and not crying, unlike any new baby *I've* ever seen. There was a Lord's Supper that he had copied from somewhere, because I know I've seen it in magazines. Those pictures weren't any more real than the big sunny smile I wear when I knock on a door. You could have those pictures in your living room for ten years and not even notice them.

But there was another group of pictures that didn't look copied, and I don't know how they could stand to sit in that room with those pictures and not stare at them all the time. That's how real they were. I looked over my right shoulder, and there above the couch was some prophet who looked like a bas-relief instead of a painting. His hair was blown back, like he had just whipped his head around to glare at someone in the crowd who had called him a name. His head was bald and mounting up his forehead were deep wrinkles which looked like grooves you make with a knife in soft cheese. The cords in his neck were swollen as if he had been shouting. His eyebrows were bushy and threatened to hang into his eyes, but his glance was so bright that it would have scorched the white hairs. There were about five pictures he had obviously done out of his own head, and they were all of angry men condemning someone. When you look at a picture like that it makes you ask yourself if you've done anything wrong recently. But there was something funny about them. You never see anybody like that in real life. They were so real, they weren't real. You know what I mean?

I figured I had a real mullet. Anybody who is that religious must be pretty sentimental. If they swallow all that Bible stuff they're a sure thing to swallow a sales pitch. So I said to his wife, "Well, I guess you're wondering what I'm here about."

"I'd better go and get Jim," she said.

Jim was carrying the baby when he came in. He looked the way Elijah would have looked at age thirty. Tall and gaunt and wearing a tee shirt which showed his slim arms almost to the shoulders. His hands were extremely large, and cords of muscle stood out on his forearms under a light coat of long black hairs. His neck was thin, and the sinews stood out on either side of a large Adam's apple. His head was large, with thick black hair greased and combed straight back. His forehead had the same lines as the prophet on the wall. His long face, slack jaw, and dimly flickering eyes made him look stupid. I stood up, thinking what a typical country jake he was. "I'm Nick Orange," I said.

"Glad to meet you sir. Jim Davis." He folded himself like a carpenter's rule into a low chair.

"Mighty cute little baby you got there, Jim," I said. I've gotten into the habit of using people's names a lot. No matter how religious a guy is, he loves to hear the sound of his own name. "Is it a boy or a girl?"

"He's a boy."

"Gee, I bet you're proud. Were you hopin' for a boy or a girl?"

"A boy. I told Linda here, I ain't got no use for a girl. If he ain't a boy, I don't want him. And the reason I want a boy is, I want him to be a preacher or a missionary. Yes, sir."

"Well, well. I know both of you are mighty proud," I said. He held the baby in his huge hand, and I thought of how a Chesapeake Bay Retriever can swim through the water with a dead duck in his powerful jaws and drop it in your hand and you won't find a single feather out of place on its back.

I decided I'd establish a little common ground before I went on with my pitch. "I was looking at your magazine, here, *The True Word*. It looks pretty interesting. What's it all about?"

"That magazine is by a man out in California. He reads the Bible and interprets from the book of Revelation what is going to happen, and he prophesies it in his magazine. Shore does."

"Oh, I see. I thought maybe this was one of your church publications. What church do you go to?" I said.

"We go to Free-Will Baptist Church. Yes, sir." These people I call on are always saying "sir" to me because of my coat and tie.

"I see. What do you do? Are you the minister there?"

"No, I'm a deacon. I preach sometimes. For my living, I'm a carpenter at the hospital," he said.

"I was noticing your art work here. Your wife tells me that you never went to school to learn how to paint."

"That's right. Sure is."

"That's mighty good."

"Yes, sir. Taught myself. A man doesn't need no education to glorify God. Take our preacher for instance. He was fifteen year old, and the Lord came to him and called him to be a minister of the gospel. And that man couldn't read or write. But when he come up to take his preacher examination what they give him, the Lord he'p him. The Lord he'p him to pass that test. He shore did. Yes, sir. Praise His name. Now he can read and write pretty good. His wife teach him a lot. 'Course, he can't read nothin' that's writ too fancy. But he can read his Bible pretty good. And a man don't need no education to praise the Lord, and to do the Lord's work. Shore don't."

"That's the truth," I said. I would have said "amen," but I couldn't quite get it out. I was afraid it would sound funny. "You know," I went on, "the disciples weren't educated men."

"That's right," he said. "A lot of those professors out at Duke, now," he went on. "They've got a lot of education, but it shore don't do 'em much good."

"Uh, oh," I thought. "I've got him started now."

"No, sir. Doesn't do them any good. You know why? Because they don't know people. Shore don't. A man can have all the education in the world, and he won't be happy, because he don't know people. But if a man knows people, even if he don't have much education, that man can be happy. Yes sir. Shore can. And the Lord be praised."

"That's the truth," I said. I thought to myself, "That's how you can tell a real ignorant bastard. They're always proud of being ignorant." But before I could start my pitch, he interrupted.

"A lot of people don't pay much attention to their religion. Now, if I miss church one Sunday, then the next Sunday I don't feel as much like going to church. And if I miss church two Sundays, then it's mighty hard to get up and go to church that third Sunday. And that's just the chance the devil's waitin' for. The devil is on every street corner. And he's quick to catch you when you slide back."

"That's the truth," I said. Then I hurried on. "Well, Jim and Linda, I'd better tell you what I'm here about." You can't spend all day talking to these people. My job is to get into a house, sell the album, and get out as soon as possible. I don't have time to listen to sermons. I've got all the religion I need. Anyway, these holy rollers can bend your ear by the hour if you let them. "You see," I went on, "I'm sent out to do advertising for the company. We'd like to sort of butter you up, try to get your future business. Now, here's the first thing you get," I said as I bent over, opened my kit, and pulled out the big leather album. The album is the come-on. It always makes their eyes light up. "Now, this album is bound in genuine top-grain cowhide and stamped in twenty-three carat gold. The gold is inlaid so it can't get rubbed off. And you know how rough babies can be on things." Usually I get a smile from the mother at this point, so I looked at Linda. She had about as much expression on her face as some potatoes I've known. So I went on. "Now this album is washable from cover to cover. We call it 'peanut butter and jelly sandwich proof.' You'll find out what that means in a few years," I said, smiling at her, but she seemed to be looking at the empty doorway.

Jim interrupted me again. "I don't mean to be impolite," he said, "but the man selling albums has already been by. Linda, go and get the album, and the paper we signed. I want to show you the paper just so you'll know we aren't deceiving you. I'm not saying you're suspicious now. You understand."

Linda brought out an album identical to mine. The contract was from our rivals in town. "Yes," I said, "this album is a lot like ours, but it's not from our company. I know you'll enjoy it, though." "Well," I said to myself, "I knew he was a mullet. I just wish I had gotten here first." I got up.

"To tell you the truth now, and not meanin' no offense, we're kinda sorry we signed up for the album now," said Jim. "Sixty dollars is a lot to pay, and we got a lot of bills. Carpentry don't pay too well, neither. I reckon we'll pay it, though. We're honest folks, and we always pay our debts. Not meanin' no offense to you, now, but I wish fellas like you wouldn't come around sellin' stuff. Now this other fella that was here, he sold Linda the album when I wasn't here. She signed for it and everything. I called him and tried to cancel the order, but he said that he had already turned it in and that it was out of his hands. So I reckon we'll have to pay for it. I'm not sayin' that we won't enjoy havin' an album full of pitchurs o' Jimmy here. I'm not sayin' that at all. I know it's somethin' we'll treasure in our hearts in years to come. But I swear, I don't see how we're gonna pay for it now. Not meanin' no offense to you, now. I know you gotta make a livin' for yourself. You prob'ly got a wife and kid, too. We been pleased to talk to you. You're a nice young fella."

I was busy packing up my case of samples. "Christ," I thought. "Just

what I've always wanted to be. A nice young fella." I headed out the door.
"Well, nice talking to you, Jim, and Linda," I said. "Thanks for your time."

"Lord bless you," said Jim.

So I left Jim Davis alone in his house with the stern and unreal prophets, the stern and unreal wife, and the little baby who was going to be a preacher or a missionary. I wondered if he had slapped his wife around for buying that album.

I walked out to my car with my kit under my arm. Another dead end. I looked at my watch. Half an hour wasted, and no sale yet today, so I decided to try the other side of town.

Guys like that irritate me. They'll talk your ear off trying to save your soul, and all the time they're feeling so damn religious and pious. Most of the time they're so poorly educated they can't even talk right. I don't go to church much any more, but I've sort of got my own religion. I believe if you live the best life you can and do your fellow man a good turn when you get the chance, you'll come out all right in the end. But you don't catch me going around and preaching to people and boring them to death like I was better than them.

I wish that Davis guy would get into the racket I'm in and go through what I go through. You go around from house to house, getting doors slammed in your face, getting put off with phony excuses, when all you're trying to do is make an honest buck. And when you finally find a good mullet, you find out someone's been there before you. If Jim Davis would go around trying to sell these damn albums, he'd change his mind about people, he wouldn't care about saving their souls. That's one thing this job does for you. You get so you can see people the way they really are.

Wallace Kaufman

A road she didn't know

With Bart's arms around her, his hands clasped on her stomach, she had leaned back against his chest and dozed. When she opened her eyes she could no longer see out of the car windows. Their warmth had fogged the glass, and the orange sunset blurred against it. Around her his big arms were so still he might also be dozing. She tried to remember the woods outside. They had driven in several miles along a rocky lumber road and parked by the edge of a steep hollow. She wished she could see the partially bare trees which crowded on both sides of them.

"Good morning, Stringbean," Bart said, tightening the scissors of his arms on her sides.

"I'm not a stringbean. I'm an inch shorter than you," she said.

"I know, you're not skinny, just tough."

She dug an elbow backward against his rib and he laughed. She was always amazed at how invulnerable he was to even her hardest blows. "Don't fight so early in the morning," he said.

She stretched and shivered. "If it's morning, I'm going to be kicked out of school. It's also a cold morning."

Bart reached into the back seat and put her sweater over her shoulders. It was her favorite sweater, one she liked to wear out of doors.

"Who pulled the curtains on the windows?" she asked.

"You like the color? It clashes with your sweater."

"Mmm-nn. They're both sun colors. Sun-orange is nice. It's sort of gold like the wool." She stared at the windshield and tested the accuracy of her description. Closed in like this her thoughts became words more easily. "Bart," she said calmly, "what if I get pregnant?"

"You won't."

"But suppose I did?"

"Are you proposing?" he teased.

"No."

"That's too bad. Maybe you wouldn't marry me."

"I think I would." She knew she would, even felt she might just now have tricked him into proposing. The weight of this new thought seemed to press them apart into separate silences. If they got married after graduation in June, she would seem to be doing just what many other girls did, but the "told-you-so's" would not bother her. If they got married, it would be something she had to do because it was the *best* thing, not just the only thing or the proper thing or the done thing. 'And besides,' she thought, 'nobody has really asked, thank God.' She didn't want to make him ask. As far as she was concerned, he would never have to ask; with them she would just know.

If she let herself go, she could imagine that the orange-gold haze on the windows was timed to hallow her new life. She reached out a hand to rub a small hole in the haze and see what the woods were like in this light.

As if the clearing touch of her hand had brought it, something broke on the outside of the glass, a shout, one word loud and clear—*HELP!*

Her hand stopped for a moment, held out with the wet fingers touching the hole she was making. They both froze, waiting for another word or the same word again, but only a purer silence surrounded them. Not a breeze nor a bird nor the motion of a dry leaf. Bart released her and straightened up, almost pushing her away. Very slowly, as if to preserve the silence, he rolled down his window. The hollow below them was already filled with night as with a cold tide. On the ridge across the hollow the sky between the trees was still too bright for them to see there. Even around the car the woods were a murky cloth of brown and gray.

She shifted closer to him on the seat, assuming he too was afraid. Also that he was her safety no matter what happened. The voice had said *help*, but very loud and not in anguish. She reached out and touched his hand where it rested on the steering wheel. It was cold. She held to his big wrist as his eyes groped the woods framed in his window.

"*HELP!*" This time the voice rose out of the hollow into the car. It seemed too loud, too distinct to mean help.

Bart's wrist turned out of her grasp, and he stepped out of the car. "*Here,*" he shouted, and the word echoed back from the rocks of the hollow.

The echo died and for several seconds silence was as strong as a command. Then what came was not a reply but a cry. And not really a cry but a loud firm call, like a hunting call—Aaiiyooooeeoo!

Trying to see down, Bart moved to the edge of the slope into the hollow. "*Up here,*" he yelled. "*Where are you?*"

While he waited she got out of the car and stood several steps behind him, checking the woods around them for any other life. She thought the woods like a room deliberately abandoned in the face of obvious danger—only not obvious to her or to Bart.

"*HELP!*" Again only the one word. And so strong. She watched Bart as he listened for some noise to locate the voice. If help were needed, they were not giving it, but who would want help out here, miles from the nearest house or road? "Ask what's wrong," she whispered to Bart.

Without turning, he raised a hand by his head and motioned her to be quiet. "*I'm coming down,*" he shouted, beginning to descend quietly among the rocks.

"*HELP!*"

"Okay," Bart answered. He stopped and looked back. "Wait in the car," he said and began to descend faster.

She looked back at the car but could not go and sit there and close the door and wait, all closed in. Standing on a rock, she followed with her eyes as far as she could, glad that he moved easily over the rocks and that he was strong. Even glad that he had not waited any longer. He was out of sight quickly and soon beyond hearing though she guessed he had gone down and to her left. She still strained for sight and sound but received none as if trying to follow a diver underwater. For a moment she even had the feeling that a long delay would indicate something as bad as drowning. She was as much alone as if he had never called for her this afternoon. If she were his wife, he might have taken her along. No, that was stupid. She should have gone, not waited to be asked.

Her own name startled her. It came up out of the hollow louder than she had ever heard it. In her first fright her mind translated her own echoing name into the word she waited for—*help*. Then she wished she had heard it right. "Vanity," she said to herself at the very moment Bart called again.

"*Here,*" she yelled back, her voice ringing like a shrill pipe in contrast to his.

"*Can you find your way down?*"

"*Yes. I think so.*" She should have said just yes. Any motion was better than waiting in the empty dusk-filled woods for someone she could not see.

She started down carefully, testing each of the smaller rocks she had to step on. When it came to climbing she was a stringbean. Too bad they didn't teach you dancing right out in the woods instead of in gyms. She was glad Bart could not see her. Finding the slope easier than she had expected and the hollow not as dark as it seemed, she hurried her descent. She twisted her ankle once but only enough to restore her caution. Halfway down she stopped to listen. Before, she had thought of Bart as a diver, now the silence made her a diver also, moving with only faith toward a guessed location. "Bart?" she called.

"Here." His answer was definitely closer and no longer distorted by shouting and an echo. "Watch your step," he called. "It gets wet down here."

At the bottom of the slope she found the creek and followed it to him. He was squatting near the water. Next to him was an old man propped against a big rock, his feet in high-top shoes almost in the creek. His khaki work clothes were soaked; and shirt, undershirt, and pants met and parted over his white paunch as he breathed.

As she approached, Bart stood up and the old man tried also. He got one foot under him and a hand on the rock but fell over when he tried to position his other leg. "Take it easy," Bart said to him as he tried again.

"Sorry m'am," the old man said. "You shouldn't have come down here."

She looked at him as if there might be some visible reason why she shouldn't have come. His voice and his motions were like an animal run over in the street, but she could find no obvious wound or broken bone.

"I think he's all right," Bart said. "He's exhausted."

"Don't get up," she said as the man tried to rise again.

"It's getting dark," he said. "I been in here since nine o'clock this morning."

They both squatted by his side. "How did you get in here?" Bart asked.

"I got two dogs, beagles. I wasn't hunting. I just wanted to see them running. I'm eighty years old. I ain't got no business being in here, but it was a pretty morning. I just felt good. I don't know. I give out hours ago and the dogs left me. They're just puppies. Still running. I can hardly walk and fell in the creek."

She looked at his wet clothes and knew he must be cold. The effort of her own climb had worn off and she was shivering.

"Why don't you go back, m'am," he said. "You're cold. I'll make it all right now."

"It's okay," she said, believing and hoping they needed her help.

"How do you feel?" Bart said. "You hurt?"

"No sir. I'm just give out. How old are you?"

"Twenty-two," Bart said.

"That's good. Sixty years ago, you believe it, I would run these woods day and night and not get tired. Day and night. My kidneys broke in the first war."

"World War I?" she asked. She knew immediately that was what he meant, but the phrase "the first war" had sounded much farther back.

"Yes m'am. Belleau Wood. But I never saw an enemy. I was a machine gunner. They told me what angle to fire at and I fired. Till a shell blew us up. Hurt my kidneys. Up at the V.A. Hospital in town they draw puss off every so often."

"They hurt you now?" Bart asked.

"Just my back," he said, rubbing the small of it with his fist.

"Can you walk?"

"Maybe we should get help," she said.

"It's getting too cold to wait," Bart said.

"I can walk, m'am. I'll be all right. I just give out. Would have froze if you hadn't heard me." He began to struggle for his feet again, this time with Bart lifting under one shoulder. With this small effort the old man's breath rasped. He steadied himself against Bart and hiked up his soaked pants. They slipped quickly below his navel and the top of his underpants. "You go on, m'am," he said, lifting the pants and holding them with one hand.

"Go ahead," Bart said.

The old man looked much heavier than Bart and she wanted to protest, but they stood waiting for her to move. She turned and began up the creek the way they had come, aware that now Bart could see if she were clumsy or afraid. The sky was no longer orange, but a deepening blue. The old man would have missed two meals, she thought. And she and Bart had brought nothing in the car. She looked back. She had walked too fast. Bart and the old man were barely in sight. The old man had one arm over Bart's shoulder, the other pushing aside brush and bracing against trees. His feet moved only a shoe-length at a step, as if he were measuring. Even above the sound of their feet, she heard the old man's hard breathing. 'Heart attack,' she thought. The conditions were all right for it. Possessed by this realization she stared at him as if he were already dead. For an instant she saw Bart struggling with the corpse of an old man.

But they came to her, and just as she said, "Maybe we should rest," the old man stumbled. He did not fall, but full in her stare his pants dropped about his ankles. Her reflex motion was toward him, to help before he tried himself and fell. But he fell of his own accord to his hands and knees to hide himself. Having seen, she turned away and let Bart help him to sit and redress.

"Okay," Bart said after she had stared at the trees for a full two minutes.

"I'm sorry, m'am," the old man wheezed. "I shoulda kept hold on them. I wisht you'd go on ahead."

"Never mind," Bart said, "you just sit here till you get your wind back. We have to start going uphill now."

"You folks are putting yourselves out too much for me," the old man said. "I'm gonna pay you for this."

"Nonsense," Bart said.

"I don't have no money now, but I'm gonna pay you."

"It's a favor," Bart said.

"Well, you're nice folks." He rested for a while, rubbing his knees so hard they might have been pieces of wood.

She had watched him as he talked to Bart and wondered why he was not shivering. "Aren't you cold?" she asked.

"No, m'am. I've worked up a good sweat. Long as it don't freeze on me I'm warm." He looked at her carefully. "I had a daughter, same color hair as you. And ten grandchildren."

"Where are they now?" she asked.

"All over. Only my granddaughter's here in my daughter's house. I have five great grandchildren."

"Quite a family," Bart said.

"It's all I need to carry on. All I need. I could have died out there and they wouldn't have needed me."

"Everybody alive is needed," she said. Right away she knew that was a lie. She looked at Bart to see if he would indicate his own need and save her from her lie, but he was not aware of what she had said.

"You're good folks," the old man said again. "I'm just an old man. I know it."

"Maybe so," Bart said, "but we're bringing you back anyway."

"And I'm gonna pay you for it too."

"We're not doing it for money," Bart said.

"You ought to be paid."

If it would not have embarrassed the old man, she would have bent down beside him and kissed him. For a moment she was happy to imagine herself his daughter, his youngest who had not yet borne children. 'I would be his last promise to the world,' she thought, then added, 'If I could be anybody's promise.' Half in fun she looked at her arms and legs to assure herself Bart couldn't really think of her as a stringbean.

As if to remind her she was being frivolous, Bart spoke gently to the old man. "Can you go again? I don't want you to get pneumonia."

"Okay. I can go." He braced his hands on the ground as if to get up but waited for Bart to lift from one side before he moved his legs. Once standing, he began breathing as heavily as before he had rested. He stood with his arm over Bart's shoulder as if not knowing how to take a step.

She waited for them to move before going ahead. The old man was looking at his feet, also waiting. Bart adjusted the man's arm over his shoulder and his own arm behind the man's back. If anyone were close to belonging to the old man, Bart was. Not her. She was neither fruitful nor innocent.

Nor was she helping. The old man's feet moved, but even with Bart lifting he could not walk uphill. "I can take one side," she said coming to them.

"No, you don't have to," the old man said, straightening up. "You couldn't lift much on me."

"I can try." She waited awkwardly at his left side, then reached for his arm and clipped under it. He was cool like the earth, and when her other arm touched bare flesh at his waist, the skin was slippery with sweat but equally cold.

Supported evenly, the old man could move. They shuffled upward, pausing time after time for the old man to lift a foot over a vine or rock. The weight on her was not the almost impossible burden she had expected and it gave her no trouble. Bart, who was on the downhill side, was the main support. The old man's arm did not pull hard on her, and his hand, she noticed, refused to grasp her shoulder as the other hand grasped Bart's. She tried to see across the old man to Bart but couldn't walk with her head turned. The old man was like a live corpse that had grown between them. She shuddered and the old man stopped. For a moment they stood there, and she was sure he had stopped to die, after all these years finally felled by a shell that had exploded in World War I. She wanted to take his arm from her neck but realized Bart was quietly supporting on the other side.

"Sit down," Bart said. The sound of his voice relieved her as if the words were addressed to her. The old man was breathing too hard to answer. He stood up until he could. "You rest, m'am," he said.

At first she wanted to plead with him not to think she was so weak. She was not at all tired. The three of them stood yoked until she followed Bart's lead in slipping from under the old man's arm and helping him down. She held his arm to try to feel his pulse. He pulled away before she could count, but she could see nothing in his face to say why. She only knew his pulse beat much faster than hers. When she caught Bart's eye over the old man's bent head she patted her hand to her heart. He shook his head. "How can he be so sure?" she asked herself. She looked at him questioningly, but he only puckered his lips and nodded a kiss to her. She tried not to kiss back but she had pursed her lips before she could gain control. She was aware of the old man, maybe dying beneath their kissing. She looked down, then back at Bart, but Bart was already looking up the hill.

'I'm not hurt and I'm not doing any work either,' she thought. 'Yet I'm the one who's getting hysterical. I'm almost wishing him to die.'

When the old man raised his arm over Bart's shoulder, she quickly reached out and took the other.

"You shouldn't," he said hoarsely and without looking at her.

"It's just a little ways," she said. She had wanted to say, "You need me." Pressing her arm against the cold back and gripping the wrist on her shoulder, she tried to lift some of the weight from Bart, but she could not rise high enough. He was Bart's, or Bart was his. Except that the old man used her for balance, she could be a rag trailing behind them. She told herself that to be angry was childish. But if only Bart would see how weak the old man was, she would not feel so stupid and useless.

They found level ground almost at the car, but the old man suddenly sank between them. The weight fired her fear but only as long as it took for the old man to reach the ground and for her to see that he did not crumple but held himself against Bart's leg. She stooped beside him quickly and had touched him before she realized his hard breathing was not suffocation but crying. Her touch stopped him and he turned his face momentarily into Bart's shirt, Bart having also crouched, but very deliberately looking at the man's head and not across to her. When she did catch his eye, he looked away quickly and would not meet her.

When the old man looked up he studied the car while he regained his voice. "Is that your car?" he asked.

"That's it," Bart said. "Ready to go."

"I wisht I'd known you was up here. How long were you here?"

"A couple of hours," Bart said.

She thought back to those hours and wondered how they had slipped so easily to the back of her mind. 'A couple of hours,' she thought, 'I have already lost them. No wonder Bart can forget me.'

"I was down there. I didn't hear nothing," the old man said.

"I guess sound carries out of that hollow but not into it," Bart said.

She was trying to think of her and Bart in the car and of the old man crawling out of the stream in the hollow, starting very slowly to freeze to death. She wanted this God's-view to make cosmic sense, but it remained only a weird painting.

"I'm glad we heard you," she said, glad that she had heard first, or that her hand clearing the window had seemed to bring his cry for help. Yet what they had given didn't seem like any real help.

"Yes m'am, I'm glad you did too. I'm gonna be all right now."

The confidence frightened her. It was too easy. 'You are not all right,' she thought. 'You are too old.'

"Let's get you in the car where it's warm," Bart said. He helped the old man up, and she tried to take her position again, but the old man would not have her.

"Open the door for us," Bart said.

She went ahead and stood holding the door like a chauffeur. Bart helped the old man into the back seat. When they were all in and the motor running, the smell of sweat and creek water filled the car. She wondered if the old man's skin was warm now. He sat in the corner of the back seat so quietly she wished they had put him with them up front.

Bart turned the car slowly and began up the lumber road. The old man groaned as they pitched over rocks and ruts. When she turned to him he said, "I'm okay. It's just my kidneys acting." But she saw his face was pulled with pain as it had not been during their climb.

"Go slower, Bart," she said softly. He did not answer but the car slowed.

"This is a new road," the old man said. "You never could drive in before. I knew all this country before they cut it over the first time."

"It's a good thing we can drive *out*," Bart said.

"It sure is."

She sat back staring into the tunnel of the headlights, trying to see the trees which she knew were crowding them.. 'Why,' she thought, 'should we suddenly be driving an old man out of the woods for the last time in his life? Why us? Why today?' She knew there were no answers, but she thought back to the morning, searching it for something overlooked that might have been a clue. But this morning she had awakened with the sun in her eyes, sung in the shower, read her political science text on the Supreme Court and fussed with her hair. She had finally decided to wear it down. The girls in the dorm said that she was sensual wearing her hair down. After that she picked out her sweater. And when she had met Bart in the dorm parlor she had blushed because she could not control a smile even before he said, "Hello Stringbean." Since then, or rather since she woke up with the windows fogged, he had hardly spoken to her. She sought for something to say to him immediately but found no words.

When they stopped at the paved road Bart turned to the old man. "You have to give us directions now."

The old man leaned forward to look out the windshield. "I don't know the road," he said.

"I think they call it the Jonesboro Road," Bart said. "Isn't it?" he asked her.

She shrugged helplessly.

"We go left," the old man said. "It's about ten miles. If you could stop somewhere, I could call and have my granddaughter come get me."

"We'll take you right there," Bart said.

After waiting to hear if the old man would reply, she shifted toward the middle of the front seat. "Bart," she said quietly, "what about a doctor?"

He sat for a while staring ahead, then shook his head no.

"It wouldn't hurt," she mumbled.

Bart looked at her and arched his eyebrows noncommittally. When the old man told him to turn onto a dirt road he did. Another mile and they stopped in front of a small house. Bart turned the car out of the narrow road into the dirt yard. One more car length and they would touch the front door. The house was a rectangular box set off the ground on cinderblock piers and barely large enough for four rooms. The plate-glass window to the right of the centered door and stoop was lit from lamps inside. There was no light at the door.

"I'm gonna pay you good folks," the old man said, straightening up.

"You're home," Bart said, "that's good enough." He got out of the car, tilted his seat forward and reached back to help the old man.

She watched from the front, waiting a chance to say good-bye. Bart was being very gentle, she noticed. She tried to see his face but was blocked by the roof of the car. As they stood up together two brown and white dogs came wriggling up, pushing between their legs and leaping. The old man tried to reach them with his free arm but could not bend far enough. "Scamps," he said, "got me in there and left me. Now look at 'em." He shook his head at them as if they were babies. "They don't know I'm eighty years old."

A light came on beside the opening door. A woman in a loose housedress stood behind the screen door. She shielded her eyes with one hand and with the other swatted at a naked baby who pulled at her dress. The baby began to wail but did not let go. "Who's out there?" she said. Then almost as loud, "Shut up baby!"

"It's me," the old man said.

"Who you got with you?" she asked, still not opening the screen door and swatting again at the crying baby. A bigger child was staring out from behind her now.

"Some nice folks who got me home," the old man said.

She opened the door and stood on the threshold holding it open. "Where the devil you been?"

"He's pretty tired," Bart said. "He's been way back in the woods."

"I been there too." She laughed curtly and pushed back the baby again.

Not until Bart had helped the old man to the door did she move. Then she stood aside to let him in. Bart helped him up the one stair and he caught hold of the door frame.

"Gramps, where you been, Gramps?" shouted the bigger child, a boy. "We ate a'ready, Gramps. We ate."

The woman slapped him and he bawled and ran back into the room.

The old man turned to Bart and said once again, "I'm gonna pay you. You tell me where you live."

"You ain't got any money, Dad," the woman laughed.

"It's all right," Bart said. "We just wanted to help him home. We'll see you."

"Sure. Come on, Dad, I'm holding the door."

The old man pulled himself into the room and turned to Bart. "I can't pay you now," he said, "but I thank you for getting me home."

"It's nice of you to do it," the woman said, letting the door shut between them.

"Take care of yourself," Bart said to the old man and turned back to the car, the old man's dogs still circling his legs.

As they picked up speed on the dirt road Bart reached over and stroked her neck. "He's home," he said. "A long afternoon."

She slid up against him and his arm reached across her shoulders as the old man's had but held her upper arm.

"Why didn't you take him to the doctor, Bart?" she asked.

"I don't know. It just wasn't the right thing somehow. He wanted to go home."

"Weren't you afraid he was going to have a heart attack?"

"I wasn't afraid, no. If it happened, it happened."

"I know, but . . . Well, it just scared me."

"I didn't even think of being scared until I saw that woman," Bart said.

She leaned against him more heavily. She felt his hand lightly squeezing her shoulder and looked carefully at his face. She knew he was not as unmoved as his words. "I didn't help much, did I?" she said.

"There wasn't much to do."

"Don't you think I'm useless?"

"Stop feeling sorry for yourself." As soon as he said it he squeezed her.

"Just think," she said, "those screaming kids were his great grand-children."

"We could be his grandchildren," Bart said.

"That woman *was*. They were all his. He started it when my mother wasn't even born and he's still here."

"Just barely."

"Bart!"

"I mean he wouldn't be alive if we hadn't been there."

"Have you ever been there before?" she asked.

He smiled. "Nope, never. You inspired me."

She stared out into the headlights, thinking that this trip was just part of a lifetime of going. She wished she could see the sides of the road better. She wished Bart knew he wasn't just driving a car. "You know," she said, "he came out of the nineteenth century. He was in a war before I was born. He's an antique." She laughed at her own foolish image. "He is older than most trees."

"Eighty's not that old," Bart said. "Don't panic."

She sensed a certain irritation in his voice, but she continued. "I know, but he made me feel so helpless. I mean he's going to die soon. They killed him in the war, didn't they?"

"Who knows when we're killed," Bart said.

She was still not speaking what she felt. She wanted Bart to tell her why anybody had to die, but that was a stupid question. Maybe she wanted to say, "Bart, I'm dying, are you?" No, what she wanted to find reason to say was, "Bart, I can help you." But there was no way he needed help.

He withdrew the arm from her shoulder to turn into the college gates. The people walking under the mercury-vapor lights along the road and on the walks seemed ghostly to her. She could hardly believe she had been one of them this morning.

In the parking lot she leaned against Bart for a long time, his arms around her. She did not want to go back to the girls in the dorm. They were all, including her, just the age of the old man's granddaughter.

When the lights blinked for closing she said suddenly and firmly, "Don't walk me in."

Bart paused with his hand at the door handle. "Don't you want to get kissed on the doorstep like all the others?" he said.

"Kiss me here."

He kissed her and she was glad he was not urgent and rough.

Wallace Kaufman

Mid-ocean dark

Snow still falls at midnight.
Outside there is no world
but squares of window light
on unmarked snow. Inside
no sound unless we speak,
but we have watched the fire
two hours now.
As through mid-ocean dark
here in this house we ride
the night. Afraid to speak.
We are like voyagers
run out of talk. The words
which daily make us one—
working, eating, walking—
fail.
They melt like dreams pursued,
they fly like wind-crazed flakes.
Each in our own thoughts
toward our own ends we go.

Jane McFall Wiseman

All thy many blessings

She bit her lip when they all bowed their heads. For one fraction of a
second, she held herself rigidly upright, unbending, and that on Christmas
Day, when they all must bow themselves down to the Lord. It seemed to her
that in one flash of her eyes around the table, she took measure of her life
as it was and treasured it up as it never would be again. She at the bottom of
the table, her father at the top with his wife Grace beside him. On his other
side, her grandmother. Next to her grandmother, her Great-aunt Edna. And
then she herself. On the other side, her Great-aunt Flora. And back again
to her father's wife.

For a half-second her eyes met her father's, dark and fine under their dark
brows. "Frances,' he said. She dropped her eyes and bent her neck. She was
bending once more in obeisance to the King, as she was used to bending
three times a day to Him, but especially now, especially on the day of His
birth.

Her father cleared his throat. "The Lord make us thankful for these and
all Thy many blessings and save us at last, Amen."

With a genteel little commotion, the great-aunts and the grandmother
and the second wife settled back in their chairs, unfolding their napkins and
straightening their lace mats. She, Frances, had laid them askew.

She barely noticed. "And save us at last, Amen," she said out loud to
nobody in particular. "You know, when I was a little girl I always thought
Daddy was saying, 'And save us *for* last,' like we were some special family
that the Lord ought to pass over on Judgment Day until the very last, the
absolute last, so that He could savor the judging and the receiving of *us* into
Paradise as completely as possible."

"Well, you know, Frances," said Great-aunt Flora on the other side of
her. "You know, we *are* a very special family, when you come to think of it,
now aren't we?" She looked around for approval.

"Well, Flora," said Great-aunt Edna, "you know I think the world of
this family, I wouldn't take *money* for it, but I think that attitude—well, it
isn't humble enough for Christmas, I think today we ought to make a special
effort to humble ourselves before the Lord, after all, it's Christmas Day."

"Mm-hm," said Frances' grandmother. "Mm-hm."

"What's that?" The wife leaned forward from across the table.

"She said she thought we ought to worship God on Christmas Day, honey. Cut out all this commercialism on Christmas, mm-hm," said Frances' grandmother, who didn't hear too well.

"I agree," said Great-aunt Flora. "I agree absolutely. All these street-corner Santy Clauses."

"Well, I don't mean just that, honey. I mean all this using Christmas to sell things, that's what *I* mean."

"Oh. Yes, of course."

"Mm-hm," said Frances' grandmother, looking up the table to her son, who was carving the turkey.

"Well," said Frances' father, skewering the bird firmly with the double-prong of the fork. "Well . . ." The table leaned forward, collectively waiting to hear what he would say. He compressed his lips and inserted the knife in the white side, drawing fine slices that toppled over, dry and crumbling, to lie on the platter alongside the rich, steamy dressing scooped from the cavity he made.

"Well," he said. "I think this is a fine family, too; moreover, it's *my* family and I have a sense of loyalty toward my family; and I thank Heaven for it. All Thy many blessings. This table is my many blessings." He looked around at them all, his eyes resting on Frances.

"Amen," said Great-aunt Flora. "Amen, Richard. You always were a fine man, why, I remember even when you were a little boy . . ." She stopped because the man was at her elbow with cranberry sauce. "Thank you, John," she said, taking a helping.

What a contrast Frances' bare city apartment would make to this dim house with high-ceilinged rooms where John served real cranberry sauce, dark red with dimpled jelly and round berries in it. Next year, far away, she would have cranberry sauce in a can; a can she would take to the can-opener in her apartment; which she would insert in the metal clamp and grind around until the tin top came off it, and out of which, into a cereal bowl, she would shake a can-shaped, homogenous goo. But the cranberry sauce of this year was the real thing in a real cut-glass bowl, a wedding present that had belonged to Frances' own mother, who was dead.

Next year Frances would be heating up the slices of turkey she might have bought at a delicatessen. Or maybe, since it wouldn't matter, she'd spread two pieces of bread with the cranberry stuff and have the turkey in a sandwich. An unblessed turkey sandwich. How could she, merely Frances, hope to say "The Lord make us thankful for these and all Thy many blessings" over it? It wouldn't work, that's all.

She would wander over the two-rooms-and-a-bath of her apartment, her heels clicking on the uncarpeted floors. Undoubtedly her father's wife would want to send her away with a couple of the old rather moth-eaten ("But still good. Still good.") oriental scatter rugs that her father and grandmother brought from their cruise to the Holy Land, "just to make things homey, Frances dear," but she'd say, no thank you, she didn't believe she'd take them just the same, she was going so far away to lug those heavy things along and she thought maybe they wouldn't go with the decorating ideas she had in mind, but thanks anyway, Mother (Capital M).

Not that she ever meant to be offensive to that inoffensive woman. A stepmother could have made all the difference in the world to her, coming as she did when Frances was eleven years old. But the new wife had dropped like a stone into the pool of the family, had sunk like a stone down into it with hardly a ripple to show the intrusion. "An ideal adjustment, that girl has made an ideal adjustment to Richard and all his clan," the town had said, pretty much surprised.

Frances sighed and looked around the table. In imagination, she went to the cabinet in the corner of her city apartment's living room, the corner with the minute built-in stove and refrigerator that the landlord called a kitchenette in his advertisement. A projection of herself, the Frances of next year, opened the cabinet and took out a cranberry can. Then she got turkey and a package of frozen—hmm—Brussels sprouts out of the refrigerator. She put them on the stove beside another can, her one secular concession to Christmas Day. It was a can of pickled artichoke hearts, and *they* would go into a cereal bowl also. No cut-glass dish for them. And no Great-aunt Edna to coo over them, as she was cooing now,

"My, my, John. Artichoke hearts! Art-i-chokes. Christmas Day wouldn't be Christmas without artichokes, now would it, John?"

"No, ma'm, it sho' woodin."

"Of course," she added, "I'm not saying that the food makes Christmas, not by a long shot. We mustn't forget the *real* reason for Christmas, must we, Richard?"

Frances' father looked down the table at her while he helped himself, then his mother, to fried oysters from a platter in front of him.

"Have some sauce, Dick," said his wife at his other elbow. "It's only a little ketchup and tobasco sauce and lemon juice. I made it myself, I know how he likes it," she said to Great-aunt Flora.

"Mm-hm. Mm-hm, you're real good to Richard, I know you are, Grace,"
said Frances' grandmother. "He's a lucky man. When that one's mother
died—" she poked her loaded fork in Frances direction, then guided it into
her downy little sickle-shaped mouth and chewed slowly. "—mm-hm. I
guess you saved my baby. Both my babies!" (A beam for Frances) "—from
loneliness and I don't know what-all."

Frances squirmed in her chair. It always embarrassed her to hear talk
like that—but it didn't seem to embarrass either her father or his wife. *She*
was nodding at every adulatory phrase, not out of any conceit, Frances
knew—just calm acceptance of their approval and good opinion, calm
acknowledgment of the qualities that peculiarly fitted her to be her husband's
wife. As for the father, he was oblivious of the chatter of his women. As far
as Frances could remember, she herself was the only female he'd ever con-
sidered worth the effort to listen to.

That was what made it so hard.

"How is school, honey?" said her grandmother to Frances.

"What? Oh—"

"Yes. Tell us ol' ladies how it is at that big school up there, Frances,"
cried Flora.

And Edna, of course. "Frances, you know it's such a sacrifice to your
father to send you to that fine school. I don't mean the money, of course not,
why, I remember Richard put his own two brothers through school without
any problem, without blinking an eye, I may say. Your father, child—why,
he can just sit in that chair of his and snap his fingers and he makes money;
never seen anything like it before nor since. Now, you take Tommy. *That*
boy, dear as he was and as much as I loved him, he—"

"Mm-hm. Honey, all in the world Edna's trying to say is—it's a sacrifice
for your father and for us, too, just having you away from home," said her
grandmother, nodding her head.

Frances looked around at them sharply, wondering if they'd been
primed. But no. It's what they would say anyway. A mere two hours away
from home was like another world to them. What would they say when they
heard about the apartment waiting for her to move into? The apartment that
was eight hundred miles away, not one hundred?

"Yes, well," she began, "I wrote a letter to Daddy—"

"Grace," said her father. "Pass me those biscuits, if you don't mind."

Silence enveloped the table, except for the tiny scraping noises of six
people cutting their turkey and daintily piling their forks with green peas
and mashed potatoes, with salad and fried oysters and slices of Smithfield

ham that John brought out on a platter to supplement the turkey.

Frances' father took a biscuit and was carefully buttering one half of it. She watched his hands with their deliberate movements. The fingers were long and blunt. The joints were flat, the skin pulled tight across them. They were clean, capable hands, well-taken care of. But her own hands were like her dead mother's. ("She has her mother's hands.")

It was Flora who broke the silence, laughing nervously as she looked from one end of the table to the other. "I declare—look there, Edna, Grace— I declare, as alike as two peas in a pod—"

That's what everybody had always said about them, Frances and her father, except for their hands. Always, merely by going to a mirror and knitting her brows, she could strike the fear of God into herself; and next year, next Christmas, she would still be able to do it, even so far away from him—a distance that would be greater than the miles and the twelve months of their physical separation.

All at once, right there at the table, she had a weird picture of how she could somehow inversely bless next year's canned goods, taking them to the mirror next Christmas and saying "The Lord make us thankful" over them. Maybe, by rigging up two mirrors—she laughed uncertainly. It was almost as if she carried her father around with her, almost as if—were she to flee to the "ends of the earth," as he put it—almost as if he would be following her around in her body and in her mind. As though she weren't going to be on her own after all.

She remembered the first day of Thanksgiving vacation a few weeks ago, the first time she'd seen him since school started. Through some compulsion, she had run into the bathroom and clicked on the light, leaning passionately over the basin, her forehead cool against the mirror; her father's straight nose nearly touching hers, her stubborn chin wrinkled the way his must have wrinkled that time (her grandmother said, but she half didn't believe it) —that time, when her mother was dying, that time he was supposed to have broken down and cried. At the funeral, now—and she still remembered it— he had kept his eyes fixed on the ground the way he did when he was severely annoyed.

Well, the dessert. She actually had a hard time remembering what they were going to have. Since September and her first taste of a curtailed kind of freedom, she had pushed these things down inside her. It seemed like it had been so long. Well, not so long. Only since last Christmas, but then in terms of life lived, it had been an extra-long year, the longest one she'd had; almost as long as all the others put together. That was quite a while. Nineteen—no, twenty next month. Twenty years in one.

Plum pudding, that was it. Twenty years since they brought in the plum pudding, John and Mary (Mary always came out to help John hand the dessert around, and everybody gave them money). It was only plum pudding from the store, but Mary made a special topping to go on it that was, Flora said, hard to beat.

When everybody had been served, Frances' father picked up his dessert fork as a signal for everyone else to start. Frances picked up her own fork, then laid it down again. Her hand was shaking. She knew she must put on an appearance of normality. If she acted as though everything were perfectly all right, as if she were their little Frances, the Frances they all loved for her cheery smile and her thoughtfulness to the old people and her contentment with the family, which was the center of the town which was the center of the world—

"You know," said Great-aunt Edna, "when Richard was a little boy we were afraid he'd be 'most spoiled to death, we were. You know, he seemed to think he was the center of the family, and the fact is, he *was* the center of the family. A little king, a little god."

"Edna!" The grandmother was scandalized. "The idea, talking like that. Why, I never heard such nonsense in my life. We raised Richard to be a fine Christian boy and if—"

"Why, Sarah, I never—"

"Oh, Sarah, she only meant—"

"Mm-hm. Yes, I know what she *meant*. But the way she *said* it, honey, why, it was downright blasphemous."

"What I meant, Sarah, was that none of it ever seemed to go to Richard's head, he was always a perfect little—"

"Sweetest-natured child I ever knew," said Flora.

"Mm-hm. Yes." Frances' grandmother sat back in her chair, respreading the napkin in her lap, her sickle mouth turned down, the corners twitching. "Yes, he certainly was. And let me tell you, Edna, I—"

"Grace," said Frances' father. "Pass me the pitcher of syrup. I think I got cheated when Mary poured it on."

"Of course, Dick."

The pitcher was by Frances, and she started it up the table to her stepmother, who would personally ladle it out onto her husband's plate. Frances looked around her at the room, avoiding her father's eyes, which were fixed on her with an intensity unusual even for him. So she wasn't getting out of it this time, was she? Somehow the issue had been avoided over Thanksgiving, only a few weeks back. This whole Christmas vacation had been a carefully planned series of maneuvers to be extra-agreeable, extra-superficial, and not long alone with him at any one time. But the letter. Well, it was a pretty rash letter, and no amount of maneuvering was going to get her off the hook this time.

The walls of the dining room seemed to be closing in on her, holding her prisoner in the very heart of the house. This was its mainspring, this was where its big issues were settled, where many blessings were invoked. Let all mortal flesh keep silence.

A gleaming length of table reflected the dark, expensively papered walls hung with dingy forbears. Old Matthew, her grandfather who had made a mint during the Depression. Frances, his sister she'd been named for, thin-lipped on the wall. And their mother, a matriarch in rusty silk.

"We've got you here with us now, Frances. You've come home and we're thinking about keeping you here forever. We don't think we're ever going to let you get away again."

Frances blinked. "What?"

Great-aunt Flora simpered at her. "That's right. Don't think I'm even going to let you out the front door."

"Oh—yes, ma'm." She laughed a little.

"Come down to earth, girl," grunted her father. "Look like you're a million miles away. Now pay attention to what's being said to you."

"Yes, sir."

"Eat your dessert. You haven't touched a bite."

"Yes, sir."

"Honey, go on and try to eat some, even if you aren't hungry," said her grandmother. "Mary's feelings will be hurt if you don't eat your dessert."

"Yes, ma'm."

"Mm-hm. That's right."

She forced her slice of pudding down, bit by bit. They were all waiting for her to finish, because they had already eaten their desserts, every one. It wouldn't do to hurt Mary's feelings. She'd been with them forty years—

"Longer than you have, Frances!" said Great-aunt Edna with a little trill.

—and that made her a part of the family, too. Now, John. John was a Johnny-come-lately. 1957. Frances could remember when there wasn't a John, but a Henry instead. Henry died and they all went to the funeral, every one of them. This family doesn't quit on you 'til they bury you.

And in your grave, cool and light, would you finally be quit of them?

It was funny—at first the pudding stuck in her throat. But as the slice steadily disappeared, as she tilted the last crumb onto the end of her fork and lifted it toward her mouth, she began to wish she'd never finish it. If this moment could be frozen, if it only could—Where were the fairy godmothers her mother used to tell her about? the gentlemen who cantered up on white horses to save you at the last minute? Where were they, hm? They were false gods, unreliable in a crisis. No competition for a father.

But soon Frances would be laughing at herself, safe in her own apartment. She could see herself in its living room, shaking her head in mature amusement. The big moments of our lives, how foolish they seem, looking back on them. There you are, silly girl back from a mere hundred miles away, a three-months' separation, eating Christmas dinner surrounded by doting relatives. What an odd time to feel your palms damp on the waxed surface of the table, to be staring hard at an empty plate, biting down on the insides of your mouth, waiting for some kind of psychological axe to fall.

But you aren't safe and alone in your apartment, not yet. You're here, this Christmas, now. The moment grew and grew and swelled and swelled until it made you want to stand up and shriek. It seemed to sprout tentacles snaking backward and forward and sideways into time until there seemed to be a network connecting it to all the other moments in your whole life, and this the node of them.

That's why it surprised her when she realized that nobody else but her father felt the tension that literally seemed to crackle between them. In an atmosphere so charged that, should you dare so much as to pass your hand between those two—the father and the daughter, the alien girl and the straight-backed deity at the other end of the table—you'd be thundered and bolted off the face of the earth; in such an atmosphere, the young woman connected by the thinnest and yet the thickest of threads to that girl felt only a numbed kind of amazement that the great-aunts could be talking of anything so prosaic as breakfast. As a matter of fact, she was just as astonished that what they were talking about penetrated through to her at all. Except that, in such a crisis, feeling the doom hanging by a hair over your head, you seemed to drift aside, leaving your body sitting there to receive the blow alone. And during the brief period of your cowardly desertion, all your senses seemed to be heightened and concentrated, as if realizing that the moment would be forced over and over again through the fine-toothed comb of the mind for years' worth of sleepless nights to come, and that they had better soak up as many details as possible, so that later they would be able to eke out the insomniac hours as fruitfully as they could.

She supposed she must be the very picture of outward calm, her eyes level with her father's, her hands cupped patiently in her lap. And in one sense, the calm hung over her like a consecration, as if she were receiving some kind of blessing before embarking on a stern but sanctified ordeal.

Piercing through it all, the chatter of the great-aunts.

". . . Well, if you ask *me*, honey, one egg is plenty. I say a light meal is better for the heart or at any rate for my particular heart—of course I can't speak for yours, Flora."

"I guess you've been criticizing my big breakfasts for fifty years, Edna, so I don't believe anything I can say will convince you. All *I* know is, I find a piece of toast and juice mighty insufficient to start *my* day."

"She *said* an egg, honey," put in the grandmother.

"She *said*," said Flora, "but I've never seen her eat one. Now, me, I take two eggs. Sometimes I even have *three* eggs. And coffee and—"

"Breakfast," said Grace, making one of her rare but momentous entries into the conversation, "is the most important meal of the day." Her tone was so final and her pronouncement had the ring of such truth that it ended the matter forthwith. But it had the happy faculty of convincing each great-aunt that her particular argument was being upheld and her sister's, soundly defeated, at one unanswerable blow.

In the silence following the exchange of universally victorious, then universally puzzled glances, the table first became aware that Frances' father was about to make a statement *ex cathedra*.

He cleared his throat.

Get on with it, then, she thought.

"My daughter," he said slowly, "has written me a letter. I received it the day before she got home for her vacation."

Everyone looked at Frances, then back at her father as he fumbled in his trouser pocket and pulled out an envelope, rather crumpled and smudged. He settled back in his chair and opened it, extracted the folded white sheet of paper, unfolded it, smoothed it out. They waited while he put up his hand to his shirt pocket and removed his glasses case. From the case he produced his glasses, which he laid on the table beside his empty dessert plate. He replaced the case in his pocket and then, with precise movements and precise, metallic little clicking noises, he unfolded the temples and settled his glasses on his nose.

Frances watched in fascination as he ran his eyes over the opening sentences.

"I'll only read a paragraph or two to you all," he said. "Only a little of this letter concerns the whole family. Oh, yes. Here we are.

" 'Daddy, I have something important to tell you. I've decided to leave school after this year and you all can't stop me. I'm going to get a job somewhere far away, and it's going to be in a big city, too. In fact, I went all the way to New York last weekend and looked at apartments. One of them is just right, and I can have it in June. All I have to do is find a job now. I want to live my own life . . .' " he trailed off. He moistened his lips which were almost imperceptibly trembling.

With the detachment of a criminal about to be executed, Frances caught herself wondering whether they were trembling because he was very angry, or because he was very hurt. Probably both. Well, she wasn't giving in.

She was going, and after all, what made her want to? This stifling little Christmas dinner, that's what. Last year, the year before, the year before *that*. She couldn't remember a year when Christmas dinner wasn't exactly like this Christmas dinner. Oh, sure, some of the people had gone, but others just like them were snapped into their places like spare parts.

Only not my mother, who died.

But all the rest were like that. And they were all blessed. Blessed, of course. Three times a day. That makes it all right, doesn't it, Daddy? What better occasion for one of these little performances of yours?

She had been sitting there mute, her teeth clamped together. In a minute her father began reading again. " 'Being away from our town and our family, so closed in, has opened up a new world for me, and I can see there's more to the world than you and our safe little house. It might be big enough for you, but—' " He stopped again. "Well, there's a lot more that all says the same thing."

There was a shocked intake of breath around the table.

"But my dear!"

"Frances, how could you—"

"My baby Frances, what do you—"

She felt a flush rising slowly up her face. "I'm sorry I hurt your feelings, but I meant what I said."

"Frances." This was her grandmother.

"Yes, ma'm."

"Frances, your father's worked and slaved for you. Did you know that?"

"Yes, ma'm."

"Yes, mm-hm. Worked and slaved. Bled over you and broken his body."

"Yes, ma'm, I know and I certainly—"

"Why, Frances, you ought to *thank* your father for everything he's given you and done for you. He did it all out of love, honey. You ought to thank him and not treat him this ungrateful way."

Edna nodded her head vigorously. "You ought to *thank* your father for everything he's given you."

It is meet and right so to do. "Yes, ma'm," said Frances. "I do. I mean, I'm certainly grateful, but—" she stopped, perplexed.

Another silence, longer than the first, measured itself out over the table. Pretty soon she imagined her father would unleash the full force of his wrath. His face would darken over and his eyes would begin to glint even more fiercely.

Yet she realized she welcomed finally getting it out in the open. Then it would be over with and she'd be glad, not wretched and miserable, knowing she should be crawling at his feet begging for pardon but then, not penitent in the least. The guilt that was pressing down on her so hard was that greatest guilt of all, the guilt attending the carefully nurtured child of the Lord who suddenly discovers that he does not feel guilty; the immeasurable guilt of feeling no guilt at all.

But the explosion to come would be her expiation. He would wreak his vengeance upon her; it would be over with. Exonerated, blessed, washed white by the hellfire of his wrath, she would go away to independence and excitement in some large city. It would be Life! So she welcomed the violence to come, she embraced it as the holy rite of passage to adulthood.

"Frances—" It was her father. She set her chin stubbornly. Here it comes!

It almost seemed as though a shudder passed over his body. He looked at her, then down at his plate. It was a cunning look she had never seen on his face before. "Well, then. You can go next month if you like." He stood up abruptly, muttered something and walked out of the dining room.

They all stood up. Frances stood as though she were stunned.

And even next year, standing in the middle of her city apartment with its peeling paint, Frances knew she would still be able to feel the wave that washed over her in that moment. That retreated, leaving her pale and gasping, the skin of her face tingling as the blood drained from it.

They had all left the room, but she stayed at her place. She stood with her head bent, ashamed to let them see the tears starting in her eyes; furious that she had fallen for her father's little ploy, but ashamed nonetheless.

He thought he could get her that way. He might not be able to keep her physically in his house, but he thought he could worm himself into her life. Well, she was an intelligent girl, wasn't she? She wasn't going to let herself be fooled, was she?

Frances stood there with her head bent. After all, she didn't begrudge him the tears. She even smiled a little, in the deluded belief that it was the last obeisance she'd ever pay him.

Wendy L. Salinger

Five poems

Notes: 7–8/67

1

Least visible
in Colorado, this:
the line between mountain
and sky.

Inaudible
alto
line of Colorado,
deceiving the cadence
of sky and
mountain.

Line of most secret writing.

2

Colorado, there is worse
than these mountains
we climbed: the mind: no-man-fathomed.

Hopkins, who said it,
knew landscape
inscape
no escape
                there is none.

The field mice

With the first killing frost,
they inhabit the walls. Mornings
the cat licks clean her fur and the small corpse
is stiff, already a museum-piece.

Then the truckload: the carcasses of deer;
the bucks point their dark bare branches.

Well it is that time. The set table
brings us together another season—
the napkins folded like hands in our laps,
our tongues honed and ready.

A poem in which Heine appears

1

The hands disbelieve but sometimes
they unglove, stretch their real fingers
and then, all night—*schreiben, schreiben, schreiben.*

2

Mattress Grave, soaked
with these last sweatings, dreams back

the blue planet, infant eye
before the worlds undreamt us
into the one dimension: *There,*
where you are not, there is happiness.
You were
everywhere. Objects loved you. Your hands
danced where music, quanta of light,
met them and no leverage cried,
here motion ends! Dying was effortless.

3

Are you afraid?
Your heavy hands choose
paper! pencil!

4

Nights when none of us
can sleep, I read to the books
the bed
the chairs:

*It may be that energy dissociating
here, assembles somewhere else*

but they are not comforted;
they breathe insistently
against the air.

A poem about Schoenberg

1

(disastrous immortality). He laughs, the notes
reconvene space against sentence, syntax.
(Beethoven's impatient fingers
reach out
threatening suicide
blaspheming Newton
and tonal logic:

2

Damn causality. I keep
happening, there are no
consequences but to accuse.

They call it deafness but I have put on
the ears of a dog. They turn me around
to see the applause, not knowing that I am
an anarchist, a dancer.)

3

Heretical mathematician. His answer
strips angels of their spheres:
Earth spun without governments
Sun, moon in simultaneous eclipse
Clock without hands, the heart.

4

As if earth were matter, I wear the old clothes.
Sit to write as if gravity
held me.
At my wrist the old escapement
still turning for me night into day
and again back. My lips compose
the same lie, the cadence.

My Lai

This is where the poem ends
itself, lies down in the ditch
with the other children.

Ann Saalbach

Cello concerto

Cello Concerto was the bone-skinniest go-go girl in Massachusetts, but she kept right on dancing on those table tops, losing weight and turning twenty. In the blue room filled with people's smoky heads and clanking waiters, Cello watched balding piano players through half shut eyes, and danced until the hair floating past her eyes wasn't hers any longer, and her head swirled until the music played inside her, the people ran warm together, and she could bend her body around them all, and hold the tight universe in her arms. Cello felt as if she were surfacing after a lifetime under water.

Then it was over somehow, and slender-limbed Cello was left standing inside herself, under a yellow floodlight on the low ceiling. She climbed down from the table, and walked barefoot across the tiles, working through people's hands, voices, drinks, and the eyes of the college boys; inside herself she was tired and lonely, empty of the world a moment ago there, yet she was breathless and laughing, finally free.

Now her need to love did not have to be feared, would not turn her into a hovering smile, make her strong beauty tremulous, and leave her with empty hands before the rushing freedom of her own later children. Ever since the soldier had ended the night drunk and lost, his head held close to her chest, she had become, Oh Jesus! what a beautiful woman. And growing still within her arms, he had let her be the calmest of answers to despair, made her into an entire world which held solace and peace for the saddest of wild-eyed boys. She thought now that perhaps she would grow up happy, needed, and strong: O hold on to me, I will take care of you.

She leaned against the bar and talked to the haggard black-haired man behind it, wondered where all her other summers had slipped to, and he told her about his children, while clanking ice into glasses, plopping golden liquor on top. It made her lonely to hear him talk, as he sweated in the crowded room, and slipped his sentences between noisy orders.

"Son's going to be a quarter-back next year," he said, his stick-like arms juggling ornate cut-glass bottles, and pausing a moment to smile fully at her. Then he shook his head, slapped change on the bar, and said, "Good built fellow, real good built."

I won't have good looking sons and be lonely, watch them turn silent and myself clinging.

Still strong and only nineteen, Cello had claim on confusion and freedom, was allowed to be desperate and permitted to believe in the love she felt inside her, reaching and tearing. But soon but soon I will be grown up, there will be my own children, and can you carry on Cello? No longer able to wrap up the world in your own long arms, what will you do then?

Cello strode back to her table, intermission over and the drummer still adjusting his drums, climbed upon it again with sure motions. She had looked back at the college boys, unafraid, and had not shrunk from the older men. Standing above everyone and waiting for the first falling piano notes, she thought of her own mother under the yellow light at home, still thinking Cello's name was Jane, and waiting in the corner of the couch for letters. Dear mother, you know I too remember the tiny thimble cakes we baked for the dollhouse weddings, and the dark stairway on Christmas eves when we were still a kitchen family inside away from the snow. It could never be the same now, tiptoeing home from her new world each spring, when all her sweet new strength, passionate confusion could never be shown, had to be buried under more regulated love, and those very hard attempts to erase silence and separation. I had to leave, I had to leave, she begged, because of these things that scare you, make you sad.

Forgetting, she danced, and she had promised herself this always, saying, "Soon, soon," as she grew beautiful in a world too full of daytime. Had traveled away from duty to summer Massachusetts, forget about turning twenty, and it's really not your fault if other people miss you, count on your letters. For once not failing anyone, Cello now was separate and happy, belonged to herself, the falling falling piano sounds, shifting drums, and the eyes of the soldier: I will be everything to him.

Cello rode home over the Massachusetts beach roads in her old big bumbling station wagon, and then down the highway to her two rooms. She climbed into the car, the springs pressing into her bare and thin legs, and she patted the dashboard, saying, "Hi, hello," so that it would not fall apart quite yet. She knew she would never be able to hold it together until she returned home, but she thought that she and the car liked each other then, in that time right before she turned twenty. Down on the night time highway, there were the summer top down gleaming little sports cars, flashing their twin lights up and down, dancing across the white dotted lines, and she knew how it must be at seventeen, feels so good, feels so good to be pretty and flicking your ashes all over the place, knowing the solid wall guys from the same lunch table . . . ah, but these are tricks I've only recently learned, and Cello smiled her serene smile, laughed because no one would be waiting to question her tonight. (Oh and Cello had never been able to enjoy flying down the highway, boys in the back seat coming into sight in the rearview mirror, screaming laughter, because perhaps this is one of the things to produce straight line mouths, worry and aching silence in her tender mother, waiting to ask, Is he a nice boy? Coming in on time, she stood on the worn rug, waited to know, Have I failed you again, made you sad?) She shared sudden freedom with the smaller and bigger and newer cars, that lit the highway beside her, and flashed into hamburger stands, gravelly parking lots in wide arcs, landing in parking spaces, engines roaring. She looked at them, wondered where her other summers had slipped to, wondered how they did it: Oh, exactly what *did* the bartender's son say when he went to parties given by sweet girls, threw up on the lawn, and left with most of the careful Japanese lanterns under his coat? No, you didn't feel your father thinking of you, as he wiped the bar counter, worked over Singapore Slings, and waited for you tall and strong to change the blue room somehow.

At the last stop light before her two rooms, Cello leered out her window at a middle-aged man, turning her radio up there at two o'clock in the morning, as a last fling before maturity. Almost twenty . . . but I will always be laughing, dancing on table tops somewhere way up north.

She climbed up her stairs, that sounded hollow, and no one else even knew where she was, what time she stepped into her own doorway, or how long she looked at her room. Dear Home, I even have this broken coffee table all my own. She crossed the floor, sat on the couch, beautiful and white, alone, and very separate at last. I'm so strong, I'm so strong, she thought, I can take care of you all at last! She felt her mother's pain, but was not guilty for it, found there was room inside her now for these tears and her own climbing laughter. She remembered all the more recent years of strain, wiped her mother's tears: I never took the hubcaps off your car to look cooler, and that's the truth. Having learned to gently wrap herself inside until needed, she could never be broken again.

Strong thin Cello slept very soundly, filled with soaring love and in her mind she held the sea, booming all night down the street.

In the early light, the soldier silently opened the door, said, "Hi, little girl, hi, woman," and she opened her eyes. They crept down her stairs, let the outside door bang as they ran for the beach, and then they were walking by the edge of the ocean. White and silver, Cello and ocean, watched as the soldier strode before her, the wind gentle in his hair. She watched him safely, no longer in danger of growing tight inside. Then he turned, smiled, and they were running through the silent gray morning.

They slept on her couch in each other's arms till noon, filled with happiness.

Cello left him asleep, getting up just in time for her summer classes, and, turning twenty, she loved driving her car, alone and purposeful. She thought, Tonight I really will try to describe the sunrise in my letter. Dear Home: A very special thing is my sunrise, I am part of it, but it does not know me. But, as always, indifferent red sunrises were ignored, and she was urged to be good, meet boys, and make A's. Today this did not matter, and she went on loving the sun anyway, went on driving, and dancing on her safe and most dear, most secret table tops, erased sorrow for her mother thinking about her, waiting for her to return white and slim. (Although they do not know, I am sure I'm not in danger, am ok; it's good to dance up here, I'm sure.)

But returning from class, climbing her own stairway and laughing, for the soldier would be waiting sweetly, Cello did not yet know all things. She opened the door, and saw the soldier facing her; he said, "Your mother was here! Found me."

Cello looked at her room; all her books and magazines, brave earnest letters, lay on the floor; the coffee table must have broken again, flooding the room. The red sun lay in strips across the wide floorboards. The soldier's jacket was neatly across the ladder-backed chair, and the high ceilings would surely echo still when he and she laughed, cooked dinner. He was in a tangle of sheets on the couch, and she suddenly went light-headed, and blind.

"Cello! What's the matter? Open your eyes," said the soldier.

She didn't though, and stood there slim and white, limp-limbed, and she thought: I will never cry again, I will never cry again. Oh, had it made him feel ugly, awkward? Had her mother been polite, tiny, frightened? Cello could feel her own children tear out of her body, race past her in time, to other arms and stranger beds; Come back, it is not safe! she cried, and knew the pain her mother must feel. Oh my high ceilings, my wide-floored room, and all the silent mornings when I rode home over the highway among the other cars! Oh, it was safe, it was safe, she pleaded. Dancing, hadn't she seemed to become the drum itself, its sound in her ears, moving her slender limbs? The music reaching the ceiling, until Cello herself had grown straight and tall, touched everyone.

The soldier had walked across the room, and his hands held her shoulders. She knew how his face would look, his mouth open just a little in worry, and then there was the way he had always strode before her down the beach, the tender morning wind in his hair. But she couldn't open her eyes, look at the room again across her own history of hope, knowing now that it had not been safe, she had not been holding the world close, giving it answers. She had been a skinny dancer, before the eyes of the college boys, and she found herself searching and searching for her own departed children, waiting for them to return, and she wondered hopelessly, Will they know me? Has someone changed them to foreign people with strong eyes, who will not feel me watching, waiting?

Please do not ask me to change back, it was so very hard! Do not prefer me round and warm, nestled under your arm, making everyone laugh at dinner, crying easily. What can parents do but wait empty-handed, hope to be told pieces of the truth? Not I, not I . . . She had thought that now at last she was large enough, sure enough to wipe all tears away, but instead she had been lost, and her mother must have stood here, wondering how to lose Cello, how to keep Cello, and speaking in careful words. Failed again, huh? Haven't I?

Oh God, said Cello, and she feared the love inside her once more, saw herself grown helpless. Never again could she be the slim guardian of love, and she leaned her head on the doorway and cried.

George Young

Fourth of July, corn knee high

He was approaching the sleepy river at last now, and small puffs of fog
swept toward and past his car. The fog grew thick, swirling in his headlights,
as he drove down the hill into the valley. He could not see the water or its
movement for the fog, but he felt the river chill and smelled the river air,
and across the way, as if through a whirling shroud, he saw the strange,
blurred glow of the lights of his home town.

He passed Oscar Purvis' souvenir stand, and as the hand-lettered sign
of misspelled words whirled in the fog, he began to remember the names
and faces he had not thought about for years.

He wondered if, while old Hump hammered and sawed, Nasby still
stretched himself out under a shade tree, snoring, a bottle of water cradled
to his side; and he wondered if Otis still leaned against his broom and
practiced, on some new young boy, those interminable sermons on women,
drink, and cards. And he wondered if his father still had to step out of
the office now and then and say something, or clear his throat, or maybe even
just cast a shadow, so that Otis would cut his sermon short and try to pretend
that he had been sweeping all the time, and Nasby would somehow slink
to an upright position and slowly, scratching all the while, find some light
board or other that might need moving from one pile to another.

And he wondered if that new young boy, if there was one, ever paused
in his work sometimes to watch in silence as old Hump slowly raised his
left arm, which was nearly twice as thick as his right, and brought it down
quickly, powerfully, driving a nail into solid oak as far as an ordinary
man could drive one into pine. And he wondered if Otis still looked at the
old giant with the curved back and the hundred-year-old eyes, and said,
shaking his head: "You know, you can tell by his shoulders that he was
some man at one time—but just goes to show you how whiskey can
ruin a man."

For Hump and Nasby had always been the bad examples in Otis' practice
sermons. Those two had attended Saturday night poker almost as
regularly as Otis attended church, and, the story went, one Sunday
morning, just as Otis was driving a whole church bus full of children past

the gas station where the Saturday night games were played, a chair came crashing through the window of the station, followed first by Nasby flying backwards, then by Hump charging forth, all accompanied by such a long and loud string of ill-chosen nouns and adjectives that Otis had to bear down on the bus horn with all his might to protect the innocent ears of the children from all those uncouth words.

But many years had passed since he had first heard that story, and now as he drove across the bridge into his old home town, he wondered what was truly memory and what was simply fog.

"That you, Boy?" his father's voice called, as he shut the door.

"It's me," he said.

"Drive straight through?"

"Straight through."

"Well. Welcome home."

His father stood at the top of the stairs, looking thin, wrinkled, and gray. Three years ago, his father had not looked old.

"See you've put on some weight and lost some hair," his father said, shaking his hand. "Don't let it bother you, though. Hell, mine was the same when I was your age. Thought I was going to be bald as a rock, then it stopped falling out, just started getting gray."

"Well, it's good to be home."

"Good to have you home," his father said. "Let's get some sleep now, and we'll talk in the morning."

The bright sun shining through his window did not wake him until noon. Downstairs, in the light, his father looked even thinner and more wrinkled than he had the night before.

"Hungry, Boy?" his father asked, and, knowing that boys who came home were always hungry, he called to Anna, the cook, without waiting for an answer: "Bring this boy some chicken, Anna. He's hungry as a bear." When Anna brought the chicken, his father put three large pieces on each of their plates. "Well, tell me how you like that city life. They keep you running most of the time?"

"I get to sit down once in a while," he said.

"You got that big raise, didn't you?"

"Yes, I got that one last year, then they gave me another one just last week."

"Good. Just keep it up, Boy, and first thing you know you'll be president of the whole damn company."

He smiled. "Well, that's a ways off." He looked at his father carefully.

"But how are you doing, Dad? That's what I came home to find out about. How you feeling now?"

"Oh, hell, I feel fine. You know those doctors, always getting alarmed about something. I told them not to write you. I feel fine."

"I hear they're going to open you up to have a look."

"Well, that's what they say, but I just may not let them. Hell, it's my body. If I don't want them poking around I don't have to let them. Anyway, I feel fine now. You want another piece of chicken?"

"No. Well, look Dad, you ought to let them have a look anyway. They probably won't find anything, but even if they do, you know they've got that radium and that cobalt. You know what they can do these days."

"Well they're not going to do it to me—Anna, bring this boy some more mash potatoes, he's hungry as a bear—now let's not worry about me any more. I feel fine. What did you make this boy for dessert, Anna?"

After lunch, he lit his pipe, and he noticed that his father's brown stained fingers shook as he lit a cigarette.

"Well, how are things over at the lumber yard?" he asked. "I was just thinking about old Hump and Nasby and Otis as I drove in last night. Wondering if the two of them still loafed all the time while Hump did all the work."

His father was laughing. "Didn't you read about it in the papers?"

"Read what?"

"Hell, Hump shot Nasby last Fourth of July and they've had him up in Liberty jail ever since."

"You don't mean he shot and killed him, do you?"

"Naw, you know Nasby's too mean to kill. Hump shot at him five times and hit him twice. The first bullet hit Nasby in the head, up behind the ear. Well, you know how thick Nasby is up there. He just reached up and picked it out the way you might pick a tick off a long-haired dog. The next bullet got him as he was running back to the house—hit him in the ass and worked its way up so close to the spine the doctors were afraid to take it out. So Nasby's still sitting on that one. They say he doesn't even notice it any more, except the day before and after a rain. The third bullet hit either Nasby's little boy or a tree. The boy says it hit him and the next day's paper carried a picture of the boy holding up his shirt and pointing to the scratch, but I've checked into it and what that boy calls a bullet wound looks a lot more like an average sized mosquito bite. The fourth bullet punctured a watermelon, and the fifth blasted a hole in the sidewalk. All told, it was about a dollar and a half's worth of damage."

He shook his head. "It's just hard to believe. I can still picture Hump hammering and sawing—but shooting Nasby. I just can't picture it."

"Well, I guess a lot has changed around town since you worked at the yard. I guess I'll have to catch you up."

As they moved into the next room, to get more comfortable, he noticed how slowly his father now walked. And he noticed again how in lighting another cigarette before beginning the story, his father's brown tipped fingers shook.

Much more had changed than he could have realized. As his father told the story, he could only shake his head in wonder.

Hump had, it seems, a few years before, at the age of sixty seven or eight, fallen in love with Sugar Yancey. Now everyone knew that Sugar Yancey was the richest woman in the county. But she weighed almost three hundred pounds, had greasy, matted hair, and always had about her the strong odor of old sweat mixed with Piggly Wiggly Jungle Flower perfume. Women in the town always used to tell their little daughters: Comb your hair and brush your teeth or you'll look like Sugar Yancey.

"Hump moved in with her about three years ago," his father said. "And at first they were just like a couple of honeymooners. I used to drive by Sugar's house sometimes of an evening on my way to the bank meetings, and there they'd be, sitting together on the porch swing, their feet both propped up against the rail, sharing a bottle of Old Grandad. And the way they'd be looking at each other—well, it was just like Romeo and Juliet."

But after a few months things seemed to start going wrong. Sugar's natural laziness and stinginess came out, and soon it was Hump who had to buy all the groceries with what money he had left after Saturday night poker. Sugar refused to spend a cent of her own or lift a finger to help herself. Hump even had to water her when she was thirsty because she wouldn't leave the T.V. long enough to get her own.

"I figured Hump was having problems," his father said. He lit another cigarette. "Because some mornings he would show up for work late and other mornings he wouldn't show up at all. Hell, you remember how reliable he used to be. And he seemed to be drinking more. Used to be he could just look at an angle and tell whether it was square or not, but now when he tried that he'd be off two or three degrees. And now and then, he'd even miss the nail he was driving at. But worst of all, he was losing bad at cards, mostly to Nasby. The other boys would always quit when Hump got down to his whiskey money, but Nasby would take even that.

Poor Hump was turning into a henpecked wreck. But finally it all came to a head over a lightbulb Nasby was keeping on over his watermelon stand all night."

Nasby, he was surprised to learn, had quit working at the lumber yard some years ago, and had opened a watermelon stand.

"He liked the contemplative life," his father said. "He had the women unload the watermelon truck every week, then, the hard work finished, he would lie down against the stack of watermelons until the women sold them all." His father puffed on the cigarette. "He was going to open a bait stand, too, but none of the women would dig the worms."

And the women, it seemed, were not two now, but three. He remembered Old Rose, and Old Rose's daughter Mary, but sometime last year Mary's daughter, Little Hazel, had moved in with them too. Before Little Hazel moved in, Sugar had been slipping across the street, while Hump was at work, to meet Nasby, it was rumored, behind the watermelon pile. It was just after Little Hazel moved in and promptly got pregnant that Sugar began to complain to Hump about the all-night light over the watermelon stand.

"Now it's just a yellow, hundred-watt bulb, and it doesn't make much of a glare, but Sugar said that the way it glared in her window at night she couldn't get any sleep, and finally she told Hump that unless he did something about that bulb she would throw him out of her house for good. So Hump went over to the stand and asked Nasby in as nice a way as you can ask a man who's been taking your whiskey money every week if he wouldn't turn off the light at night. Nasby snapped back something about a free country and how it was his own property and he would burn as many damn bulbs at night as he wanted to, and he said that if Hump came back to complain again he could expect a knife to be waiting for him. And you know Nasby's as well known for his ways with knives as he is for his ways with women.

"Well, Hump didn't take kindly to Nasby's words, but, as he said, he wanted to go home and study on it for a while. I spose he must have burned about a gallon of midnight oil, ninety proof, because the next morning, the Fourth of July, he came out red eyed and staggering. I had just gone over to the office to empty the dehumidifier, and I was locking up when I heard Hump shouting: 'Nasby Purvis, if you ain't the son-of-a-bitchinest yellow backed coward that ever lived you'll come out and settle with me right now!' I'd got just about halfway up the street toward Hump when Nasby came out of his house hitching up his pants. Hump was standing there in the middle of the street, holding a rusty looking old pistol with both hands, shooting, then pausing to wave a car through, then shooting again. That old pistol had just about enough power to sort of arch the bullets across the street, I guess. And by the time I got there Nasby was crawling back toward his house on all fours as fast as he could go, but at the same time he was looking back over his shoulder and howling and swearing at Hump with every breath. All eight or nine of Nasby's children, plus his three women, were standing there, jumping up and down and screeching at Hump like a bevy of flushed bats. And while people in the backed up cars were staring and everyone else was running around screaming, Hump just walked calmly as you please back to Sugar's house.

"Someone ran off to get the law, and after a few minutes Oscar Purvis— believe it or not they made him town marshal last year—well, Oscar Purvis came strutting down the street with his pistol drawn. He told everyone to stand back, but when he got up to the door of Sugar's house he didn't know quite how to go about it. Finally he started hammering on the door with the butt of his pistol and shouted: 'This is the law. This is the law. Hump, come on out of there with your hands up.' Nothing happened for a minute, but just as Oscar was getting ready to pound on the door again, Hump opened the door and just stood there, smiling around at the people outside. Oscar stuck the gun in his stomach and marched him out to the street backwards, and all the time Hump was telling him: 'I wouldn't hurt you, Oscar. I wouldn't hurt you.' But Oscar had forgotten the handcuffs, so he told Hump to stand still and not move, and he loped up to the souvenir stand for the handcuffs. While he was gone, Hump just stood there with his hands up in the air, looking around and smiling at everyone, and all this time Nasby's kids were throwing sticks and dirt at him and people in cars were stopping to stare. Then finally Oscar came loping back with the handcuffs and they put Hump in that old '48 Hudson Hornet of Oscar's, the one with all the spotlights, mudflaps, and foxtails, and while Oscar was fretting with the starter, Hump was chuckling out loud: 'Huh huh, I shot the sumbitch. Huh huh, I shot the sumbitch.' Then somebody got the car started, and with the siren screaming and the tires squealing and the oil smoke clouding up behind, off they roared toward Liberty jail. And that's where Hump has been ever since."

His father lit another cigarette and looked at his watch. "Hey, my foursome was supposed to tee off five minutes ago," he said. "Got to run." He put the cigarette in the ashtray and went to get his golf shoes from the closet. "Would you like to play with us?" he asked.

"No, not today."

"Sure like to—" His father's voice broke into a long, hoarse cough. "Sure like to have you join us."

"Is Doc playing?"

"Yes, he's playing."

"Then maybe I'll come out and meet you after the game. I want to talk to him—I don't like the sound of that cough."

"It's nothing." He rushed back into the room with his golf shoes in his hand and a silly hat on his head. "I'm healthy as a horse. Don't hit them as far as I used to, but I can still give it a pretty good knock. See you later. Sorry I got to run, but we'll talk again later. Hell of a thing about Hump, isn't it?"

He nodded. After his father had gone he leaned back in his chair and stared at the cigarette still burning in the ashtray. He was afraid of what they would find if they opened his father. And Hump. It was still difficult to picture Hump in jail. Nasby, yes, that would have been easy to imagine. The Nasby he had known as a boy had even then been capable of cheating and cutting. But this shooting—it was just not the sort of thing that people you knew well and admired did. Shootings happened in newspapers, in movies, on television screens. But an old carpenter, whose skill with nails and boards and saw had helped angle a growing boy's mind toward long, constructive aims, was difficult to picture aiming a pistol at a man. He had to see Hump in Liberty jail.

On the way to Liberty he drove past Nasby Purvis' watermelon stand and saw the yellow light which he had not seen last night in the fog, but which, he now agreed, could not cause much of a glare.

For gas he stopped at Edgar Purvis' station, where the Saturday night games used to be played. When he went in for tobacco, he nodded to the loafers sitting around the fan.

"Well drat burn, Boy, if it ain't you after all!" a very familiar voice rattled at him. He turned.

"Otis!" he said.

"Yes sir, drat burn, I was just telling the boys here: 'Blamed if that don't look like that boy,' and you come in and sure enough it is you. How you doing, Boy. Looks like you've gained some weight and lost some hair."

"Fine, how you Otis?" he said. He looked at the other loafers and saw, on the floor, among them, Nasby, leaning back against an old tire. "Nasby. Boys."

Otis, holding a batch of revival announcements under one arm, was still pumping his hand, grinning at him, and repeating: "Yes, sir. Drat burn, you're looking good, Boy. You're looking good." Otis looked at all the other old boys sitting and squatting on the floor. "Now ain't he something, ain't he just something now!"

He looked at Nasby. "Understand there was some excitement around here last Fourth of July."

Nasby, busy picking his nose with one hand and playing with a long, open knife in the other, looked up but said nothing. Otis grinned. "That's right, Boy. That's right. Old Hump figured there wasn't going to be no fireworks for the Fourth, so he worked some up himself." Everybody chuckled at this except Nasby, who, leaning back against the tire, had stopped picking his nose and had started picking his fingernails with the long knife. "I always knew Hump was bound to do something like that," Otis said. "I used to tell you so, didn't I, Boy. I knew he'd show his colors sooner or later. Why the way he drank, and chased women, and played cards—I told you it would happen, didn't I, Boy."

"That's right," Nasby said, and as he spoke everyone looked at him. He picked his nose again, then looked at his fingers as he pressed them together and pulled them apart. "And if that sumbitch dares to show his face in this town again, he can expect a knife waiting for him." Nasby looked straight at him and held up the knife for him to see. "He's one of them mountaineers—had no business coming to this town in the first place. Things is different now than what they used to be." Tobacco juice was trickling from his chin, and he paused to wipe it on his sleeve. "Used to be folks knew how to take care of a sumbitch like that. When my daddy was a boy, why any niggers or mountaineers moved in, the nightriders seen they didn't stay long. Nowadays they let just anybody settle in here, and all it means is trouble for decent folks. But let him show up again in this town and I'll take care of him the way they used to take care of his kind." Nasby raised the knife again for him to see.

"So that's the way it is, huh Nasby," he said.

"That's the way it is," Nasby said.

He nodded, bought his tobacco, and walked back to the car.

In Liberty, he drove down the main street, past the rows of dirty little houses with the junked washing machines, sunflowers, and automobile parts in the front yards, past these houses to the jail. Leroy, the jailer, was sitting with the loafers and whittlers who were perched along the courthouse wall. When he saw who it was, he waved, favoring his perpetual game leg, limped over to the jail. "How are you, Boy?" Leroy said, in his high, friendly voice. "Something I can do for you?"

"I'd like to see Hump," he said. "I brought him some chewing tobacco."

"All right," Leroy said. "Just a minute and I'll get the key." Leroy pulled out an enormous ring of keys and began to sort through them. All the old boys perched along the wall had big eyes on those keys, but Leroy calmly shuffled through them, holding up first one, then another to the light. "Got so blame many keys I can't hardly keep them all straight," he said, inadvertently raising his voice so that it carried out to the courthouse wall. "Oh, here it is," he said, going back to the first key he had raised to the sun. "Sure you'll be all right in there, now?" He said, opening the door.

"I'll be all right."

"Well, I'll be back to get you in a little while." Leroy closed the door, puffed up his chest, and half-limped, half-swaggered back toward those wide-eyed old boys perched along the wall, unavoidably jingling that big ring of keys as he went.

It was a dark, smelly, one-room jail with stone walls and earth floor. Hump was sitting on the cot against the back wall, squinting at him, not knowing who it was walking toward him. Finally, when he got closer, Hump smiled and rose stiffly from the cot.

"Well, Boy. So it's you," he said. "You're looking good, though I think you've lost a little hair."

"Hello, Hump," he said. He shook the huge, yellowed hand, and stared at the old, grizzled face. "They been treating you all right?"

"Guess so," Hump said. "It's jail, but it could be worse."

He stared at the old man who had now moved into the light of an unshaded bulb hanging from the ceiling, looking for some sign of the powerful giant he remembered. The corners of Hump's eyes were so red now, the muscle in his left arm looked so loose and flabby, his skin looked so yellow and wrinkled. "Do they let you walk around outside some, Hump?" he asked.

"Well, I spose I could if I had a mind to," Hump said. "But you know—all those old boys out there, they'd stare at me like I was the monkey in the zoo."

"Well what do you do with your time, Hump? Do you read—you want me to send you some books?"

"Boy, you know I can't read. I couldn't even read what they wrote about me in the paper. Leroy showed me the clippings, and when he said I could have them I kept them till I ran out of wiping paper. No, Boy. I can't read. Mostly I just sit and think."

"What do you think about Hump? You decided what you're going to do when you get out?"

"I'll never get out, Boy. Oh, at first I thought I might move on to some other place, maybe do some more carpenter work. But they won't let me out now. They know I'm too mean to let out. They found out I killed a man down in Bell County—that was before I come to this town. Nobody ever knew about that around here, but after I shot Nasby they started checking in and opening things up and they found out about that fellow I killed. They'll never let me out now. And even if they did, Nasby and I would get into it again and I'd probably wind up killing the sumbitch."

"I didn't know you'd killed a man."

"Of course you didn't. Nobody around here knew till I shot Nasby and they started checking into things. But hell yes, I killed a man, and I'd kill Nasby if they let me out. It ain't that I hate the sumbitch—I don't. But you know—one thing would lead to another, and first thing you know I'd be shooting at him to kill him. It's better they never let me out."

He stared at the floor. "I didn't think you were the kind to kill, Hump."

Hump stared at the floor too, and for a long time neither of them spoke again. Something, somewhere in the cell smelled dead and rotten. He wondered, was it a bird, a rat, something that had gotten in, couldn't get out, had died, and no one had bothered to remove. He looked around the room, wondering what it was stinking, and wondering what he could say to cheer Hump up.

"Oh, here," he said. "I almost forgot. I brought you some chewing tobacco."

Hump grinned. "Well thank you, Boy. Thank you. You want a chew?"

"All right," he said.

Hump broke a pinch off the plug for each of them, and they began to chew together in silence.

"I'm dead inside already, Boy," Hump said. "I'm dead as last year's leaves. Just waiting for a wind to come along and blow me off. It'll be better for everybody when I'm gone."

"You're not dead, Hump. It's just this jail getting you down. You ought to get out and walk around some. I don't know what it is in here—a bird, a rat. But something's dead and rotten and stinking in here. That smell would get anybody down. You ought to get out and get some fresh air now and then—make you feel better."

Hump shook his head. "I smelled it too, boy. But then I looked all around and I found out there's nothing stinking up this jail but me."

He looked at the floor again and wanted to say something, but couldn't think of what. He chewed his tobacco for a while, spat, and chewed a while longer. Finally he heard Leroy at the door, jangling all those keys.

"Well, Hump," he said, getting up. "Got to go. Got to meet my Dad."

"How is your Dad?"

"Don't know. The doctors are going to open him up."

Hump nodded. "Well, he's a fine man. Give him my best."

"I will. Good-bye, Hump."

"Good-bye, Boy. Thanks for stopping in."

He nodded and turned to walk away before Leroy closed the door.

There was a place halfway between Liberty and home where he often used to stop the lumber truck and step out for a stretch, and he stopped at that place now.

Before him stretched a rising crescent of color, a cradled half-spectrum: first the yellow-brown earth; then the yellow at the base of the ripening tobacco plants, which darkened into the soft green of the leaves. Beyond the tobacco lay grasses, and then small oaks, shading into the blue-green hills, the hills shading into the sky.

Across the road stood corn: straight, ordered in rows past the range of the eye; green, the leaves free and streaming down the constant breeze; tall, reaching far higher than the head of a man. He watched as tassels and leaves, yellow and green, moved back and forth freely as a breeze moved slowly over from the left, pushing out across the field as far as he could see.

Farmers always said that if the corn reached knee high by the Fourth of July it meant a bumper crop. And now, looking out as far as he could see, he gazed at the fulfillment of a promise others had beheld on gazing out on Fourth of July. All of him was drawn into the wonderful sense of movement, the weaving back and forth, the yellow and green, the freedom with which each leaf and tassel moved. Yet in just another month or two it would all be plowed under again to prepare the ground for another spring. And the ground he was standing on would be the spot from which new promises and forecasts would be made, new fulfillments gauged, new harvests plowed under again. And he, whom they called "Boy" was getting bald, and they were going to open his father up, and Hump, who had looked inside himself, said he was dead inside.

It was nothing to be frightened about, he thought. It was nothing new or strange, and neither Hump nor his father had been the first to know the feeling he now had, nor would he himself be the last. What he now saw had been there all the time, in the cards from the beginning. It was in his father now, and would still be there when they opened him up. And it had been in Hump all along—he just hadn't seen it until Liberty jail.

There was nothing to do, he guessed, but do what nearly everybody seemed to be doing, that was, living on with it and in it and not lose a sense of humor. And though his hands were still shaking slightly, he lit his pipe, looked once more across the road at that rising crescent of color and out at those ordered rows of moving corn, blew out the match, and drove on toward home to join his father.

Angela Davis

Mr. Rudishill

"Get me a cup of hot water right now," Mae said.

Mrs. Carson never swore out loud. The water spigot burped and sputtered, then gushed muddy-colored water.

"Hotter than that," Mae said. "It's for my gas."

Mrs. Carson let the water run full force and leaned against the windowsill. Light rain fell against the window bars and splattered Mrs. Carson's back. She thought barred windows silly; in this building, the women were weak and so old they smelled and felt of death. She hated to bring them from the ward to this room each day, for they leaned against her and she could feel the brittle bone beneath the papery skin of their wrists and fingers and smell their loose, unwashed bodies. Their eyes trembled in shrunken faces as they looked at her, pleading.

Mrs. Carson looked at the small grey room, the glass-front cabinets which lined one wall, the picture of braided Gretel made from cloth (Hansel had fallen to the floor), and on the wall opposite her, the mirror bordered with a ruffle. In the mirror she could see the bottom half of her white uniform and athletic legs crossed at the ankles. Her ladies were seated at two tables, Annie, Ruth, and Mae at the one closest to her, Mrs. Conner and Susie at the other. All but Mae were bent over their sewing, their shoulders hunched as they labored their needles through bits of cloth.

Mae sat idle, neglecting her scrapbook. One arm lay on the table; the other rested akimbo on her hip, Mrs. Carson felt, in defiance. Mae stared at her, a mixed expression of anger and defeat on her tilted face. Mrs. Carson put the cup of water before Mae and sat down at the table.

Mae had brought a doll with her; it was an ugly nude rubber one. She poked it in the eye with her scissors.

"Why, Mae," Mrs. Carson said, "don't hurt your sweet baby."

Mae belched, as a prelude. "I'm no mental patient," she said, "so don't take that tone with me, Mrs. Therapy-worker."

"I think I'm mental," Ruth said. She had a sweet, placid face. Mrs. Carson liked her.

"That's a cute dress you've got on, Ruth," she said.

Ruth smiled, "Yeah, isn't it. Look, it buttons and unbuttons." There were two brass buttons at the top of the bodice. She carefully unbuttoned and buttoned them.

"Brass?"

"No!" Ruth looked shocked. "Gold. If they was brass I'd throw 'em down and go 'bout my business."

"See," Mae said, "she's mental, I ain't."

"How come you're not?" Ruth said.

Annie dropped her embroidery and looked down at the floor. "Don't you talk back to me, John Chatham," she said to the tiles.

"How come?" Ruth asked Mae again.

"Shut up. How can I talk when you butt in like a mental patient?" Mae began tearing whole pages out of a magazine.

"Now quit that, Mae," Mrs. Carson said. "A new magazine!"

Mae regarded her stonily, then looked at the glass-front cabinet. "That cabinet looks like a hurrah's nest," she said.

Mrs. Carson laughed. Mae was always saying that; she had been a housekeeper and couldn't stand a mess. The shelves were disorderly, piled with cloth, paints and other supplies, but she hated to poke around in them for fear of cockroaches and spiders.

"You haven't told us why you're not mental, Mae," Mrs. Carson said, to make peace.

"Well," Mae said, "I wouldn't try to get away with some things the mentals do. I'm here for somethin' else. Ruth now . . ." She pointed her scissors at Ruth. "Ruth walks around stark raving naked," she whispered.

"Only in the john." Ruth slammed her hand on the table.

"Uh uh. Everywhere. In the hall, on the ward, and in my lady's chamber. And with Mr. Rudishill around. You gotta watch Ruth," she told Mrs. Carson. "Since you're new, I'll give you that tip, you gotta watch her." Mae ran her tongue over wide, slippery lips. "That Mr. Rudishill," she said softly, "he's sumpin' else."

"Thread my needle," Susie said in a whining voice. Mrs. Carson moved to the next table in relief. She had not heard of Mr. Rudishill and didn't care to. Mae had irritated her from the first day she had worked here, a little over two weeks ago, but she had enjoyed Mae's stories for a while. They made her feel knowledgeable and understanding; they were so obviously the result of the classic persecution complex she had studied at college several years ago. She could remember the page in the text where the complex was described and could remember studying it for the test but here she found a living example. So at first she looked forward to the stories eagerly, but soon discovered they almost all began the same way.

"I used to be paralyzed," was the most frequent. "Yes, that's right, paralyzed, all down this side." Mae would touch her sagging left cheek and draw her hand all the way down the left side of her body to her feet. She would watch Mrs. Carson, not the body she was touching. "An attendant done it. I's just standin' there next up to the ward door waitin' to be let out, just mindin' my own beeswax and the attendant whomped me one on the hip. She's fattern you can imagine," she would say, "and she done it the next day too. That's how come I got the stroke the next Sunday. Eatin' some grapes, sittin' on my bed, and pow the stroke hits. Musta been on account of the attendant took me so by su'prise. An' at first I wouldn't tell the doc on account of they might make it hard for me on the ward. But finally I said 'Could a lick have done it, doc, could a lick have done it?' and the doc says 'Why Mae? Why Mae?'" In this story, as in all the others, the enemy was punished. The attendant was stricken with gonorrhea and fired: Mae's favorite denouement. Mrs. Carson tried to be attentive; she was afraid not to be. But after all, she reasoned, there were the other ladies who needed attention and understanding too.

Mae belched suddenly, this time very loud. "Hey," she said, after deciding Mrs. Carson wasn't going to respond to the belch, "Hey, you going to sit over there all day?"

"I'm helping Susie." Mrs. Carson began sorting embroidery thread into piles. It bothered her that she had made an excuse; she should have said something firm, yet consoling.

"Lord God have mercy on us," Mae intoned. Her voice was high and chant-like. "Lord God have mercy on all the people in this room worth the saving. God have mercy on me. God have mercy on Ruth. God have mercy on Annie Chatham. And Lord God at the next table forgive and have mercy on two only. God have mercy on Susie Murray. Lord God please have mercy on Eva Conner." Mae turned and looked at Mrs. Carson in triumph. "Lord God save five out of six of us in this room from Mr. Rudishill." Mrs. Carson, feeling awkwardly silent and embarrassed, looked back at her. Mae laughed suddenly: a low rumble and a twitching of shoulders. "Ain't I a mess?"

"How's that scrapbook, Mae?" Mrs. Carson moved to the other table and looked at the picture Mae had clipped from a magazine. It was another frothy blue-eyed baby and a mother bending over, rich brown hair falling across her cheek. "How sweet," she said.

"You don't know 'em from a bunch of turnip greens," Mae said, "but I know 'em all too well. You won't know nothin' till you've had and lost."

Mrs. Carson smiled and nodded.

"Hey," Ruth said, "your teeth are clean. Mine usta be too but see I only have three now. Brushed 'em all away." Mrs. Carson raised her eyebrows and Ruth nodded emphatically. "Brushed 'em all away. Can't hardly eat now. I've only had three meals in the last two years."

"Oh, Ruth, that's not so."

"Yes, ma'am." Ruth grinned, then became serious. "A veal cutlet, a grapefruit and uh . . . an egg." Her eyes were glazed in reminiscence. "A cup of coffee once too, I believe. That's on accounta no teeth. Usta have an eye tooth here and an eye tooth here . . ." She pointed carefully.

"That Mr. Rudishill," Mae said, "I bet his teeth bite like a hoss."

"All right," Mrs. Carson said, "who in the world is Mr. Rudishill?"

Mae's mouth began to work violently. She dropped her scissors and looked at Mrs. Carson. "That Mr. Rudishill," she said, breathing heavily, "that man is after me."

Ruth locked her hands under her armpits and cackled. "If any man is after anybody, it's me."

Mae gave her a scalding look. "Just you hush your mouth, MISS nudity. You might try as you will, look bug-eyed at every man on the bus ride and carry on like you do, you'll never get one if you live to a hundred and ten." She turned to Mrs. Carson, one hand dramatically on her bosom.

"I know plenty plus somethin' when it comes to sex," Ruth said. "But me and my husband didn't marry for that. Only went to bed three times in thirty years."

"How'd you get so many children?" Mrs. Carson said.

"He just touched me on the arm and ping it come out my nose."

Mae threw her doll across the room. She looked at it on the floor. "Elsie, honey." She heaved herself from the chair to retrieve it, then fell back in her seat and turned to Mrs. Carson. "That Mr. Rudishill's got more in mind than touchin' me on the arm." Mrs. Carson drew away from Mae's intense face and her smell of unwashed clothes. Mae leaned closer, her eyes large and full and hypnotic. "He's been watchin' and slurpin' at me for I don't recollect how many months. Everyday I go on a walk, see, up by Brown Building, and there he is, just lookin' from behind the corner."

"Sex is dirty," Mrs. Conner said from across the room. "I'm getting out." Mrs. Carson watched her collect her crochet needles and wool and push open the door.

"How do you get outside, Mae?" Mrs. Carson said smiling.

Mae looked at her steadily. "Like I tole a judge once, that's for me to know and you to find out, if you can. But don't you worry 'bout him none. He's after me." She wiped her mouth with the back of her hand.

Susie trembled against the table's edge. She had wet her dress. "Back to the ward, please, Susie," Mrs. Carson said. It was almost time for lunch anyway, she thought, time for them all to go.

"Are you going to pay me mind or not?" Mae's hand clenched Mrs. Carson's wrist. "If I am paralyzed again," she said slowly, emphasizing each word, "If I am, it'll be his fault. That man, Mr. Rudishill. You wouldn't save me from him if I was on my deathbed. You wouldn't even give me a piece of candy if it would save my life, you'd just rustle around in that prissy white dress an' say no, Annette Mae Hensley, no candy, you have diabetes. Even if it would save my life you wouldn't." Her face was distorted, sucked in as if she had eaten a big lemon.

"Now Mae," Mrs. Carson said. "Mae, don't be silly."

Mae sighed and released Mrs. Carson's arms.

"Now, Mae," Mrs. Carson said, "you know you don't go outside. Even if you did, there's no one to hurt you."

"Oh yes. There's Mr. Rudishill." Mae nodded slowly and looked out the window. Her eyes were vague, focused on a distant point. "Just yestiddy I found out his name. I crep up to his corner at Brown Building and peeked around and I could see him lookin' at me, his eyes all glittery and his nose runnin' and I says 'what's your name man,' an' he says Rudishill. The sun was bearin' down so hard I could barely make out anything but that and his glitterin' eyes. An then he says real low, 'Woman, I don't even *care* what your name is.' And then he shook out everything he had, with me just standin' there like that and he laughed and laughed you never heard the like. I ran like the devil was clutchin' at my shoestrings an fell on my bed to pray to the Lord God our Saviour in Heaven."

Annie slapped her thigh. "Don't you bring no more Bufferin in *this* house, John Chatham."

"He's after me, all right. And me such a frail thing." Mae touched Mrs. Conner's arm and looked at her sadly. "I don't know what I'll do if he gets me."

"You ain't so frail, honey," Ruth said. "You're just afraid he *won't* get you, that's what." She plucked at her buttons.

"I'm not comin' back in here again," Mae said. She walked across the room and stopped at the door. "This place is a hurrah's nest," she said, without looking back. She slammed the door behind her and thudded down the hall.

Mr. Rudishill's appearance in Mae's mind frightened Mrs. Carson, frightened her the more because she didn't know why. She often thought of him at home, brooded over Mae's piece of fiction until it ceased to be fiction and she could see Mr. Rudishill and his glittering eyes and she shuddered, feeling dirty and sinful even though repulsed. She might be doing some little thing, like making the beds or reading her Sunday School lesson, and Mr. Rudishill would come to her like a slap. At work, however, she made Mr. Rudishill a joke, a basis on which to re-establish a rapport with Mae every day so as to avoid lame silence before her stare. "How's Mr. you-know-who these days?" "Who?" "You-know-who. Starts with an R." "Rogers?" "Nooo . . ." Some days Mae would clench Mrs. Carson's hand and say, "Mr. Rudishill, he's sumpin' else. Shakin' out everythin' he's got with me just standin' there." But usually she would say "Mr. Rudishill, who's he?"

One morning about two weeks after first hearing of Mr. Rudishill, Mrs. Carson arrived at work late with a headache. A sullen nurse watched her enter the building, then looked pointedly at the hall clock. Mrs. Carson hurried the ladies from the ward to the room, avoiding the nurse's eyes. The ladies settled down to work happily, turning their old faces to the window, to the flood of April sunlight and the comfortable noise of workmen talking on the lawn outside.

Mae was electric: giddy and sullen in spurts. Mrs. Carson straightened a shelf in the cabinet, then sat at the table with Annie, Ruth and Mae.

Mae looked at her, waiting, paste brush poised in the air.

"Well, good morning, sunshine," Mrs. Carson said.

"Good morning, cloud," Mae said. She laughed and laughed, holding her side with one hand.

Ruth scratched her grey head. "A thief came last night. Stole three of my pink silk dresses and threw lead down my throat."

Mrs. Carson wished she had brought her aspirin.

"Men's always been after me," Mae said. She moved her mouth happily and folded her arms across her chest. "In Norfolk one day a sailor looked at me on the bridge so I started walkin'. I walked alla way from that bridge to Gramerley's Shoe Store. Well! I tried on shoes and he tried on shoes! I was in W. T. Grant's and he was in W. T. Grant's! Finally he comes up an' says 'honey, meet me at six-thirty at the Eatwell.' So I smiles an' says 'sure thing' and beats it home. That night I was washin' the dishes and watchin' that clock and laughin'. Mama says 'what you laughin' for, Mae Hensley,' and I tells her. She says 'honey, you done the right thing.' " Mae laughed again and Mrs. Carson laughed with her. "I's a mess then, just like now, and a good lookin' mess, too."

Annie walked to the mirror and bent down to look, her arms folded behind her back. She looked at her face as if it were far away and someone had just pointed it out to her. Her eyes were narrow slits behind her glasses; she rocked forward and back gently.

"Weren't you married then, Mae?" Ruth said.

"Huh?"

"Married. Weren't you married. Before, when you told that you were married."

"Yeah. I reckon I was married once. Me and Bill had some time in bed. Uh *huh*."

"Sex," Mrs. Conner said, "sex, sex, sex."

Ruth patted Mae's hand. "That's all right, dearie, you just have a dirty mind."

Mae's face turned stony. "It's men what has dirty minds." She looked at Mrs. Carson a long time. "My husband did."

"Where's your sweet baby, Mae?" Mrs. Carson said.

"Dead. Stone stiff. Tried to kill me, she did." Mae clutched the table edge. "Tried to kill me." Mae's voice cracked.

"Don't be ridiculous, Mae," Mrs. Carson said.

"Ri-dic-u-lous. You're ridiculous. You'd try to kill me if you could, you'd deny me candy on my deathbed if you had the only piece in the world and the doctor begged and begged." She rapped on the table with the scissors. "You don't know A from bullsfoot cause you haven't lost a baby that tried to kill. That man done it. Mr. Rudishill. Mr. Rudishill." Mae was screaming now.

"Stop." Mrs. Carson slapped Mae's hand. "Stop it right now." Mrs. Carson spoke carefully, trying to reason. "Mae, we don't want to hear about Rudishill today. My little boy is sick and we missed a payment on the car . . ."

"My cataracts are actin' up," Mae said. "I swear. I swear I've been through H E double L and drug up and down the chimney twice."

"Mmmm." Mrs. Carson looked out the window.

Mae belched. "That Mr. Rudishill. My heart palpitates. I'm gettin' nervous."

"It's the change of life," Ruth said. "That's all, dearie."

"I may not look it but I passed that, so shut up. It's that Rudishill." She banged the table with her fist.

"Mae," Mrs. Carson said, "Let's not hear about him today," Mrs. Carson's palms were wet; she felt suffocated. She walked to the window and looked out at the lawn and the trees in the distance. "Just please be quiet."

"No," Mae yelled. "No. Do you know what it's like?" Mrs. Carson turned around and saw Mae rip a button from Ruth's dress and run across the room to the glass-front cabinet.

"Mae now . . . sit down, honey."

Mae thrust her fist through the pane and held her arm there against the jagged glass. "Mr. Rudishill will get me TODAY," she screamed.

Mrs. Carson ran to the cabinet and jerked Mae's limp arm from the glass. She looked down at it, looked at the blood on the limp wrinkled arm.

"Today. His eyes glitter." She began to cry.

"Calm down now, Mae." Mrs. Carson tried to push her towards the table.

"Lookit Mae," Mrs. Conner said, "her eyes glitter."

"Let's go get a bandaid," Mrs. Carson said. She thought perhaps she should call for the nurse.

"No no," Mae said, "I've gotta tell you." She pulled her hairnet down over one ear. Her old face was wet with tears. "I wanta tell you somethin'. I'm no mental patient. I'm in here for threatnin' to kill. But I didn't cause like I tole the judge threats like that are dangerous."

"Come on, Mae, honey."

"NO." She held Mrs. Carson's arms, pinned her against the cabinet. Mrs. Carson felt weak, nauseated by Mae's close hot smell and the blood from the old arm on hers.

"The judge sentenced me to a work farm. I says judge I'm not a goin' cause I didn't threaten. He says how you gonna get out of it. I says that's for me to know and you to find out, if you can."

Mrs. Carson looked at Ruth, who winked and said, "It's Mae's change of life, dearie."

Mae pressed harder on Mrs. Carson's arms. "That afternoon. The trial was on a Wednesday morning. That afternoon I got on the top of the double-decker bunks and put a belt around my neck, just for foolin'." Mae threw back her head and laughed wildly. "Talk about unlockin' a door and gettin' in there quick that sheriff sure did." She laughed again, then became solemn.

"My husband tole me to do somethin' dirty an' me his wife! So dirty an' horrible I only tell it when I have to. I told him I'd knife him and I meant it, by sweet Jesus. I threw a kitchen chair through the window to attract attention. He deserted an' my daughter run off an' I haven't seen her since she was fifteen." She began to cry again, this time softly. "That's why I have my baby doll."

"Baby doll," Mrs. Conner echoed.

Mae cocked her head and looked at Mrs. Carson through bright tears. "Don't you never . . . don't you never feel like you're in a hurrah's nest?"

Mrs. Carson looked at her and Mae's face became vividly clear, as if it were etched and cut out and pasted on the rest of the room. She saw Mr. Rudishill's evil grin, the glittering sunlight on his hair and eyes and teeth and saw Mae, her face heavy with sadness.

"Yes, Mae," she said.

Gail McMurray

Magdalen

"This is the way it is sometimes," Anne thought with a little breath like a sigh, muffled (her breath colder than her hands from the November wind in the streets outside). She looked around at the four, brown-stained walls, at the cracks playing along the ceiling. Inside the walls was a scattering of cheap veneer furniture: desk, chair, bed. The room smelled like an old cigar.

She dropped her coat on the chair and mechanically pulled open one of the desk drawers, touched the neat pile of hotel stationery. (When she was a little girl and she went to Baltimore with her mother, she always looked in the drawers and cubbyholes of the hotel room, under the bed, always surprised that no one had left and forgotten treasure. Or a fur muff. She had wanted just a small one, white, warm to hold like a small rabbit or like the one in the picture of Katrina and Hans with the silver skates. Her mother wouldn't let her have a fur muff; she said muffs were cheap). This dresser didn't hold treasure either, just a complimentary shoeshine cloth, the stationery, Gideon Bible. She looked again around the room. "This is not a bad place to be," she thought. "It is not a bad place." Peter was bringing in the suitcases, putting their suitcases down together on the rug. He didn't have any books with him. "Why do you bring so many books?" he had always asked her when he met her at the station. She always said she studied on the bus, which wasn't true. This time she didn't know if she had brought books or not. They might be in her suitcase. Her suitcase wasn't heavy, she remembered. She didn't know. Anne looked at her red suitcase beside his on the rug. "I love you, Peter," she said because she should have.

"I'm glad you're here," he said as he always did, walking to her and holding her shoulders. His face never looked the same as she remembered it. His eyes were light, almost no color. He looked at her very hard until she had to smile and throw her arms around him to keep from looking in his face.

"I am too," she said, wondering if she was. "It's such a long ride from Banham. It's on the ride here that I miss you most of all, get so lonely for you." He held her and she looked over his shoulder at the painting over the bed of a shepherdess with two lurid, magenta roses in her hands. Her eyes traveled up the pattern of cracks to the ceiling. You close your eyes, put your finger quickly on a page in the Bible to protect you from every crack. She pulled away from Peter and walked to the window.

Anne tugged on the cord dangling beside the faded print curtain and it yanked open. "We're on the twelfth floor," Peter said, coming to stand beside her and looking down with her into the city streets. He unlocked the window and shoved the window up so that the cold wind shivered against their skin.

"There's no screen on the window," Anne said. It seemed an impossible thing.

Peter shrugged, leaned his two hands on the window sill and looked out. There were Christmas lights up already on the store fronts, stringing together the almost deserted streets; the other gray-fronted buildings looming high across the street. Anne came nearer to the window, touched the sill with her hand. Night outside was a cold and gray cloud falling over the lights.

"But no screen at all. What if someone fell?"

"No one falls," he said. He put his arms around her and she tried hard to believe she wasn't standing there alone. I am so alone, you can't touch me, she thought in panic, but saw that he was touching her.

"But they could fall," she insisted, frightened at how wonderful and far it was to the street. But if someone fell from the window (into that surge of space and street, she thought, feeling dizzy) then they could grab for the flagpole, hold by their hands over the street. If they could only reach the flagpole. The streets were very quiet, the cars that passed could not be heard over the wind. "If someone could touch the flagpole, Peter, they wouldn't die then, would they? They could hold on there?"

"No," he said.

She stared down into the street, following the cars, the policeman on the farthest street with something under his hat. She strained to see; ear-muffs, maybe. It was very cold. Peter turned away from the window, touched her arm. "Come on," he said.

"No," she said. (His face was very close to her. She tried to look at him.) "I mean, it's really wonderful to see so far down." She looked again out the window, into a dozen streets at once; a woman with a package hurried a little boy along the sidewalk. Anne rubbed her hand against her cheek. The cold was making her face ache. The wind whistled around the edge of the building. "It makes you want to jump, doesn't it. Just because it's so high."

He laughed. "Don't," he said, "you didn't bring your wings." He moved away a little so that he was not touching her and she was standing alone again.

"But I know just what it would feel like, don't you? That rushing feeling, the fear." But when death came, how would it feel against your skin? Her eyes sought the flagpole against the brick front of the hotel. Below it was a round canvas canopy. "I don't know how strong that canopy would be," she said. "I don't know why they have a window so high without a screen."

"For God's sake, close the window." He looked at her annoyed and pulled the window closed. It was still cold in the room; she shivered, looked down into the street. Everything that moved was so far down, so small and busy. Peter pulled her away then, like she was a stubborn child. She looked at him and laughed and thought she did love him and was glad. But when he turned the television on to cover the sounds they made in the bed (she didn't think she made those little screams, but maybe the walls were just so thin), the room was ugly again and she wondered why she had forgotten that he always smoked a cigarette afterwards. She felt heavy, distant from him, and he leaned his head back against the headboard and held a cigarette between his fingers. She thought again about the window.

It was dangerous, she was sure of that. Doors shouldn't have screens, she hated those screens with initials or flamingoes, but windows and a window so far up . . . What if a child crawled up to the sill? The air in the room was still cold. She wondered if death could seep into an open window. It would be cold. She looked at Peter's face, his eyes not looking at her, but staring at the wall, his pale eyes. Kind eyes, she thought. I do love him. There was such an ugly painting on the wall. She turned, looked at it over her head, the shepherdess like a china statue, painted red lips and cheeks and too-red roses. There was once a girl, she thought, very slowly, saying the words in her mind, and she wore my clothes and used my green towel and then someone she loved died and the clothes were too fearful, touched by too much death, and they had to be burned. She was very far away from people in the street; she wondered why.

Peter put out his cigarette in the ashtray beside the telephone and turned on his side to look at her. She was pressing the wrinkled sheet down tight over the narrow mound that was her body. She moved her foot slightly under the sheet to make sure. If Peter held her it might not be true about the window.

"You look like a mummy," he said, touching her face and brushing her hair from her cheek.

She smiled at him. We belong together, she thought. His eyes *were* kind, she was sure of it. "You love me, Peter?"

"Yes," he said, pulling her to him so that she felt his heart beating beneath his chest. She was sure he was holding her, she could see his arm around her and his long fingers resting on her arm. With his free hand he began touching strands of her hair and fanning them out in a circle on the pillow around her face. "No," she said, and tossed her hair back into the tangle over her shoulders. "It's not a good feeling, being arranged like that. Like I can't move," she said apologetically and smiled at him, not knowing what made her say the words she did.

He kissed her and when she closed her eyes she saw the little girl looking in the desk for the white muff. It was somewhere, I always knew it was somewhere. Her body was lying still and sweet-smiling on a pillow, the white muff was in her hand, and a crowd of people walked by her and cried and said how small and beautiful she was. She laughed and picked up the muff and started to get up, but they wouldn't let her. They wrapped her tightly in a sheet so she couldn't move. Peter moved away and she opened her eyes. He got up from the bed and started pulling on his clothes. Anne lay very still and watched him.

"Hungry?" he asked her, not looking at her, but buttoning his shirt. His shoulders were too thin, she thought.

"Uh-huh." She watched how he moved in the room, picking up his watch and some dropped coins from the desk. There was an ashtray with his finished cigarette, the blue bedspread that had fallen wrinkled to the rug. Behind her (without looking) she knew there was the shepherdess, simpering; the plastic roses. If they loved each other they and the room were not ugly. She did love him. It was good to be with him, not separate. She noticed that a knob was missing from one of the desk drawers. It was dark outside the window. "I am living," she reminded herself, looking from one bare beige wall to the next, to the closet, the vinyl chair, the ashtray.

"What do you want?" Peter asked her, his hand on the door.

She started and pulled the sheet tighter around her.

"What kind of sandwich, I'll go find someplace that's still open."

"Anything. Whatever you like. That delicatessen on the other street maybe." If people didn't get hungry, they would die. She had eaten a big lunch at the bus station. Chicken, potatoes, carrots too. That was the only reason she wasn't hungry now. "Thank you, Peter," she said.

She did not get up, but stayed where she was, lying under the sheet with her pale hands still over her flat stomach. She looked at the wrinkled pillow next to her and long after Peter had closed the door and she had heard his footsteps moving down the hall, she kept trying to imagine his face next to her in the bed. His high forehead, pale eyes. She was sure he would come back. Through the wall from the next room she heard a faint song from a radio. The song was vaguely familiar. She tried to remember where she had heard it before but could only remember sitting in a restaurant and looking out a window into the street. I'm glad I'm here. I love Peter.

The room seemed warm now, almost too warm; she kicked the thin blanket off her feet. The cold outside in the streets was only a little whistling sound against the window; the radiator clanged and rumbled in the corner like a complaining stomach. She closed her eyes and saw she was walking down the hotel corridor, the doors were all closed and the rooms quiet and she carried a red flower in her hand. It was a long corridor and very dim, flickering like candles. Outside it was November and cold and bitter and she quietly walked to the end of the corridor and opened a door and walked into a room that was so cold her footsteps made hollow echoes on the floor. When she walked in the room the men put down their knives and scapels on the tables with dull, clanging sounds. They all looked at her but did not speak or move, stood in half-ritual. She walked to the straight body on the first table. There was plastic wrapped around the face, a gray-white cloth under-neath it, loosely opened to show the straight open body, the silence and the veins and muscles and strings of bone and yellow fat lying open. Death was a sick-sweet smell on all these tables, ice colored. Her eyes looked at one foot twisted to the side, uncovered. Skin, toes, toenails. Just like my foot, she thought. There is this foot and it is cold. "Great and staring death," she said, "white-eyed," and she reached down and touched the fine-spun silver hair of the head beneath her. The face was tight and stretched and horrible, open-mouthed, the teeth dark and uneven, but the hair, sweet pale grass, covering the head was softer than anything her fingers had ever touched. It is so soft, she wondered why the mouth was open and not moving. She faced the white-clothed men looking at her from behind the twelve tables. "I am in a rage at you," she screamed. "I am in a rage." She ran from the room and opened her eyes.

"It is important not to die," she thought, looking around the room, seeing her suitcase on the floor, the desk, the mirror over the desk reflecting bare brown wall. "It is one thing to remember."

She could see the black outside the window. She got up, turned off the lamp and went to the sill. The colored lights cast harsh red-gold shadows over the darker shadows. She raised the window and stood naked, shivering, in the darkness. She could see the flat roof of the parking garage, and the post office with the gray, silent pillars like fingers in front of its face. There were still a few people walking down on the sidewalks. A tiny man put a letter in the box outside the post office. A couple walked together, their arms clutching each other against the night and the cold. She was too far away to see their faces. It is very lonely to see people who love. But I love, she reminded herself. She wondered if they would go to a room together out of the night. Anne watched them until they turned the corner behind the bank building. It was very far down to the street; the city was a toy, but she knew it was not a toy but lived. The wind was cruel and cold on her body; she folded her arms over her chest. She was more thin and naked than she had ever felt. Her hair tangled and loose over her shoulders seemed too much for her bones and skin. She would have knelt and touched that dead twisted foot with it. The lights in the street turned green and yellow and red. It was so far and dangerous to the ground.

When Peter came back she was still standing in front of the window. "Don't turn on the light," she said. "I'm not dressed."

"Pimento cheese or ham?"

"Either. Peter, stand with me and look down there. Take off your clothes, no one can see us."

"Close the window," he said, handing her a sandwich, "you'll get pneumonia."

"Keep the window open, just for a while. You can lean out and see much farther." Peter's face was quiet and dark in the shadows, she couldn't see what color his eyes were. (We shouldn't be separate from them, she thought. Those people living in the street. We are not separate.)

"You're shivering," Peter said.

"Please," she said, "let's sit by the window. It's wonderful to see so far." (We are not separate, you and I. It was true, maybe.)

He dragged over the chair from the desk and sat down beside her in the dark. They did not speak for a long time. It was still and cold all around them. "Pretty good sandwiches," he said finally. "Here," he said, making the paper bag on the floor rustle, beside him, "eat this one too. You're getting skinny as hell."

"Too thin?" she asked in real alarm. (You must think I'm beautiful. If you love me it is so, you have to.)

"Nope, I love you. Let's watch the news," he said.

"No, see those people down there. They're so small and you can see them walking down the block, and feel how the wind is in their face, but they don't know you can. They don't know I can see them at all. I wish I could touch them, let them know."

He laughed. "That's how snipers start out. Just wanting to touch people who didn't know they could."

"That isn't it at all. They're alive, you know they are and they're so small and walking. And you could be down on the street with them in a minute if you jumped, but then you couldn't be like them. Living, I mean."

He got up from the chair and kissed the back of her head. "I love you," he said. "You're impossible. Let's watch the news." He reached up, pulled the window down on the wind. "Still hungry?" he asked her, pulling on the cord and drawing the curtain. She didn't answer, remained naked in front of the closed window. He switched on the lamp and went to the television and fumbled with the dials until a measured voice spoke in the room. A helicopter flying over South Viet Nam showed on the picture tube; the helicopter exploded.

"I'm going to take a bath," she said. She went into the bathroom, felt for the switch and turned on the light. She closed the door, then locked it. She took one of the white towels from the rack and turned on the bath water full force, the water splashing on her cold hands like needles. Waiting for the water to fill the tub, she stared at her reflection in the mirror over the sink, rubbed under her mascara-smudged eyes with a tissue. Peter's shaving kit was beside the sink. A package of razor blades had broken open and lay scattered loose over his shaving gear. Anne picked up one of the blades very carefully and felt the sharp edges through the red paper. It is so dangerous. You could just move it against your skin and you would die. Death is so easy. It is very hard to belong to something enough.

She turned off the running water and eased into the bathtub. The water was warm, comforting, over her body. She leaned back until the water soaked the tips of her hair. There were black and white checked tiles on the floor, small squares; she studied them. The sound of the television came from the room. She wondered if death came like water or wind. Or like fire, she thought, considering the helicopter.

I don't know if I'm tired or not. (It was dangerous for the window not to have a screen.) She looked at her legs under the water. They looked so far away she moved them, sloshing water against the sides of the bathtub to be sure they were hers. When she was a little girl she put her face down under the bathwater and blew loud bubbles. Her mother said no, it was dangerous to hold her breath for so long. She had had a rubber doll she played with in the bath. She closed her eyes, held the doll by the window. There wasn't a screen, it was not her fault but the doll fell to the street. It was beautiful to see, she fell so very straight. The boy and the girl walking on the sidewalk picked the doll up. They held her in their arms and walked away with her. "Come back," she called to them.

The water was getting cold. Anne grabbed the soap from the soap dish and began scrubbing it over her arms. Peter called her from the other room. "I'm coming," she said. She watched the water run away from her and down the dark drain.

Peter was already in bed when she came from the bathroom. She looked at the bedspread still lying on the rug. "I'm tired," he said, "you too?"

She nodded, looked at his face on the pillow. He had a wide straight mouth, he looked like he should always smile. She crawled awkwardly in her night gown over his feet, he pulled the sheets aside for her. "I love you, Peter," she said.

"I love you, too."

He reached for the lamp beside him and turned off the light. "Good night," he said. The room was very dark, except for the paler darkness underneath the curtain. Anne stared into the dark, waiting to feel sleepy. Her arms and legs didn't seem to feel anything, not even tiredness. Hold me, she thought. The sheets rustled slightly beside her as Peter turned over, shifted position. She smoothed the blanket over her. Outside in the corridor someone laughed softly, then everything was quiet, very still. "I am not alone," she thought, reaching out her hand and touching Peter's shoulder. "Hold me," she asked him. "Quiet, woman," he kidded her. He moved his arm underneath her back. "Can't a man get any sleep?"

She moved closer to him and lay listening to his breathing in the darkness. His arm felt awkward and uncomfortable against her shoulder blades. "I love you," she said, listening carefully to her voice. It is true, she thought. "Love *you*," he mumbled. "Peter," she whispered. "I'm glad the window's closed." She couldn't see his face in the dark, she reached out and brushed his hair lightly with her hand. Do I belong to anyone? she wondered. She closed her eyes, tried to sleep. She was touching the dead face on the table.

The old man's hair was soft grass around his horrible face. His mouth moved. "You've touched me," he said to her in a dry, rasping voice like leaves moving. "It's the same as dying." "Peter," Anne said aloud.

"Anne, my arm's going numb." He gave her a sleepy kiss, and pulled his arm out from under her. "Go to sleep."

"Peter."

"Uh-huh."

"Peter, I do love you."

"Good night," he said.

She lay on her back and stared into the black pit of the ceiling. By the even breathing beside her, she knew Peter was asleep. If I went to sleep, I might wake up and find you gone. I would be lying here all alone in this room. And there's no screen on the window, no one knows I'm here. (Would it be a sin, then, she wondered if they knew?) But I love Peter. Please don't leave. I love you, you make me not alone. She leaned on her elbow and looked up to see if she could make out the painting in the dark. She could not. I love Peter. She was holding her hair in her hands, it had grown to the ground and she was wiping all the twisted feet with it. They were dead, all those people, the silence thick upon them was cold and ominous. She had to touch them, she had to. The old man had such beautiful silver hair. It was not dangerous to touch him. His hair was just soft, very white and soft. "It is important not to die," she thought. We are not separate, Peter and I; I am sure. The room was so dark and the closed curtain hid the square of gray. It's so far to the street.

Anne pushed off the covers and got out on her side of the bed, close to the wall. Her feet made no sound on the rug. She went to the window and pulled the curtain open, very quietly. There was no other sound in the room but the curtain jerking slowly open. She looked out. A thin moon wandered aimlessly now over the city, everything else was very cold and still. She didn't open the window, but pressed her face against the glass, looking down far below to all the deserted streets. The window pane was hard and cold from the wind outside. She shivered in her light nylon gown and drew her fingers close up into a fist. I am alone. No one can see me so high and in the dark and I am alone. The buildings across the street threw looming shadows into the dark streets. A man walked far down the sidewalk. Anne could see him when he came opposite a street lamp. He moved very slowly, his head looked down at his feet. "I wish I could touch you," Anne whispered. I am so far up here. (The window. I wish I could touch you.)

She was so far above the streets, in a room alone and just as dark. There were no night sounds but the wind rushing cold against everything. I am here, she thought. It is so dangerous. She touched her hand to the window. The man crossed the street and turned in the direction of the hotel. His feet moved very slowly along the sidewalk. The clock on the bank building said it was almost three. There were no cars on the street, only the Christmas lights and the black buildings and store windows. The man walked slowly to the front of the hotel. Anne could see him far down on the sidewalk almost directly beneath her window. He wore no hat and his pale hair stood out in the light of the street lamp. Anne breathed against the window glass. There is no one else but us, everything is so lonely. I wish I could touch you. The man was walking beneath her window now. "It is so far," she said. "It is dangerous to open the window. I am up here so close to death. You don't understand," she said "It is so high here; there is no window screen."

The man stopped walking, glanced around him and stood straight with his hands at his sides. He slowly lifted up his head as if it were very heavy and looked up at her window. "I wish I could touch you," she said. I don't belong to anything enough. He looked at her in the room. The room was darker than her shadow. "You think you can see me," her hand quickly adjusting the strap of her gown that had fallen down one shoulder. "You can't," she said. "No one can. This window is very dangerous."

The man looked at her, slowly lifted one hand to her like a wave. She backed away from the window, back farther into the dark. Peter was a gray shape in the bed, she listened for the faint, even sound of his breathing. "Peter," she said, very softly, wondering if anything could penetrate the darkness. I love you; it was true, we shouldn't have been separate. Separate, it is too easy to die. It wasn't a sin. "Peter," she said. Far down on the sidewalk there was a man standing beneath the window. He looked at her. "I can't see your face," she whispered, "there are too many shadows." She touched her own face slowly with her fingers. There is a statue in the park, she thought; there never is anything. There was no sound in the room. A man was standing on the sidewalk looking at her black window. "It is so dangerous here. The window doesn't have a screen."

She went to her suitcase on the floor, groped in the dark for her clothes. She dressed quickly, pulling her dress on over her gown, feeling for her shoes. Closing the suitcase, she grabbed her coat from the chair near the bed. Her breathing seemed very loud, she glanced out the window. The moon was pale and high, higher than the room. Her hair was loose around her shoulders, she pushed it back impatiently from her face. The man was still standing on the sidewalk.

Anne walked to the door, hesitated, looked at the dark bed. This is such an ugly room. The painting, the unlovely roses. Too red. She unlocked the door, turned the knob carefully. She hesitated a moment and went back and picked up her suitcase. "I must remember," she thought. "It is too easy otherwise."

The corridor was narrow and dark but for a red exit sign hanging from the ceiling at the end. She walked very fast down the hall, counting the soft thudding sounds her feet made on the carpet. Her mother had said not to walk alone in buildings at night. It was too dangerous. She came to the elevator, pushed the down arrow, waited in panic for the elevator to come. The coke machine made a sudden whirring noise like flying birds, everything else was very quiet. The elevator came and she walked in, pushed the lobby button hard with the palm of her hand. "You cannot be separate," she thought. "It is too dangerous." She felt a slight pressure in her ears as the elevator sank down. The door opened and she hurried into the lobby.

The clerk at the desk looked up at her as she walked across the lobby and down the stairs. There were a handful of people waiting around the desk or sleepily reading newspapers on the sofas against the wall. Through the glass door, it looked very dark and quiet outside. She leaned on the revolving door, pushed her suitcase ahead of her. She turned and walked quickly toward an old man standing at the corner. The side of his face was turned toward her. (Are we not alone? she asked. I don't know.) He was looking up to the top floor of the hotel, his brown muffler flapping against him in the wind. He had gray hair; it was very white under the lamp and the moon. The Christmas lights touched his face.

Anne walked up to him. He turned and they looked at each other, neither of them moved or spoke. It was cold and still; somewhere Anne heard a car passing in the street. It was a sin, she thought. Someone knelt down and touched the old man's shoes with her hair. No one spoke. It is important to remember not to die, she thought. She shifted her suitcase to her right hand, touched the old man's wrinkled hand with her other. "We will live always," she said. The light turned red and they crossed the empty street.

Katherine B. Taylor

In the home

"You know, we've got my mamma in a rest home,"
sighed Hurly Maybry, gathering up his nails.
I'd had him check the lock on my front door,
after that crazy man tried to attack
Miss Archer, down there on the river road;
and, while Hurly was by, I let him hang some pictures of my children.

He wanted to know all about the children—
how they were doing, how often they get home.
He looked to be about to hit the road
when, pulling out what he calls his "coffin nails,"
and lighting up, he frowned, as if he wanted to attack
some deep dark subject. Standing by the door—

his thin gray head high as the top of the door—
he had his say: "Some one of us children
could've kept Mamma, if her last attack
hadn't been so bad. She don't take to the home.
She tells me that she never bit her nails
before she lived near that noisy road.

And I know how she feels about that old road;
I heard four sirens whoop right past the door,
just while I was doing up her nails—
she gets a manicure every time her children stop by—nails filed and polished
pink. There in the home,
no one'll do it for her—they'd as soon attack

a nest of water moccasins, 'cause she'll attack
any poor attendant about the road,
about the food, 'bout anything and everything in the home.
I bet they're scared to get too near her door.
But she's still mother hen to all her children,
won't have us do a stitch for her, 'cept fix her nails . . .

They found the old Jones girls, dead as two door-nails.
Miss Jane fell down after Miss Lynn's attack,
it looked like—out there in the boondocks. None of us children
would hear to Mamma staying on the river road,
for fear she'd end like that.—Miss Jane's fists bruised with
     pounding on the door . . .
Besides, Mamma's mind's going. While I was at home,

painting her nails, some truck screeched on the road.
She jerked, like after an attack, made for the door,
and whined out, 'Where's my children? Where's my home?' "

Burke Davis III

The inmate, returning to the asylum

1

Older than any of us within,
Rising higher than I can shout
Out of the earth to the shielding sky,

This stone wall
In keeping us in
Keeps worlds' torments out.

2

Days ago they packed me home:
A fretful trek
A task through unpeopled desolation.

It was less home than here.
It was no more than knowing
Which floorboards creak,

The pictures frozen on familiar plates
The same stains mapped like rusty continents
On the sterile sink;

The dark allergic rooms
Of my dust-mote particled youth
The ghoulish spirits of past trauma.

The folks were faceless fixtures
Organs functional in the belly of the house,
Less loving of me

Than dreadful of some scandal
My next foaming rage against blood
Might provoke among the neighbors.

3

I left as I went, stuffed on a bus
Among flesh wrapped machines,
Braced for peril

Watching the kaleidoscope
Bloom beyond the pane
My pupils pressed against.

4

I returned without having been.
The cosmos convened in my heart
I felt the pulsars throb.

5

The limits of this life
Are the confines of the grave:
Promise of an easy peace.

But the mind wielding past
Like a life-seeking sword
Perverts holes on every side

And chaos spurts in
Like ghouls' black blood,
Putrefying the sanctuary
Wall and sky and solid soil had made
And these are particled to suffocate dust
And my naked heart trembles
With the roil of worlds upon worlds.

George R. Wood

Two poems

The watch

Opaque morning fills the mist.
Dumbfounded, enraptured, a soldier sits.
Nothing is clear. Emotions
age and waste to twist
his lengthening line of sanity.
Waking people punctuate the day
of his quoting existence: things to say.
Conversations, looped interlaced lines
leading irrelevantly tangle behind.
He has his peace as best he can.

Inconsequently they wear the day,
laden, with human moves,
and cross the land.
Common, the scene lasts deep into
the calendar, mindless of its men.
The day ends. Scorched, the soldier
awaits another death of dark,
ruminating a dark death.

At the war

"I lead a lonely life,"
she writes. "Billy,
the paperboy,
will arrive soon.
He is a fine boy."
Which brings to mind
my boyhood route,
and all the old ladies
I'd forgotten about.

"I have been going for walks."

She has been going for walks . . .

Nancy Rottenberg

On Route N.C. 54

N.C. 54 opened like a fan
before him; tires hardly fastened to the road,
his motor drowned the raging dogs that ran
beside. The bucking bike plunged more quickly
with its load; and then the dotted middle line
swung left—the whistling cycle went straight,
struck the leaning branches with a lowering whine,
left half an arm upon the tree that broke its gait.
And just before he landed: thought how the moon
and forest toppled by; remembered then how, young,
he rang the chapel bell, rode the rope
down and up again; remembered how he hung
midway above the floor. He had a sudden hope
the bell might sound—listened—but he hit the ground too soon.

Anne Tyler

The feather behind the rock

In movies, they still held hands, although Mrs. Hopper had arthritis by then and her hand would rest in her husband's without moving, swollen and lumpy. When something important happened on the screen, her fingers tightened one by one, in slow motion. "Look," she would say to Mr. Hopper. "There above that ridge—do you see that pony? Yes, the Indians are there. They've been watching all along. Now that first one is coming down to parley. I told you this would happen."

To Joshua, their grandson, who sat on his spine in the seat beside her, it sounded as if Mrs. Hopper thought her husband was blind—or worse than that, feebleminded. He felt heads turning in the dark toward the sound of her voice as she went on describing what was there for all to see: "He's carrying a white flag, you notice. A sign of peace. I don't know how much faith I would put in it, though. Do you see the yellow marks painted round his cheekbones?"

The more she talked the harder Joshua ground his teeth, until the hinges of his jaw were sore and a headache had sprung up from the back of his neck, but Mr. Hopper only said, "Yes, that's so. They're bent on war, I would say"—not just pretending patience but really interested, considering her words in his mind.

"The leader of the wagon train looks tired," Mrs. Hopper said. "I wouldn't like *his* job. Not at all." Then there was a silence.

Joshua turned and found them both smiling at each other, ignoring the screen altogether, although it was they who had wanted to come here. He sighed and slid down farther in his seat.

They were travelling the width of the United States that summer, going from east to west. The point they had started from was Wilmington, North Carolina; the point they were headed for was San Francisco. There was no reason for the trip. The first Joshua had heard of it was in April, when he came home from school one day to find his grandfather drinking iced tea with his mother. Mr. Hopper was a small, round man in his seventies, as exactly matched to his small, round wife as if they had been a couple of gingerbread cookies. Ordinarily, they visited on weekends. They lived in

Duppleton, about seventy miles inland, and they had a standing invitation for Sunday dinner with their only daughter. But this was Wednesday, and Joshua's first thought was that something was wrong. "Where's Grandmother?" he asked.

"She's at home," his mother told him. "Grandfather's got something to show you, Joshua."

Joshua was puzzled by her eyes, which looked as if she had just asked a favor of him, although she hadn't. He said, "What is it?," but Mr. Hopper only shook his head and went on drinking iced tea, meaning that this would have to be seen to be believed.

When the tea was gone, the three of them rode in Mr. Hopper's rickety old Pontiac to the outskirts of town, to a trailer camp. Women in dungarees and metal curlers swept their tiny dirt yards, and children chased in and out of a grocery store that was covered with metal soft-drink signs. At the far end of the camp was an unpainted aluminum trailer, so short that it seemed almost round. An old man sat on its doorstep smoking a pipe. When he saw Joshua's grandfather, he rose and said, "Well, hey there. Hey," and Joshua's mother got the favor-asking look in her eyes again. Joshua still didn't know why. He understood from what followed that Mr. Hopper was going to buy the trailer and make a tour across the continent with his wife, and that Joshua was invited to come along. But when he said, "Oh, sure, I'd like that" (and saw his mother silently thanking him), he didn't feel he was doing anyone any special favors. The summer would be his last one before college, and he had been wondering what he would do to fill it.

They started out on the sixteenth of June—Mr. Hopper and Joshua in the front seat, Mrs. Hopper in back, with a sweater handy in her lap, although the temperature was in the high eighties. That was the seating arrangement throughout the trip. Mrs. Hopper got carsick if she sat in the front, and Joshua couldn't shift over to the driver's seat because he had had his license suspended after a minor accident. He had asked his grandfather before they started if he remembered that (in case they had invited him to help with the driving), and his grandfather had said, "*Yes,* boy, yes," impatiently, waving the subject away with his small, veined hand. It was too great a distance for one man to drive, Joshua thought, but his grandfather sat behind the wheel day after day, his shoulders very straight, making a steady thirty-five miles an hour. It felt like three times that, with all the racket they made. And Joshua's narrow side window, half covered over with masking tape to mend a crack, framed such tiny parts of the landscape at a time that everything seemed to be whipping along too fast to be seen—fields, towns, and fields again—leaving him with a sense of tremendous, wasteful speed. They whirred and sputtered and choked their way along, with scarcely a stop from morning to night; yet his grandfather never mentioned feeling tired and he never complained about Joshua's not being able to spell him.

Nor could they have invited Joshua because they wanted new conversation; his grandparents did all the talking. They flooded him with words from both sides at once; they interrupted each other without noticing and sometimes they talked simultaneously, their voices keyed to a crisp, factual tone that Joshua had never heard them use before. Subjects seemed to come to their minds so fast—comments on the countryside, stray memories, unrelated facts—that they would leave one subject in midsentence and dart on to the next without pausing. Joshua listened, nodding, lulled nearly to sleep by the flow of words and by the broken lines down the center of the highway, which stretched long and then were swallowed by the car over and over again all through the day.

He liked the trailer, which smelled like a musty tin can and rang hollow wherever you rapped it. He liked stopping in the camps every night, pacing out the barren, bottle-littered ground that reminded him of circuses and country fairs and then returning to the trailer, where his grandmother would be frying food on the tiny gas stove. He didn't even mind the endless riding, or all that talking. But he did hate the movies.

It never failed. After supper his grandfather would say, "Well, now, I think I'll take a stroll." But he only strolled as far as the camp's grocery store, and then he bought a newspaper and strolled back. " 'Apache Warrior' is on tonight," he would tell them. "We saw that in Emmaville. How about 'Hondo'? Didn't you enjoy that? Shall we see it again?"

Sometimes there were good movies playing—not often, because the towns they chose to stop at were small—but his grandparents ignored those. They liked Westerns, and occasionally a war movie. They liked plots where the villain was obvious, though they never seemed to realize he was obvious, and Mrs. Hopper would point him out with pride, right at the start of the movie: "Do you see that man with the cigar? Oh, he has a mean face. Look, he's yanking the horse's straps too tight. He's going to cause trouble, Charles, I can tell you. Do you see him, Joshua?"

At the beginning of the trip, she told Joshua everything she told her husband, all through the movie. She would tell Joshua first, usually, and then she would nudge her husband and say, "I was just pointing out to Joshua, here . . ." But gradually she stopped, because Joshua never answered her.

In the first place, he didn't know why they were there at all. They had started out to see the country, but all they saw were highways and then, at night, the insides of movie theatres and the half-familiar faces of heroes drawing six-guns. They marked towns by the Indian battles they had watched there, and almost the only people they saw were the shadowy forms in the rows of seats ahead of them. It was true that Joshua didn't have to go where his grandparents did; some sense of responsibility that he couldn't explain seemed to drag him along, even after he had told them he wasn't interested. "Why don't we take a look at where we're at?" he would ask, and his grandfather always said, "Oh, we will. We've plenty of time for that."

But they never had any time at all. In the morning, when Joshua's head was still not cleared from last night's movie, they rose out of mildewed blankets and munched cold rolls and took to the road again. They never stopped for anything. They travelled steadily all day, calling out for Joshua the sites of historical interest, along with the printing on the marquees of drive-in theatres, and then in the evening it was time for supper and "Tall in the Saddle."

One night—in Kansas somewhere—his grandmother said, "I don't like that man's face, Charles." Her voice carried clearly to the farthest rows. "I don't trust the look in his eyes."

Joshua sat up straighter in his seat (they always sat too close to the front, so that he had to crane his neck back and squint) and said, "That's Jack Palance, who's the villain in this and every other picture, as *any* fool could see." Then he got up and walked out.

As soon as he reached the sidewalk, he was sorry. He had had, all during this trip, a sort of protective feeling toward his grandparents, and now he felt as if he had ruined the summer for them—all those movies, all that flood of words entrusted to him. Instead of looking around the town he went back to the trailer, and when they returned he was fast asleep on the couch, with moths circling the table lamp.

In the morning, neither of the Hoppers mentioned what had happened. There was even a chance that they hadn't understood, or that they had passed it off as something he had eaten. Mr. Hopper said, "Today we will cover more ground than usual, Joshua. We'll have lunch in the car—no dawdling on the way."

"Oh, fine," Joshua said, for he had the feeling that this was some kind of gift to him, although the lunch stops were what he looked forward to all morning. He helped his grandmother wash up the breakfast dishes and put everything away, so that it wouldn't rattle around on the road. Then they climbed into the car and set off, with Mrs. Hopper beginning the day's conversation before she had even got well settled.

"In school, they called the Midwest the breadbasket of America," she said. "Or of the world—I forget."

"The world," said Mr. Hopper.

"Was that it? Oh, they told us how much grain they produced, and it was staggering—more than I could imagine—and think what it is *now*adays. Twice that, I should think, maybe more. What with science coming in—"

"In the summer of 1913, when I was in college, I roomed with a boy who came from right in this area somewhere," said Mr. Hopper. "A farm boy. Joshua, you should be interested in this. In his school they had a project, each of them—a piece of livestock to raise or an acre of land to cultivate, which they would follow from beginning to . . . His name was Harvey Stample. One hot afternoon—I should tell you this—just before exams, we were sitting on the dormitory lawn, not a penny to our names. 'In all this world,' Harvey said, 'if I could wish for just one thing, I'd wish for a man to drive up right this minute and unload a case of beer on the lawn.' Well, Joshua, no sooner had he said that than up drove a man in one of those unpainted wagons they used to use for delivering, and unloaded a case of beer on our lawn. I'll never forget that. Turned out it was a wrong address, but by then we had drunk it all and were not made to pay. I think that might have been the happiest day of my life, all in all."

"Why, Charles," Mrs. Hopper said.

Mr. Hopper turned to smile at her, and then he winked at Joshua. "Oh, there's some close seconds," he said.

"Now, Charles, don't you tease Joshua," Mrs. Hopper said. But it was she who was being teased, and the conversation was between the two of them alone.

Joshua felt as if the shift had given him a breath of fresh air. The talk seemed to be flying faster than usual this morning, so that words were all run together, and the car was going faster, too—telegraph poles whipping by, fields gone almost before they appeared, all of them directed somehow at Joshua. "We surely are making time," he told his grandfather.

"Well, we don't want this trip to get boring. It's what I told your grandmother—keep things flying along, I said."

"The happiest day of your life, Joshua," Mrs. Hopper said, "is your wedding day. Don't you forget I told you that."

"Lucy, your mind is failing," Mr. Hopper said. "That's what your mother said to you fifty years ago—I heard her. 'This is the happiest day of your life,' she told you, and then when Charlotte was born you turned around and said, 'No, *this* is, isn't it? Mama was wrong,' you said."

"Did I say that? Well, maybe so. Charles, we seem to be coming on a real interesting old house up here. Will you slow down a bit?"

"Should have spoke sooner," Mr. Hopper said, and the house whizzed by. Behind them the trailer bumped and bounced, sounding as if it was surely going faster than trailers were allowed. What if they were really speeding, and a policeman ordered them to pull over? "Can't stop *now*," Mr. Hopper would say, and he would rush on toward San Francisco, where they were only going to turn around and head back again.

"There was something I was going to say," Mrs. Hopper said. "I'll think of it in a minute. Yes. That house reminded me of my aunt's, where I was raised. Joshua, that house was just covered with wisteria—you should have seen it. If I smell wisteria now, I can close my eyes and go back— Oh, so long ago I'm ashamed to tell. . . ."

She stopped, apparently out of breath, and Mr. Hopper said, "There were bees buzzing around it—millions of them every year."

Joshua took his eyes from the road in an effort—his lids were getting heavy and the heat had grown stifling. "Oh, around the wisteria," he said. "Did you know Grandmother back then?"

"Know her? Why, Joshua, I—"

"Was my childhood sweetheart," said Mrs. Hopper, still getting her breath. The words, which reminded Joshua of a lacy old valentine, sounded strange when they were gasped out in the stuffiness of the Pontiac. "The first boy who ever came to call on me. Only not the last, because I went to New York later on—"

"Jilted me," Mr. Hopper said, smiling. "She got engaged to a fellow up North while she was taking voice lessons."

"Oh, I didn't know that," Joshua said.

His grandmother sat forward and touched his shoulder with one finger. "When I came home again, Joshua," she said, "who do you think was the first person I saw as I was getting off the train? Your grandfather, carrying flowers to some other girl. I called out, 'Why, Charles Hopper, is that you?' and he turned right around without seeming to look and handed over the flowers to me instead. 'These were going to Mary Abbott,' he told me, 'but I reckon you can have them.' 'Thank you kindly,' I said—acting cool, since it was my own wedding I was coming home for, but I must say when I saw him I had the strangest feeling. I was almost scared of him— I didn't look him in the eye."

"I have always said," Mr. Hopper said, "that it's a shame we lost all that time. Two whole years, when we could've gotten married right off and saved all that hide-and-seek. But *Lucy* says—"

"I say it's a good thing I did jilt him," said Mrs. Hopper. "Joshua, that boy I nearly married was as handsome as they come. Oh, no handsomer than your grandfather, but in a different sort of way—dark when Charles was blond, blue-black hair but light-gray eyes. If I had married Charles right off and then seen Edwin some other way, I would have thought, Oh, my, what am I missing? What have I given up? But as it was, I had my pick of both and chose with a clear head, and I chose Charles."

They seemed to have laid some case before Joshua—speaking his name so often, setting out the facts so clearly. Joshua cleared his throat and said, "Well, I didn't know all that. It's very interesting."

"And I've never regretted it," Mrs. Hopper told him. "Those two years were the best thing that could have . . ." Then she stopped, out of breath again, and when she resumed speaking her voice was more ordinary, like the days before this trip had begun. "Charles, I think I'll have to stop for a glass of ice water," she said. "My, this heat!"

Mr. Hopper glanced back at his wife and nodded. "Yes, you're looking pale, Lucy," he said. Then he turned to Joshua and said, "Mary Abbott was a girl we had gone to school with, Joshua. I never took a flower to her in my life and never planned to, but I wanted to keep face in front of your grandmother." And in the back seat Mrs. Hopper gave a little chuckle that sounded whispery on her indrawn breath.

Within the next mile they came upon a drive-in restaurant—hardly more than a shack, with two teen-age boys in white working behind the long low window. "I'll just run on in myself," Mr. Hopper said. "Will you be all right, Lucy?"

"Why, of course," said Mrs. Hopper. "I have Joshua here, don't I?" She smiled, but her face was still pale and filmed with sweat. When Mr. Hopper had started toward the shack, she said, "Joshua, it might do us good to stretch our legs a little."

"Yes, Ma'am," Joshua said. He opened his own door and came around to help her out. The ground beneath them was cracked and dry, the air shimmering with heat. For a moment he thought of home, where there was always water nearby and where people he knew—people his own age—would be lounging on the sparkling beach.

Beside him, his grandmother said, "Your grandfather wanted us to live in Kansas at one time, Joshua. Did he tell you that?"

"No, he didn't," Joshua said.

"Oh, yes. Not that there was any *practical* reason. Just, you know, a whim he had . . ."

Joshua felt a sudden weight upon his upper arm, near his shoulder. He turned and saw that his grandmother was leaning her head there; loose strands of her gray hair floated near enough to his face to tickle him. But just as he was explaining this to himself—she seldom touched people, even her own relatives—he saw that she had merely slumped sidewise as she stood beside him. In the next instant she slid on down and away from him, until she landed on the ground with her face twisted to one side and her hands outspread and slightly curled like the hands of someone sleeping. He looked around frantically for his grandfather and saw him just advancing, carefully bearing three paper cones of water. "Grandfather, something's happened!" he called. If he hadn't caught himself in time, he would have added, "I didn't do it, I swear it. I was just standing here minding my own business."

But his grandfather came on as calmly and steadily as before, with his eyes fixed on the paper cones. "I saw from over yonder," he said. "Take the water, Joshua. I thought I'd use some of it to revive her." He handed two of the cones to Joshua and then bent down with the third one, dipping his fingers into it and patting cold water onto Mrs. Hopper's cheekbones. "It's the heat," he told Joshua. A muscle in Mrs. Hopper's eyelid fluttered.

By now, other people had started gathering around—one of the boys from the drive-in, a couple from a parked car at the other end of the lot. They stood looking at Joshua's grandmother, who had taken on the dry, papery look of a stranger and seemed not to be any relation to Joshua at all. "Can't we get her out of here?" Joshua asked his grandfather. "Can't we take her away?"

Mr. Hopper only went on patting water, saying little soothing remarks in a singsong voice. "There, now, Lucy, you can come round now. Come on, now, Lucy."

Then a man said, "Let me see her. I'm a doctor." He had stopped by the side of the highway, apparently, when he saw what had happened. Behind him, his car door was still swung open. When he bent down, already unlatching his black bag, the bystanders moved a little farther away, but Mr. Hopper stayed where he was, hunched over his wife.

"Thank you, but she's coming round now, Doctor," he said. And sure enough, Mrs. Hopper's eyes flew wide open—round, glass-blue eyes in very deep sockets. She looked at Mr. Hopper a minute and then shook her head and began trying to sit up. "Now, now, take it nice and slow," said Mr. Hopper. "Thank you anyway, Doctor."

The doctor nodded and put one hand beneath Mrs. Hopper's elbow to help her up. "I would get her examined right away, though," he said. "How long has it been since she had a checkup?"

"Oh, only last April," Mr. Hopper said. "She's got a special doctor at home, you know. He said he thought this trip might be all right."

"Well, maybe so," said the doctor. But Joshua saw his frown, and later, when they had refused the restaurant's offer of a free meal and had walked Mrs. Hopper gently to the car, holding her under the arms, he said, "Look, Grandfather, we should be turning back."

"No, I want to go on," Mrs. Hopper said.

"We should even *fly* back—pay someone else to drive the car home. We can't go on driving."

"I want to go *on*," Mrs. Hopper said. She settled herself in her seat with a little flounce. "Start the car, Charles."

Joshua looked at his grandfather, but Mr. Hopper only nodded, and turned the key in the ignition. "She's made up her mind," he said. "Nothing I can do about it. Your grandmother, Joshua, is as stubborn as they come. I don't think you ever heard about this, but in the summer of 1916, when your mother was only so high . . ."

Joshua gave up. He relaxed against the sun-warmed seat cover and drifted away on the tide of his grandfather's words, and he didn't try after that to change their minds—not all that day, when they sped along straight, unchanging roads that always sloped downward at the horizon, rounding the curve of the globe they travelled, and not even in the evening, when Mrs. Hopper sat holding her husband's hand in the darkened theatre and said, "That last wagon is dropping too far behind. Yes, there. I see a pony on the ridge, I see a feather behind the rock. I expect the Apaches are lining up now, Charles. I can hear the war cries."

Katherine Humphreys

Weekend home

This was the day she'd planned over and over, so that now it had come,
it was like a present she'd poked and peered into, and maybe ruffled the paper
once too much, and she was afraid to let it begin. Her sister would be there,
beautiful Louise, whose hair streamed down so clean and smooth, you fairly
begged it to stop, but it never did. And her eyes. Why was it some people
got the large doe eyes you could drown in, and others didn't, but could
only watch, and know how they would let the lids fall lazy half way, half
sleeping, if they only had them. She wasn't jealous; you weren't jealous after
twenty years of watching. You gave in and loved her.

Jeremy Round drove over the rough dirt road that hadn't been used since
last weekend, when her father had come, like he always did, to feed the
horses, and feel strong and young on the land he owned, all to himself, where
Mother couldn't tell him to leave the kitchen, that she could clean up much
faster with him out of the way, and he would go up to their room, and
read the papers and the magazines till sleep. Tasha'd given him up, along
with the rest, to Louise. There was only one hard night, when she was still
young, and had cried in her pillow till it was all wet, and the knot in her
chest had gone away. After that she could watch them, and be happy for
them, and even laugh when her father called her Julia that time, not Natasha,
or even Louise, but Julia. And who'd ever heard of any Julia?

Her heart thumped oddly in her breast, as they neared the turn-off, as
though it might take leave of her and dart free way out in the sky with the
doves that flickered like tiny bits of ash blown up from some hidden brush
fire along the road.

"Hey, wish I'd brought my gun; those're doves up there." Jeremy thrust
his curly head through the window in genuine disappointment.

"Daddy'd shoot you, if you did." Tasha laughed at the thought of her
father running across the open field to prevent him.

"You're not scared are you, to meet him?"

"Course not." Jeremy inflated his chest to show his daring.

"Hey, here's the turn-off."

He swung the car into the road, the tires catching in the dry autumn dirt, swerving the car gently from side to side, like in a boat, till it grasped firmer ground. The turn-off led to a cedar causeway over a marshy spot she and Louise called the End. There, blackberries grew, up close to the marsh, and the moss hung low from the oaks, so you could sit up close to the gray trunks, and not be seen, like behind dusty curtains, and eat the berries alone. Then they came to the circle, the road rounding a wild garden of easter lilies and daffodils, that were buried now, in October, in silky bulbs underground. The little white house, with turquoise shutters, was on the far side of the circle.

"There's one car. They must have beat us. You aren't scared, now, Jer?"

"Me?" He laughed.

Louise was slumped in the swing that hung from the oak beside the porch, her arms linked about the chains at the elbow, her head dropped on her chest, silver hair floating down. It caught in the wind, as she swung back and forth, like the free ends of spider webs.

"There she is."

Jeremy looked at Louise through the window, and Tasha thought she saw a frown begin to form on his forehead. "She's most as pretty as you."

"Yeah." Tasha was out of the car the minute it stopped.

"Hey, Louise, come meet Jeremy."

Louise jumped lightly from the swing, and walked toward them. Jeremy had gotten out and was standing by the car. He went to meet her, held out his hand, which she took.

"Well, finally. Tash's told me all about you. Come on in."

She led him to the porch of the house, and Tasha followed.

"Where's Mom and Pop?"

"In the creek. Are you hungry?" she asked Jeremy. He turned to Tasha, shrugging.

"Well, we had something earlier."

"He's always hungry." Tasha picked up a twig from the cedar tree at the foot of the steps, crushing it in her hand, smelling it, for something to do. There had been no real reason to bring him here.

"Great. I baked a cake for Daddy, but he doesn't like cake. So, maybe you'd like some." She rested her large brown eyes on his face, and Tasha thought he couldn't help feeling faint. It was almost unfair to him, to make him see them.

"Sure, if Tasha wants some. What're you doing, Tash?"

"Just smelling this. You go on in. I want to get some stuff out of the car."

She turned her back on them; she could go down to the End for a while, though the blackberries were over. She walked along the leaf covered road, her feet making their dry shuffle in the brittleness. Underneath her favorite oak, she sat, wondering what she was doing, running off, almost. She just did it, that's all, like jumping off the deep end of the pool, to make sure you could swim. The moss hung about her, sheltering, glooming the spot, so the sun dropped its gold in diamond patches. The marsh breeze parted the gray tendrils, like silent hands in hair, shaking bits of dust on her cheeks and lashes.

"Tasha." Jeremy was calling.

"O.K. I'm just at the End."

She brushed the moss aside, running back to the house. Her cheeks blazed from the wind and the run, and tears squeezed from the corners of her eyes. When she reached the porch, Jeremy had gone back in, so he hadn't really wanted her. Maybe Louise had told him to call. The old wooden steps sank beneath her feet, caving imperceptively inward, toward the dark underside of the boards, riddled with old termite holes, now dried. Even the summer's dirt daubers had deserted their nest under the blue-green eave, perhaps leaving the remains of some petrified fly all swathed with silver thread inside. She opened the door to the small front room, that took up three quarters of the house. Jeremy was kneeling on the brick hearth, trying to start a fire, with Louise bent over, watching.

"Hi. Where'd you go?" she asked, handing him the lighter fluid.

"Oh, over to the End."

"I haven't been over there in an age. Remember when we used to smoke rabbit tobacco under that tree?"

"What's rabbit tobacco?" Jeremy tilted his head over one shoulder toward Louise.

"Listen to him. What's rabbit tobacco? Where've you been all your life?"

"I guess I just haven't lived, huh? Till I have some of this stuff?" Tasha glared at him. He couldn't be flirting with her, that would be too much.

Louise threw her head back and the clearest sound, like bells, trickled from her throat, ballooned out, until she shook with laughter. A spray of hair fell over her eyes. Jeremy laughed once, glancing at Tasha.

"What is it, Tash?"

"It's a weed children around here roll in funny paper and get ill on." Her words quenched her sister's laughter.

"Oh, Tash, you used to love it. Why, you'd smoke it way longer than me, when Daddy was stalking nearer, and I was already packing my mouth with gum."

Tasha looked at her pretty mouth, remembering that she really had stuffed it with gum, though she couldn't picture her quite doing it now.

Jeremy's fire caught low beneath the stout pieces of kindling, shyly licking the pine logs on top. The three of them waited, hushed, for the flame to seize them permanently.

"Not bad," Louise said to no one in particular.

Jeremy leaned back on the hearth, admiring his work.

"Well, I was a scout for a couple of years." Tasha thought he looked rather like a puppy stroked unexpectedly.

"Did you have your cake?"

"No, I figured I'd wait for the rest." She smiled at him. The heat of the fire ate slowly away at the chilly air, warming her, like a long hot bath after a cold day in the open. Louise slouched, musing on the sofa, her large eyes filled with the liquid vacancy that comes from staring at fires, or old letters whose writing's been changed by time into the faintest of blue veins inscribing the transparent sheet. Tasha found it in her heart to forgive her sister for everything; she thought she might even be strong enough to give her Jeremy. His brown hair shone gold in the fire light, as though it were the only light in the room, and it was black night just beyond the door, and they, the three of them, were the only people in the world. It would be a beautiful gift indeed. But even as she thought these things, a bitterness crept into her chest. She knew it was tears, and the same knot that had gotten there when she was little and Louise had stolen her father away, piece by piece, until she was only left with a skeleton for a father, that she couldn't talk to, or touch. Not this time, she thought; this time she would fight, and if she lost it would be gloriously.

"Jeremy, are you asleep?"

He raised his head and leaned on his elbow.

"Nope."

"I'm just about." Louise yawned her little yawn that meant life is boring.

Tasha pierced her to the heart with sullen eyes, which probably would have brought on the hurt, innocent look she knew so well, if her head had not been turned still toward the fire.

"Let's walk down to the creek." She jumped up, opened the door, and ran down the steps without waiting for Jeremy to answer. If he didn't come, too bad. She would just know all the sooner.

The sky was the palest of blues, speckled with tiny dots of cloud, like the thin cream-blue egg shells in their attic that they, Louise and she, had found one summer, all nested in the white tissue paper. Pick one up as gently as you could, and it would still crack, spoiling right in your hand. Jeremy caught up with her as she leaned down to pick a dandelion.

"Well, how did I do?"

She blew the gray fuzz in one breath, for luck, watched the wind lift it, and sail it across the brown field.

"How did you do what?"

"I mean, did I make the right impression?"

"Why don't you ask Louise?" Her voice sounded harsh in the cold, empty air. She felt as though they had been through this before, like when you see a bluejay flutter in green branches, but don't notice really, until it flutters again, and then you have that feeling, like a dream. She was taking him to meet her father.

They walked silently toward the creek, brown shambles of dead vines pulling at their feet, slowing them, until they reached the clay path, where the black beetles rolled balls of dry dung into their holes, blocking the grainy openings.

"Her eyes were black as a beetle's back."

"What?" Jeremy reached for her hand, but she thrust it in the pocket of her coat, and shuddered before the wind that flung itself over the field from the marsh.

"Oh, nothing."

"Look, Tash, I didn't come all the way out here just to meet your family. Can't we have fun, too?"

She shrunk away from him, into the collar of the coat, away from the egg-shell sky. To be in a shell would not be hard; it would crack at a breath, at a wish.

"I'm sorry, Tash. Forgive me?"

She knew how to pull herself in, like a snail, when she needed to.

"Remember what you told me once about a man that shot his dog 'cause he was liking it too much? Was it true?"

"No."

She stopped and sat on the hard earth beneath the pecan tree, the one you could climb in and see your father in the creek, though it seemed so far away, with his white shirt blowing like a flag through the green marsh. The nuts rotted in their shells where they had fallen, not firm and green like on the tree, but cracked and dark as dirt, and only dust inside. She looked at him close, and through him, to the back of his head where the brown hairs stuck out and wouldn't stop curling no matter what he did to them. Then he pushed her back, pinning her arms gently to the ground. The world spun round and round with her so close to it, she spun too, and would never stop, till the whole thing did, and then it wouldn't matter. He kissed her.

"So. You gonna talk now?"

She sat up, brushing the dead grass from her coat and hair. It was limp grass, and if you sucked it, there was no juice, like in spring, when it stained your mouth, and you tasted the greenness, trying to whistle through the slit.

"Can you do this?" She put her lips to one brown blade, that had already split on its own.

"It's too dry."

"Well, can you do it with two fingers? Father can whistle a mile with these two." She showed him the right ones.

"Nope."

"Too bad," she said, looking out over the field, to the sky, to the woods on the other side. A lone ibis flew up from the creek bed, its voice aching on the wind. She and Louise had found an ibis once on its side in the marsh. A dead one, heavier than you might think, and not so beautiful as in the air, when it cleft the blueness, all wings. They'd washed the black mud off, and the tiny hard knot of blood on the beak.

"And why do they smell when they die, Jer, like it was something unnatural to do, to die? Birds, I mean."

He waited a moment, undecided. She wouldn't talk, even now.

"I don't know."

She jumped up, and started on toward the creek, with him following, like a dog on a hunt, that might be getting tired, with no game all morning.

"We smell, too, when we die. The hairs on your head so curly now will fall to dust, and would blow away like a dandelion, if it could, and weren't kept under there."

"Are you worried Louise and I won't get along?" He looked away, to the gray tree trunks on the edge of the field, afraid, but wanting to know.

"Won't get along?" she said.

"Yeah."

"No. I don't think I ever thought of that."

"Then, what's the matter? You're acting like a kid, Tash."

"Maybe I am."

They had come to the end of the field. Before them the narrow creek snaked toward the river, brown-green, twisted, disappearing around a bend; then only the marsh spread out, its huge moving wings of gold reaching to the river beyond.

"There's Bird Key."

His eyes followed where she pointed—a pure white sand cliff rearing its point on the horizon at the end of the marsh.

"Some kind of bird goes there to nest every year."

"I like it." She slipped her arm through his, letting her mind unwind, forgetting Louise, everything, for a moment. Then the purr of a motor suddenly entered the air, like a visitor, unannounced.

"That's Pop."

"You call him Pop?"

"No, Father."

"O.K."

They slid down the rutty embankment to the boat landing, the cold sand giving way with their weight. The boat appeared round the bend as they reached the creek. Her father sat in the back of the small outboard, looking regal in his army surplus jacket. He waved, slowly curved the boat in the middle of the creek, and ran it ashore. Jeremy steadied it while he climbed out, and they hauled it up together.

"Glad to see you made it."

"Father, this is Jeremy Round." Jeremy was a head taller than he, she noticed, as they shook hands.

"How do you do, Sir."

"Fine, just fine. Natasha check that gas for me." She pulled the handle on the motor shut. The whole thing, the gasoline smell, the empty coffee cans for bailing, the gray tennis shoes—that was her father.

"What's that?" She pointed to a brown lump under the seat.

"Dead hen." He pulled the marsh hen out by the feet. "Ever see one of these before?" He offered the misshapen bird to Jeremy.

"No, Sir."

"Good eating bird." He rummaged around in the boat, picking up a rope, the shoes.

"Is it marsh hen season?" Tash asked, to show some interest.

"Well, now, I figure it's my bird. One won't hurt anybody." He nodded to Jeremy.

"No, Sir."

"Natasha, back the car over here."

"I'll get it." He tossed the keys to Jeremy and went back to unloading the boat—the gun, the paddles. Tasha felt nervous, like she always did alone with him, as though she were guilty of something.

"Where's mother?"

"Dropped her at the Pinkneys' up the creek. We'll pick her up on the way home."

She picked up the paddles and placed them carefully in the trunk. Jeremy came around and helped with the other things.

"Here's the keys, Sir."

"O.K. I guess that's it."

They drove back to the house in utter silence. Tasha stared at the back of her father's head. She knew it by heart, the red neck, the lowest thin hairs, the full curve of the back, the abrupt top. It was like a special cup your mother might show visitors, but you dared not touch, for fear it would break, and you trembled just looking at it in the cupboard. Yet she had touched it, she must have, a long time ago, almost before she could remember. She'd sat on his chest in the big bed, with her mother there, too, and the sheets smelling crisp, and she'd kissed him. But now they drove in silence, and he was strange, for all his nearness. She reached out to Jeremy and pulled a knot of his hair, coiling it once around her finger, until she knew he felt it, though his face, like her father's, looked ahead across the autumn field.

The car made the circle, past the End to the house. Louise came out on the porch to meet them. She hugged her father, hanging on his arm up the steps and through the door. They might have been an old, old couple, she thought, who lean on each other, but have forgotten what the feel of real flesh and bone and hair can be—all that burnt up long ago, and blown away up some sooty chimney. She grabbed Jeremy before he crossed under the turquoise eave of the porch.

"Jer, let's not go in just yet."

"I don't mind, Tash."

"I know; but let's not, I'll race you."

She took off across the field, toward the woods, running as hard as she could, till she felt she would fall, the ground flashed by so fast. He passed her laughing, and she thanked something deep inside of her for him. They stopped at the foot of the woods, breathing wildly, and laughing at each other until it hurt.

"You've got tears in your eyes."

"So do you." She dropped to the ground. The wind had built ridges with the dots of cloud, cracking the sky, bringing it closer, so you could almost touch it.

170

"I'm just too much for you, Tash." He tumbled beside her, touched her hair.

"You like me better than Louise?"

"Better than Louise? Whoever said I liked Louise?"

But she wasn't thinking of Louise just then; she was thinking of herself, and of how anyone could lose their father, let him slip away, piece by piece, for no reason in the world.

"Forgive me for today?"

"Sure," he said, and together they sat beneath the leafless oaks, waiting for their breath to calm, waiting for the last dove to flicker in the cold October sky when they would go back to the house and the last warmth of the fire he'd built there.

David Young

The appointed hour

This October day on Martha's Vineyard, cold and gray. Milton
stands by the window, his back to the class, his hand cold on the pane.
Outside, wind in the nearly barren trees. The air is heavy with the
incumbent storm. Like frightened, drowning girls, trees toss wailing in the
wind, thin branches outstretched, reaching. Storm expected.

Brady knew from the tracks that the buck had been hit. The right
forefoot had been dragged, almost imperceptibly, in the snow. Then we saw
blood, mud-dark. The deer had been gutshot as well. It had been over a
hundred yards when fired upon that last time—then, when sighted again,
farther, a gray phantom on the landscape. "All we can do now is wait for
it to fall," Brady said. "We can't hurry it. The leg will become more painful,
unbearably painful. Then the deer will tire and lie down, and his leg and gut
muscles will stiffen."

In concert wiredrawn trees bend, fragile, waiting for the night storm.
Chimes across withered fields. Three o'clock. Class dismissed. Children
ascend like flocks of bats from dim corridors to the hills, embrace dazzling
clouded brightness. One small girl lingers. I am sorry sir, she says. Milton
does not smile, cannot forgive. She leaves. An aging schoolteacher on
a dreary island, I am incapable of forgiving.

Husk of a classroom. Milton sits behind his desk. My bright young
pupils play soccer on distant hills. The silence of the empty room is shattered
by a quavering voice, rebounding from the past. Good old Yeats, my
desperate, enduring friend:

Some burn damp faggots, others may consume
The entire combustible world in one small room
As though dried straw ...

This cold October, brittle, straw dry. A desperate need for rain. Dusk
now advancing softly certainly through hushed trees. But the quiet dis-
pelled, momentarily, by persistent remembered song—the Irish bard at
the harp in an empty crusty parlor. And with the old music the face of Tom
Brady, my college companion. Among the feasting men of the world he
dwelt. Brady sang in space and light, like a landscape painter—except

his medium was life itself, days of laughter. Summer dreams transcending season. The sky-diver, the motorcycle nightmare, always shouting and laughing. In love with life. Tell me again Brady tell me why invocation of oblong days. *"If you have Irish blood, Milt, you know one thing and one thing only—that sooner or later, no matter what you do, the world's going to break your heart. So you laugh as loud and as long as you can and you pinch the first ripe ass that comes along."* He projected upon an always drab Boston sky an inner world as shining as a tall draught of Guinness Stout. Leprechauns dancing in gutters and laughing potato faces, fairy shoemakers and fallen angels. And pubs and beer and jokes and ragged girls with idle smiles:

> *We galloped over the glossy sea:*
> *I know not if days passed or hours,*
> *And Niamh sang continually . . .*

I inhabited that world for a short time.

Milton rises from his desk, collecting textbooks for the walk home down North Water Street. Smoke curls upward from gutter leaves in Edgartown streets. *I was the first to sight the deer. The deer pausing in windless dead grass by a stream, in delicate poise by the stream, high in the Berkshires. Suspended minutes—the sun wound in its slow certain parabola west, in that spinning, in that perfect silence. Fragile beauty beneath crystal cloudless sky. Testimony of fallen leaves. Brady was off to my right, hidden by scrub oak. His foot must have broken a branch in the underbrush. The buck lifted his head, proud, sighted me. His eyes, black infinite pools. The deer running. I could not lift my rifle. A shot from behind the scrub. The deer sprung from the stream bank toward open fields running, whitetail flashing. Another piercing shot. Heavy treading upon my quiet peace. The buck disappeared. "I'll be damned if I didn't hit it," Brady said. The deer reappearing, leaping afar, gray blur against black rocks, bleached sky, cloudless.*

Milton walks slowly, curled smoke at his ankles, punting discarded paper cups. This really wasting place, Martha's Vineyard. Insular. A glacial morraine. Brady cut out for the land of the living, where all songs are love songs. *When with the Galway foxhounds he would ride.* I stayed behind. Afraid to tread upon this fragile earth. Afraid to laugh. Waiting. Soon now my life will begin. Where is the way now, Brady, through the dark bare trees, the dim silent woods? Brady sang with a lilt in the loud world. Shattering silence with the laughter of a young man who, terrified by the sensation of his loud pounding heart, denounces death by risking his life. By running with life. But in my solitude now a need for almost deathly silence—the silence I must break when I can no longer bear the uneasiness which comes from repeating my own name, alone, unheard. Take me to the highlands of March and June green as clover, kites cutting out for stray heaven. This October, a dry cold month, storm brewing at sea in a giant witches' kettle.

I followed at a distance, able to run and laugh only at a distance, in Brady's worn path. Never quite able to reach out. But they waited in South Boston—all of them, family and friends—for the funeral train. *"I'm afraid, Milt." His eyes and mouth bled. "You see I'm a phony bastard. I'm afraid to die."* I could not reach out, could not cry. Open casket—a mannequin with clown rouge. Secluded hill and headstones, December oaks, soiled eraser snow. *"At an early age my father chose to live only a little in order not to die a great deal. I want it all, Milt. Without the bullshit, without resignation."* But his father knelt at the gravesite, breathing hard, with uplifted solemn hands beneath the spinning sky. Clear cold sky quickly fractured that day eight years ago. They could not forgive me, Milton, the friend who watched him die. The sky has been mended but remains frail, open to attack.

Milton approaches his house. Six o'clock chimes. Wheeling arms over the black clock face high above the island streets. Jogging now. Past picket fences. Past desolate gardens. Marcescent leaves. And captains' houses with forgotten widows' walks where silken ladies waited for the boats to return from Nantucket and beyond, waited to smile softness at leather-dry, driftwood faces. Past patches where woodbine blazes scarlet against brittle leaves, brown lawns. Distinct October sorrow.

"I'm home, honey. Johanna! It's me—Milton—come from the dead." The same damn line every day. Forced fondness. She does not answer. "Johanna!"

"Hush, Milton. I'm trying to call Mama."

Try something else. "Charlotte! Emily!"

Silence. My lovely daughters watch Mousecartoons on TV. Milton climbs the stairs, advances to the bathtub, the warm water feels good. A chance to grade book reports.

My precious sixth-graders, all twenty-four of them. It's their calculated indifference that really does gall. Through the steamy bathroom window Milton sees flowing trees, rugged ballet before the night storm. I hand out lists of recommended books for reports. People worth

meeting—Oliver Twist, Jane Eyre, Ivanhoe. And the reports flood in.
Freddy the Pig and the Baseball Team from Mars. Sue Barton, Cadet Nurse,
Performs a Lobotomy. They mock me they must be mocking me.
"Why did we have to get that old fart for a teacher?"

Brady's father had fed deer at a particular spot in the vale for
several years. When tracks indicated that the wounded buck had gone
into the vale, Brady suggested that we wait on a slight bluff above the feeding
ground. "They always come back here to die," Brady said. "Like salmon."

Brady, I've decided to teach school next year. I can't leave Harvard
now to go with you to the Great Wild West, so-called. I think I can be a
good teacher."

"O.K., Milt. Fine. It's your life. If you want to dedicate your life
to a bunch of Dick, Jane and Sallys that's your business. But I'm leaving
next week—and just in time I think."

"So you're going to be an epic hero. Is that it?"

"I'm going to try everything, that's all."

"Remember, Brady, there are no absolutes. Philosophy 117, section
3. We are speaking now of the hostile forces of the world. And heroes die
young."

"Come with me if you want. Just imagine it: the sun going down
over full trees, the rich black dirt of the midwest, the cold rise of the Rockies.
Take Beauty to the fields of Iowa, braid her hair with summer leaves.
The highlands, Milt. They aren't that far. Can it be you can't live up to
your dreams, Milt?"

"What I'm trying to say is that there is a balance inherent in this
whole goddamn situation. And I haven't found it yet. But the balance exists.
I'm sure of that. Between objectivity and involvement, stillness and
motion. Between today and tomorrow. I'm going to discover that balance
someday, Brady. I really am. But the only way to find it is to find
yourself in the silence, on a quiet beach, or in a forest clearing."

"You're speaking now of life at anchor, Milt."

"No—you simply don't throw away everything you've worked for,
not for a momentary sprint—even if that sprint dashes you into outer space.
Them solar winds are mean. And the return trip is a bummer. And I
don't want to live a completely selfish life. Can't you see that? That maybe
I can do some good for someone else, someone other than myself."

"What you want is good old-fashioned security, Milt—a safe
haven—you'll get it."

"Goddamn it, Brady, it's not that simple. But you're partially

175

right. I want a simple quiet life. I never want to rush to do anything."

"It'll be quiet all right."

"I want that quiet beach to walk with Johanna—I'm going to marry her—and a small town in which to share simple pleasures with good friends and watch my children grow honest and loving. You're right. That's what I want. Whether you call it 'security' or not. You just keep running. We'll see who comes out ahead. And what will you have, Brady? When the legs tire? When the panting becomes loud and hoarse?"

"Spring comes in on a motorcycle, and I'm riding over the whole earth."

And I'm living a quiet life here in Edgartown. I've got Johanna. And I watch the faces of island children growing older day after day. The vines that hold and won't let go. But the bathwater is toasty warm in my porcelain sea grotto. I cannot cry. I musn't.

O.K., class. A few examples. I lie down. I lay the hat down. I laid the butter in the dish. The chicken laid the egg. He has lain on the sofa all afternoon. Now, Susan, give me an example of "to lay" in the past tense. "He laid the hen in the chicken coop." Giggles. The class totters on the brink of bottomless mirth. O.K., class, it's really not that funny. They won't stop laughing. A voice overheard from the back. "I laid the old bitch in the butter dish." Gushing merriment. Class, let's calm down. They continue at ease, howling. Shut up! Do you hear me? Shut up! Silence falls over the classroom for the last forty-five minutes of the school day. My precious sixth-graders have their heads on folded arms on desk tops. Milton stands by the window, sour-faced, an old blowhard, watching wind and trees engage in spirited courtly dance. Three o'clock. Class dismissed. I am sorry sir, Susan says. I do not smile, cannot forgive. I cannot forgive anyone. Johanna for her descent into shallowness, sterility. My children and pupils for their indifference. Brady for his arrogant denial of my life by the fact of his own. *That dying chose the living world for text.* And I cannot forgive life for what it has done to me. The coldness of this October twilight. Mice are burrowed in the barley sheaves. Nine and fifty swans stir tentatively, stretching their wings, threatening to fly away before their time. And Brady went with Fergus to dance upon the level shore.

"Milt, you'll never understand," Brady said. "Life without literary allusions. That's what it's all about."

The stag bellows; summer dies; winter crouches like a white panther behind hills nearby. Yet I have lain with Beauty. Even the saddest old man has had a singular passing moment when he took Beauty to the fields. The way they went down in the waist-high grass and reeds, before the wind.

Wild ducks on the pond scattered, crying. A single cloud passed across the sun. Where wheat grew red golden in a ripe wind. When all songs were love songs. Her name was Johanna. She used to dance.

"Milton, are you going to come down to supper or are you going to screw around in the tub all night?"

"Just a minute."

She used to dance. She danced in a small Indiana town where we grew up together, fiddlers popcorn hayrides and Nehi grape soda. She was Homecoming Queen, monarch of the hog belt, and I stood by graceless but proud to be the subject of her serene and regal gaze. And we were the spotlight couple. The juke played tinny—"Twilight Time" by the Platters. And the other kids stood around in a circle, in the glow of our light, clapping their hands to the music, as I whirled Johanna away from the merry dance. Away to the high bleachers in the gymnasium, above the drifting smoke of dancers below. Away to Saturday afternoons beneath the sky on clover hills. She followed me to Cambridge after I'd been at Harvard one year. And I introduced her to Brady. She used to dance.

"Goddamn it, Milton, hurry up. We're not going to wait for you. Your supper's getting cold."

Into my paisley bathrobe. Rinse the ring out of the tub. Now face the ordeal of chicken casserole and the kids. Milton gets dressed and descends from the steamy grotto to the land of the living, the kitchen table.

"Hi Daddy." Charlotte is seven. "Hi Daddy." Emily is four. Harvest wheat colored hair, like their mother's, and freckles not yet mellowed by autumn. Johanna fetches the casserole, plops a good lump on Milton's tupperware plate.

"Charlotte, you say grace," Johanna says.

"Thank you for the world so sweet, thank you for the birds we eat—"

"That's not funny," Johanna says. "Milton, make her say it right."

"Say it right," Milton says.

Charlotte is laughing too hard.

"Let's eat," Milton says.

Waiting. The buck had not come into the vale.

"*Milt, I think Johanna is lovely.*"

"*I must agree, Brady, whole-heartedly. But tell me, have you ever loved a woman?*"

"*I've had my good nights.*" *He laughed.*

"*Precisely! That's precisely what I'm talking about. You'll say good-bye to Harvard and start to run. And you'll sky-dive over the West—*"

always taking your life to the brink. I can admire that. I really can. But someday, if all your parachutes have opened, you'll tire of the present round of games. You might even become bored. And where will you turn, Brady? Have you thought about that at all?"

"Not at all, Milt. And I doubt if I ever will."

And Brady began to laugh. I thought about the balance—how it was necessary to run along the beach, laughing, each day collecting shells, yet still hold out a chalice for the future. In time a better day will arrive, free from contradictions. Can you hear me now, Brady? I'm certain—I know that day will arrive. My need to clear and fortify a small place in the forest. Pillars of dusty sunlight slanting through the woods on my huddled family in the clearing, secure and loving, in timeless celebration. And a single road leading from the woods down to the Sound, where someday I shall sit back and watch my children build sand castles and ride ponies along a windy beach. With Johanna warm, once again, at my side. I know it's possible. With patience. My children gathered at my knees in the forest, their hair brightened by the captured sun, my hand braiding the gold and red. The consonant hush of the bordering dark woods. And the green and gold pastoral—faint tuneful rondo—of uncounted hours. But children— my God—they grow so fast, hearts racing for separate distant islands, enchanted harbors of their own discovery. All this passion of fathers spent on children doomed like the fathers. And then in late October you can walk over dying fields at night and hear winter come crashing hard through cold acres of stars. Can it be? The way Brady laughed.

"You know Brady there may come a day when you are unable to stalk the most lead-footed deer."

"I doubt it."

Brady stalked confidently, never stumbling, certain of his chosen path. For awhile I thought I'd go with him. Cut loose from the vines that entangle and won't let go. I had left a note for Johanna. But, unable to say it myself, I had quoted Rimbaud:

> *When the world is reduced to a single dark wood for our four eyes' astonishment,—a beach for two faithful children,— a musical house for our pure sympathy,—I shall find you.*

I thought she'd understand.

"Milt, you'll never understand," Brady said. "Life without literary allusions. That's what it's all about."

I don't think I ever will understand. But sometimes I get so close—I can almost touch—then the balance swings back, seasons change, and the world regains her fragile poise. Unable to forgive, I can't even cry.

"Milton, will you please make your daughters be quiet at the table. Do I have to wear the pants in this household?"

"O.K., girls."

"But Daddy, Charlotte keeps making fun of my ears."

"That's a dirty fib," Charlotte says.

"Daddy—"

The buck had staggered onto the feeding ground, stumbling grotesquely, having lost the regimen of natural grace. Brady signalled for me to follow down the bluff. I followed. In spite of myself, I thought how easy it would be to shoot Brady in the back. How impossibly easy. To silence all contradictions to my tentative balance. To make quiet, for awhile, this small earth. Brady looked back over his shoulder. I was still following. And if I shot him, the only sound would be my own footfall, silent in the snow, But there would still be the wounded deer, and I'd be unable to aim the cartridge.

The buck had lain down in the snow. Brady approached quietly. The deer stood straight up. The front legs of the buck wobbled then spread apart uncertainly, shaking violently. His bloodshot eyes blazed, nostrils vomiting blood. Brady drew a bead for his heart. The deer started to run. Brady aimed the .30 calibre repeater, fired once, the deer jolted, fell. Fell in the glaring scrubbed light. The gunshot echoed through all the vale, against rocks.

"Milton, do you find it so hard to say a single word at the dinner table? Poor timid Milton. Well, please try to make these kids behave."

Emily squirms in her chair.

"Guess what I learned in school today, Daddy?" Charlotte says.

"Not right now," Milton says. "Daddy's tired."

Emily squirms again. "I've got to go," she says.

"Take her to the bathroom, Milton," Johanna says.

"For God's sake she's old enough—"

Emily farts.

"Bombs over Tokyo," Charlotte says.

Emily begins to cry. Milton begins to laugh.

"Don't cry, sweetie," Johanna says. "That's all right."

Emily looks at Milton with hurt eyes, unable to understand how he could laugh, and she cries louder. Nothing bothers me anymore. These tears—a small autumn shower on my oceanic indifference. I've got to

179

get out of this house. Upstairs to get my raincoat—storm approaching. And now for a few happy beers at the Scallop.

"Where are you going, Milton?" Johanna says.

"To the harbor."

"Do you know your daughter is crying? Do you know that, Milton? Haven't you even the decency to comfort her?"

"I've got to get some fresh air. I can't breathe. Please try to understand, honey."

"Milton, try to be a father and a man—just this once."

"Listen, Johanna, I've got to go for a walk. I've been thinking about Brady all day, and I'm falling with each minute."

"Things can't go on like this much more, Milton. I mean it. You've always been a cold person—but you're getting colder all the time. I can't stand much more of this selfishness, this lack of all feeling. If you walk out that door—"

"Everything's going to be O.K."

"It's all over Milton. You know that and I know that. We ran out of laughs a long time ago. And now there's not even decency. Milton—"

A door bangs. The hand of the harbor fog beckons. Odors of seaweed iodine. Down the hill in a land of crisp fallen leaves. Toward the moon over the harbor and the moon reflected on the bay, rising and falling, give and take. But over all is the silence of the calm.

Brady mounted the deer on top of the station wagon for the drive back to Cambridge. He would leave for the West the following day. The night came on, sad and confused. Just the thought of killing Brady made me shiver. Around the rotary into Harvard Square. Stopping for sandwiches and beer.

A voice from the back of the bar. "Well if it isn't Daniel Boone." Brady's friends gathered around Brady. The laughter commenced, but I didn't know the people, prepared to leave. Johanna's apartment was only six blocks down by the Charles.

"What's the hurry?" Brady asked.

"Nothing. I just want to see Johanna. I'll see you tomorrow before you leave."

It was undeniable that Brady had friends. He was the kind of person who would attract a following of idolaters. Undeniable. Yet I knew Brady better than anyone.

"Milt—"

"What?"

"Say hello to Johanna for me. If it weren't for you, I'd be kneeling at her door with roses every day." He laughed.

But I took him seriously. I thought he might. I left the bar.

Walking now down to Edgartown harbor. But first must stop at the Scallop for warmth and nourishment.

"Good evening," the waitress says.

"Hi," Milton says, staring at her punctuated breasts beneath a translucent white blouse. Like all the waitresses, she wears an imitation patent leather red skirt. Netting hugs her hair tight to her skull. And nice legs. "I'll have a tall Bud," Milton says. She looks about twenty-five.

Leaving Brady I walked along the Charles toward Johanna's apartment. She had undoubtedly received the card that I'd sent from the Berkshires about my plans to leave with Brady. I wasn't going to leave her but I wanted her to think so.

From the sidewalk her room appeared dark, and the window was open even on a blasting cold night. I climbed the stairs. She had become ever more real inside me while I had been in the Berkshires for the week.

I entered without knocking. The room was cold. A sharp knife wind fanned through the window. The room was dark, and the white curtains flashed about the window in the wind. Flapping in the wind. Johanna was sitting outside the covers on the bed, naked, her head leaned back against the bedpost, her long hair falling and flowing in the wind. She made no attempt to cover herself. I went over and sat on the edge of the bed, and she leaned her long white body on me, her head on my chest. I kissed her and wrapped my arms around her naked breasts.

"Is Brady leaving tomorrow?" Johanna asked.

"Yes. But I'm not really going with him."

"I knew you wouldn't," she said.

After closing the window, I undressed and slipped between the icy sheets. The room stayed cold. Johanna was near but distant and unknown.

"He said he'd bring you roses every day," I said.

She had fallen quickly asleep.

"Here you go, mister," the waitress says.

Milton smiles and pours the beer.

"Listen, mister, do you mind if I talk to you a minute? There's no one else in this crappy bar."

"No, not at all." Be nice, Milton. For once, try to be nice. She sits down. Milton drinks his beer, says nothing.

"Do you live around here, mister?"

"Yes . . . My name's Milton, and yours?"

"Alice. I just started working here two weeks ago. But I live over in Oak Bluffs. Sam lets me drive the car over there. Big deal I say. After all it's only a shitty '54 Ford. And it's olive—a color I can't stand."

"I'm sorry to hear it's such an old clunker," Milton says.

"Say mister—uh, Milton—are you married?"

"I'm afraid so."

"That's the same for me. I got a husband if you could call him that. He's a real bastard." Alice laughs then becomes serious, almost sad. "Yah I got Sam all right. He's not that bad really but we just don't have good times much anymore if you know what I mean. I think he'd rather go bowling most of the time." She hesitates. "I'm sorry, mister, I don't mean to bore you."

"That's all right," Milton says. "I mean you don't bore me. I'm just sorry to hear about your troubles."

Alice fetches another beer for Milton and one for herself.

"Well, anyway, most of the troubles—you sure you don't mind—most of 'em began when my Janie—she was only three—died of bad lungs and after that he beat me a lot I don't know why. I can see why he was upset after all but I can't have anymore kids—"

Waving goodbye to Brady that sunny winter morning. Johanna and I said we'd miss him, he gave a victory sign and was on his way to the land of the living, to ride the rapids west. I think Brady was sad. I didn't expect that. I held Johanna—my Johanna—tightly by my side on that winter day, waving. It wasn't until three years later that I learned Johanna had been in love with Brady. She told me. That she had wanted to go to bed with Brady. That she would have left for the West with him if Brady hadn't insisted that she stay behind with me. But I could never forgive him. She was all I had.

"—say, mister, if this is boring you just tell old Alice to shut up. I know you're not Ann Landers or anything. Well, anyway, thanks for listening. I gotta go now. Take care." Alice winks and is gone. Then she comes back. "Oh I forgot your check." Then she vanishes again.

The check says I owe the Scallop two dollars for four beers. And on the back is a note:

> *Meet me at 9:00 if you want to at my car*
> *in the parking lot. I get off work then.*
> > *Cheers,*
> > *Alice*

P.S. Thanks a lot for your ear.
P.P.S. The car's an olive '54 Ford, remember?

Along the streets wind has shaken branches from grace and has tossed them to the ground. Night falls quickly. Milton walks along remnant wharves in Edgartown harbor. He envisions phantom schooners rising from the dusk and fog with full sails, courses charted for unfamiliar misty islands where windchimes jangle together and the air is rich with incense after a slumberous warm rain. In the surging wind waves smack against the wharves with renewed gusto—plangent tidal songs. Slate-gray clouds boil in a black sky.

Waving goodbye to Brady that winter day. "He's the most alive person I know," Johanna said. I didn't see Brady again for four years, at which time he whirled back into Boston from the sunny West like Pecos Bill at the eye of fury. I received a post card in Edgartown, where Johanna and I had been living for three years:

> *Dear Captain Kangaroo,*
>
> *Surprise, surprise, surprise. Mackie's back in town. It's me— Brady—come from the dead. Why not come up to Boston this week- end for insufferable nostalgia, unending tales of the not-so-old West, and perhaps a few drinks.*
>
> *Happy trails to you.*

I told Johanna I had a teachers' meeting in Boston.

Along the wharf a solitary old man raises his arthritic arms toward the sky. Bells sing on buoys in the choppy wind. Chimes. Nine o'clock. Milton jogs back to the Scallop. Alice waits behind the wheel of her '54 Ford.

"I thought you'd come," she says, smiling.

Milton slides into the car on plastic seat covers. Alice turns on the radio. It's an oldie but goodie:

> *See the girl with the diamond ring;*
> *She knows how to shake that thing.*

Alice whips the horses, revs the engine, and peels out of the parking lot.

"Where are we going?" Milton asks.

"We can't stay here."

"I know but where to?"

"South Beach."

Alice guns the engine some more, gooses the transmission, and races off.

The scotch tasted fine.

"I never thought you'd make it back, Brady. I really didn't. I thought you'd get scalped in Provo or Cheyenne."

"No, Milt, I've never felt more alive, but I've talked too much already. I rest my case. And you, Milt, are you still teaching?"

"Right."

"I imagine you and Miss Frances have one hell of a good time at Ding Dong School."

Alice eases the olive bomb off the highway into a grove of pines.

"You wanna go down to the beach?" Milton asks.

Alice giggles and leaps into the back seat like Tinkerbell.

"Hop in, Brady. Johanna's been asking about you, and I think you'll enjoy the Vineyard. Edgartown swings."

The expressway south toward Martha's Vineyard. Through the reeling bewilderment of lights and horns the car flowing untouched like a toy sailboat down rapids in a creek.

"I couldn't help that, Milt—Johanna loved me. Because she needed someone to love her. But I made her stop—for you."

The back seat is cramped and smells like a '54 Ford that has been sitting in a swamp since 1954. Milton holds his arm around Alice, not quite sure when or if.

"Didn't you say you were from Oak Bluffs, Alice?"

"Yah."

"I used to take the kids over there in the summer. To the Flying Horses at the end of Circuit Avenue. They loved it so much, galloping across the evening sky, their faces flashing orange and blue and violet in the colored lights. The horses danced to calliope tunes. Someone played a harmonica. Charlotte and Emily laughed so hard, and their red hair tumbled up and down in the wind. Then we'd always get cotton candy."

"Sounds swell," Alice says.

Alice unbuttons Milton's shirt and begins to rub the hair on his chest.

"Well, mister, at least I'm honest about it." She laughs.

I hesitated then went for the brakes. The car fishtailed, hit a bridge buttress. Brady's head shattered the windshield, leaving a spider web in the glass brilliant beneath the moon. I was able to crawl out the window. My mouth was bleeding but nothing serious. I pulled Brady from the car. He was conscious but hardly breathing and blood heaved from his mouth and eyes. I pressed my mouth to his and breathed desperately. Cars began to stop.

Brady began to breathe, coughing, choking. His eyes stared out at me, past me, then back again, then closed. An incredibly clear night, unnoticed before. Full of throbbing stars. Orion stood tall, poised. Sirens. I sat with Brady in the screaming ambulance. Flashing amber lights. Traffic huddled along the guard rails with lights like cats' eyes out of the darkness. I could hear the wind rushing past the ambulance. Turn off the goddamn siren. Please. Brady reached out for my hand, whispering. "I'm afraid, Milt. You see, I'm a phony bastard. I'm afraid to die." I could not reach out, could not forgive, could not begin to reach out.

"And where do you think you're going?" Alice asks.

The walls of the car close in, irreversibly, on my naked body. But I am not really here. Never have been. I am walking over summer fields too easily forgotten—falling in meadows of Queen Anne's Lace, before the wind, sighing. Johanna folding her perfumed hair around me. I am taking Charlotte and Emily by their hands and boosting them to pink and gold flying horses. The horses gyre in the summer dusk descending. In the silence. Only the faint calliope song on the night wind. But Alice is close, breathing hard. Steam forms on the inside of the car windows. And through the steam ancient faces emerge, flat-nosed against the glass, howling with laughter. I can see Brady and my wife, my daughters and my students. In a fading circle of light by the pines a young girl dances in drifting smoke to tinny juke-box tunes. I cannot breathe. The beer buzzes in my head.

"I've just got to leave," Milton says, dressing himself. "You go on back, Alice. I'll get home all right. I'm sorry."

"If this ain't the shits," Alice says.

"I'm sorry. Goodbye."

Running through the sand. The beach is near. Frost breeds in the hollows between dunes. The beach is poised, cleanswept and waiting. Above which livid clouds revolve in the changing and changeless sky.

Milton's foot catches in the twisted grass. He falls on a slight sand warp above the beach. Refuge at last in an empty place, where sorrows are vented to this October night unheard. Monotonous waves pound the strand. Images flourish in the salt air.

Through the fog I see them. They wait on a hill in South Boston for the funeral ceremony. Johanna stands by me as they lower the casket. Smirking gravediggers toss unthawed hard dirt on the cold steel box. *In balance with this life, this death.* This life said to be mine. But Brady what I always wanted to say before—

Two girls run from the undersea in the cold night. They sit on the beach, amassing sand, building castles. Their hair flows in the wind, glowing beneath the moon as it glowed in the summer sun, gone away.

Their castles loom above the ocean, standing guard for the storm. Intruding waves flood the moats. Thunderclouds darken in the fragile stillness. I run toward them. They do not see me. Reaching for them but weakened, I fall to the cold sand and cannot move, cannot breathe to shout. And there is suspended silence—the silence of a deer at winter morning where the hunter waits huddled, hidden, crystal earth not yet shattered, before the first and last shot. The dome of the sky must hold back the storm. It must. It must protect my daughters. Charlotte wanders up the beach. Emily wades in the sea. I want to tell them to be careful. I must tell them.

Be careful I cry. Emily looks around. Thunder shakes trees on the dunes, shakes the earth. The sky falling like splintered glass, particles falling in sparkling billions along the tidemark. Cold rain pounds against my face. Dark waves cloak my daughter, her frail white body thrown to the ocean. Her hand reaching through the rain like a wind-tossed branch. Distant chimes ringing faintly on the bitter air. Ancient threnody of storm and sea. I cannot move, cannot reach further. The girl screaming. I must get to the water.

A lady in black draperies paces in the hard rain. She calls her daughter's name. Blaring waves drown her voice. The tide erodes sand empires, towers fall. The lady's ceaseless wailing on the night beach. She runs into the sea toward the small white body rolling in the waves. She seizes her dead child. She holds the limp body across her outstretched arms, the wet hair of the child falling long and swaying stiffly in the wind. It is Johanna dressed in a black robe, kneeling in the sand like a wounded dark swan. It is Johanna mourning for her lovely child.

Through the rain I stand and stretch my arms toward my wife, weeping her name. There is momentary silence amidst the fury I call her name I cry for Johanna she turns she steps then nothing she cannot see she cannot hear I begin to run toward her reaching for her but then again there is nothing then afar the wailing. I am sorry I cry I am sorry. But I cannot find her in the fog, in the rain. Somewhere near she cries. I cannot see her. Through the storm through the cold night they will come to me—they must come to me— they will—my daughter cannot be dead—they will come to me—all of them. And I shall embrace them. I shall hold them tight to my body in the certain rain.

Lost in the phantom night Milton runs along the empty beach, out of breath, calling for Johanna. The wind muffles his voice. He hears Johanna crying distant then nearer then far. But then the wind dies. The rain weakens. Milton falls wet and coughing to the cold sand. All voices have faded in the trodden night. He rolls in the sand, begins to laugh hoarsely. Greater clouds amass, forewarning another assault. Above the beach the sky spins, changing or changeless.

Susan Walker

Hermitage

It was his eleventh birthday, the day his father would go with them to
the park. The cup Joshua's mother gave him shone pale blue like the
morning itself. The whole room to his sleepy eyes had the thin brightness
of crystal. He could look directly at nothing really. Things were too bright,
without shadows or depth. He liked this because he could stay sleepy and
it was all right. Nothing moved at him suddenly because no dark corners
were in the room but only a steady shimmer of waves of heat and light. His
mother's dress was the one she wore the most often in the mornings. It had
a funny pattern that he couldn't understand with dots and crosses. They
were blue and yellow and he had never seen anything like them except on
her dress. He watched the pattern move around the room and thought how he
could keep on eating more and more pieces of toast and jelly for a very long
time. His mother could keep giving him more and she would be amazed
that he would never stop. He laughed into his milk at this prospect and
thought his mother would laugh too but, she stood still in the doorway, look-
ing up to the top of the stairs.

He watched her for a moment thinking, "My father is asleep because he
likes to sleep and he sleeps nearly all the time." Joshua often said this to
himself as a rhyme but it didn't have another line to it. He said it now softly
into his cup of milk so that his mother would look around.

She did, and she seemed to remember that he had laughed a minute
before. She laughed now in a gay way and her cheeks smiled and went into
wrinkles and her eyes were deep blue and looked full at him. He felt good
so that he didn't have to move around at all. The toast was gone and he sat
straight in his chair and thought about the present she always gave him early
in the morning on his birthday. It was a little declaration between them that
she had not forgotten it although he would have to wait until later for the
official presents and a party. He thought that what he would like best would
be a note under his plate telling him where to go and look for his present.
His mother had done this once, a long time ago, but she had not done it last
year. His fingers slowly tilted the plate up away from the yellow breakfast
cloth. A note was there. It said to go and look inside the greenhouse. He

heard his mother begin to sing under her breath while she washed the dishes at the sink, and he ran out of the room.

It was still very early morning outside. The wet grass surprised him when it stuck to his shoes. A brick path that his father had laid when they had first come led to the greenhouse. Weeds had pushed the bricks apart now and it lay tumbled and disused. He avoided it and took great leaps through the tall grass. The greenhouse door was always locked, but he knew where the key was and he liked unlocking it. Inside, it was steamy and warm. His friends thought the greenhouse a queer place, but he was used to it and did not think about it.

How would he find his present? It would be small and hidden. He began to look amongst a pile of clay pots and hoses at his feet. The search could be a long one and he was suddenly in a fit of impatience to be driving off with his parents to the park where he would meet his friends. He ran the length of the dim greenhouse, his feet soundless on the sodden floor, and caught a glimpse of red metal down a side aisle. It was a wagon, a big heavy one with "Racer" in streamlined script on the side. He stared at it in disappointment. He had had wagons before and surely he was too big for them now. His eyes stung suddenly with tears. But if he cried his mother would know and it might be that this wagon was different. He ran slowly with it clanking behind him down the damp, narrow aisle, the stately stalks of his mother's lilies rustling slightly together.

The sun was already hotter outside. It made him feel like it was that endless noontime when you worked in the yard and weren't supposed to stop. It was so much hotter there than when his mother said how hot it was in the kitchen. He always wanted to stop and go inside and sit on the cool floor somewhere downstairs but it was those times when maybe his father was asleep or didn't want to be bothered. He plodded like a laborer now through the grass with the wagon behind. He wondered if his father would be ready to go very soon. His father was often late and Joshua had to wait and wait for him a lot, but he didn't mind much because his mother explained that his father was busy and it was all right. He stayed in the yard a long time, hoping his father would appear in the window and wave to him. He had done this once, just come out of the blackness of the upstairs bedroom window and stared down at him playing on the grass. Then he had waved his hand slowly back and forth like a very old man. He could remember how glad he had been to see his father up above him like an audience. He had leaped in the grass and done cartwheels for him.

Now the house was silent as he lay in the yard, waiting. It looked very tall and blue in the shadow as the sun rose at its back. In the afternoon the squares of windows turned fiery so that you couldn't look at them, but now they were dark and easy to look at. He couldn't understand how a house could be like a forest but in the early morning it reminded him of one. Its blue stone was soft and dim. You could pass through it into clearings and lighted spaces in groves of trees. Forests were his favorite thing, more than the town streets near schools or fields. He imagined himself as a very old man who had always lived in such a forest and never left it.

In the house, he saw the silhouetted figure of his mother moving about the dining room. He was far enough away so that she seemed to him like the quiet movement of a shadow of a bough or a forest animal darting harmlessly. Then the house was still again. In the silence of the morning he could hear the grass around him unbend slowly where he had trod on it. He became aware that the dampness was soaking through his shirt to his skin. He sat forward slowly, as though he were just waking up, until he was on his knees, and saw that his mother had come to the doorway and stood, shading her eyes with her hand, looking for him.

"Joshua!" she called, "Will you come in for a while?"

He left the wagon behind him in the grass and ran toward her. His steps were thuds which said "I can run very fast, I can run very fast." He liked it that his mother did not move aside in spite of his onrush. He watched her waist come closer and closer and then she hugged him. She wore a wool sweater for going to town which scratched his face. Her long brown skirt and her heavy shoes meant they would be leaving soon.

"Did you like the wagon, honey? Please tell your daddy you did."

He looked up at her face. Her eyes looked as if she were going to cry. A red mark by her mouth showed like the whiplash of a thorn branch on her white skin. He stared at it and she let him go and told him to wait downstairs for his father.

Joshua wandered alone through the house watching the patterns the light from the back windows made on the parquet floor. He always felt that the downstairs was his. He could pick any shadowed or light spot to sit in and play a game. Today he would have liked to go into the living room, but he forced himself to stay in the entry hall at the base of the stairs. The ceiling popped faintly with the movements of his father in the bedroom, which he figured was directly above him. He often tried to discover just what was below him when he was upstairs and where the walls above divided the bedrooms, when he was downstairs. He was never completely sure that he was right about his calculations and the parts of the house remained mysteriously unrelated.

The noises from above increased. His feet began to follow a crack in the wooden floor, and he pretended that he was walking a tight wire over the ocean. He thought that by the time he had retraced his steps along the crack to the first wall his father would be starting down the stairs. Standing still against the panelling, he would greet his father. But the heavy steps sounded suddenly at the top of the stairs when he was only midway across the empty hallway. An invisible force kept him from turning and facing his father, made him keep pacing solemnly across the tightwire in the floor. An avalanche of stumbling steps at his back seemed to last for an interminable time, until he thought wildly that the person approaching him could not possibly still be coming down the stairs, might not even be his father. But the steps ignored the presence of the boy, immobile in the middle of the hall, and went past him with a great clatter to die away somewhere in the kitchen.

The silence of the house returned and he knew he could wait quietly here until it was time to go, but he went instead to the doorway. At the end of the hall he could see a slim rectangular bit of the kitchen with his father sitting blocklike in a chair. His back was turned, and he looked as he always looked, huge, too big for the chair, hunched over the table as though he were hiding a hand of cards. His mother passed back and forth quickly on either side of him. Joshua guessed she was making them lunch to take with them. Their voices rose and fell without a stop or a climax like the dull sound of waves at the distant beach. The silence of the house remained always above their sound so that the hall that separated him from them seemed the long arcade of a palace. His mother talked most and he forgot to listen, watching her clothes change to light brown and then to black as she moved in and out of the shadow.

The shoulder he had been leaning against the woodwork of the door became uncomfortable and he straightened up. His mother caught sight of him and beckoned him to come. The kitchen was still bright like at breakfast and his father was sitting, half shadowing his eyes with his hand. He waited for Joshua to come around in front of him.

"Good morning, son," he said. "You got the wagon your mother says."

"Yes." Joshua thought his father looked funny sitting at the table without any breakfast in front of him. He waited a little. "I like it a lot."

"Fine. That's just fine." He turned heavily around in his chair to face his wife. "Are you ready yet, Marjorie? I want to get started on this thing."

"Yes. Everything is ready. It's a nice day, we can come home whenever we want. Perhaps Joshua will show you around at the park. Now who's going to help me with this basket?"

Joshua and his mother loaded the car. His father stayed behind in the house looking for something.

"He'll be out in a minute," said his mother. "Let's get in the car and be all ready."

They sat and waited a long time. His mother took off her sweater and spread it over her knees.

"Joshua, I think your father feels ill this morning. I'm sure he'll like the park and he may start to feel better then. What's your friend's name who's so good at baseball?"

"Simon."

"Well, perhaps you could introduce him to your father. He used to play very well himself. His team always wore red caps and they called them the Bandits, for stealing bases, I suppose."

His father came out then, hoisting himself into the driver's seat and starting the motor almost in a single movement. The wheels spun on the gravel drive and the car shot suddenly forward, forcing Joshua and his mother back against the rough upholstery. His father drove with both hands on the wheel, maneuvering the car as though there were no road at all but instead a jungle fighting against the wheels. The hurtling of the car seemed to force unnecessary danger on him and his mother. She kept glancing at his father and he knew that she wanted to tell him to stop, but she said nothing. Squeezed between his parents in the front seat, he could hold onto nothing and could see little but the dense interlacing of tree branches which raced by overhead, gone before he could recognize any or could judge how far they had come.

The rough drive suddenly fell away abruptly behind them and was forgotten as if it had been a brief clanking over a railroad crossing. The wheels began to roll trimly down the macadam highway. His mother relaxed against the door on her side of the car and pointed to a herd of cattle grazing serenely on the crest of a hill.

"Look, Joshua."

"Yes ma'am." He was thinking of how funny it was that once you left their property the fields stretched away like somebody hated trees and cut them all down for no reason at all. Cows wandered in some places but mostly the fields were bare with nobody in sight and just weeds making a dull boundary to the road that went almost without a curve into town. He wondered if the people who owned the land were like his father or if he knew them.

"Daddy, who owns that land?"

"Men from town." His father stared down the road intensely as if he feared the sun would blind him and make him veer off the road into the weeds. He began talking again in a tone unfamiliar to Joshua.

"They don't do anything with it, the fools. Waiting to get bought up by a big investor for a fantastic profit. It's called the smart, clean way to a comfortable life the rest of your days. You know, if we'd been smart, Marjorie, I would have bought them out before we ever settled in here. What friends we would have had then."

"Yes, maybe." His mother smiled. "I've never much liked any of them. They're not real country people at all. Just small town, small town, that's all."

The car slowed to a crawl on main street. Joshua was impatient to see around him. He got to his knees and looked out the back window. The street was littered with women carrying bright, colored bags from the small department store, their children and others racing in nebulous circles around them in the street that was nearly empty of cars. The men were in groups standing and talking in front of the hardware store. None of this interested Joshua, but when he turned around in the seat he met the fixed gaze of an old man with a cane who was standing near the curb at the corner. He did not appear to be trying to cross the street. Joshua was startled that the old man had seen them, in their old blue and white auto, first before he had noticed him. The old man stared at them in what seemed to be outraged anger, his jaw clenched so that his lower teeth were exposed. His gaze was fixed and horrible. It took in all three of them one by one as they sat trapped in what Joshua had thought to be the private world of their car. Joshua's parents were amazingly in ignorance of the man at the curb. As they drove by, the man shook his cane at his father's profile.

A car suddenly honked at them, and Joshua's mother put her arm around him and made him sit right in the seat.

"There, the park's just up ahead. There won't be much more of this."

Joshua sat low in the car. He had never seen the man before. How could he know them and why would he be so angry? He was old and crazy. Maybe he just hated cars. The cane he had was awful, though, thick and long like he had picked it especially for scaring people. Joshua did not think he wanted to get out at the park. He wanted to tell his parents about the man but he could not. Perhaps you weren't supposed to pay attention when something like that happened. It occurred to him that he had no idea of what his father would do if he told him about the man. He imagined his father turning the car around wildly and going back and calling the man a fool. But perhaps he wouldn't. Still he was afraid and said nothing.

The wheels began to crunch slowly on the gravel entrance to the park. The car jolted over a hump and he began to feel sick. He leaned sharply against his mother. She looked down at him quickly and her arm tightened around him.

"Hey, Joshua, it's almost time to celebrate your birthday!"

Her voice was bright at their arrival. A group of women that had been standing just at the edge of the parking lot began to come toward the car.

"Marjorie!" they called shrilly. "Come and see the china display in the clubhouse!"

"Hello," his mother waved, releasing him. "I can't just now. Why don't I come over later?"

"Oh, come on and come!" said the tallest of the group. "We're dying to show someone through."

"You can leave them for a little while." A young blonde one with a round face was speaking, smiling at his father.

His mother laughed. "Well, perhaps I can. Josh, you stay with your father until I'm back. We won't be gone long."

The ladies took her off then, comfortably strolling in loose-belted dresses toward the clubhouse. The hum of cars on main street grew louder. Joshua thought how close they were to downtown where the old man was. He looked at his father, hoping he would say something in the way he had before about the men from town, but he was only standing by the car as if he did not know what to do.

"Let's go to the summerhouse and wait for Mother," Joshua offered in an undertone. His own voice sounded funny, high and light like a girl's.

His father only nodded and seemed uncertain of which direction to take, so Joshua pointed to the narrow path that ran over the slope to the picnic shed. He liked following his father's heavy body down the slope, watching his muscular thighs go back and forth as he tried to keep from breaking into an involuntary run on the steep incline. They were out of sight of the road now. Joshua looked back over his shoulder to see only the empty slope, its long grass waving slightly in the wind.

At the bottom of the hill a dark knot of boys broke apart and scattered away across the playing field. Two in dark blue coats ran up to Joshua.

"Do you want to play ball with us?" they asked, walking on either side of him.

"O.K. I guess it's all right."

His father didn't turn around, and Joshua ran as hard as he could with the other boys to the packed dirt of the baseball diamond. The one on his left suddenly poked him hard in the waist. Rudy had orange hair and a broken tooth.

"What's your father doing here, Joshua?"

"I don't know. He just came with us."

"My father said he doesn't think your father ought to come around here, you know that?"

"No." said Joshua. His mother had told him that Rudy was mean.

The rest of the boys came up suddenly. Two of them looked at each other and laughed. A fat one leaned over right into his face, saliva running from the corner of his mouth, and sputtered, "Your daddy's a crook."

Joshua couldn't understand. His eyes blurred and he backed away. Someone yelled "shut up" and the knot of jeering boys became a circle of aloof faces which accused him of something of which he knew instinctively he was guilty, but horribly he could not understand what it was.

Joshua turned suddenly and ran away from their silence, but it was the wrong direction. He tried desperately to circle back toward his father and felt himself running out of breath at the top of the hill. He stumbled to the crest of the slope and saw their car sitting innocently alone in the parking lot. His half-blinded gaze took in the stream of traffic behind it on main street and then swept down again toward his father in the summerhouse. Then he saw the old man with the cane from town again, outside the summerhouse, yelling at his father. The old man had followed them, he had been following them all the time. His chest worked very hard as he saw his father rise and walk slowly toward him. The old man's cane waved wildly. Then his father lunged at him and pushed him to the ground. A scream sounded high and thin up in the vast space above the empty playing field. He saw the tiny figure of his mother running and the old man lying on his side, still clutching his cane and pushing it in little spasms at his father.

It was that that he remembered on the long trip home in the twilight. He had to keep looking at the two people on either side of him to remind himself that they were no longer tiny figures distant on the playing field, his mother running, his father standing over the man. He had been so far away from them when his father pushed the old man down. The huge field opening emptily to the horizon and the sound of the wind in the grass and above his head had been so vast that it was as if he had really been alone, standing on the crest of the hill watching dolls play. He had not seen the old man after that. He had not seen anything except a policeman with his father and his mother beside him in the car. But she did not know that he had seen his father strike the old man. He had wanted to tell her before when she had taken him to the car and his father had not come yet, but she had huddled very small against the door and hidden her face from him, leaning her forehead against the glass. He had been suddenly afraid when she had done that. He had sat straight in the seat, staring out the front window of the car toward the park, feeling alone like a ship captain on watch while others are below. The little clock in the dashboard had kept on ticking and he listened to it for longer than he had ever listened to anything. He told himself that when its hands moved to a certain spot his father would surely have returned to the car and they would be gone, but the hands went slowly past his spot and still no one came.

It had occurred to him once as he had looked at his mother leaning against the door that maybe she was not going to move. That was silly and awful. Why had he thought it? After that he had been confused. All sorts of ideas like in nightmares had come into his head and then he had forgotten them all and was very hungry. His mother had turned around at last and opened the picnic basket and fed him his favorite sandwich and part of a beef one she had made for his father. He had even eaten a piece of cake, licking the icing from the wrapping paper. After that he had felt good and did not look out the window anymore. His mother had smiled and put her arm around him, and his father had come soon after that.

But now the car was moving again and he knew none of the things he had thought of during his long afternoon wait had any importance. Only his memory of what he had seen on the playing field came back to him with sharpness. But now his mother was not the tiny doll running across the huge field nor was she a huddled figure in the stillness of the parked car. In the dim light of the early evening she was very large and straight; the wool skirt spreading over her legs seemed an infinite expanse. He could see her feet in her heavy shoes resting quietly on the dirty floor of the car, not moving at all. The car was so still with only a souvenir doll of his father's swaying slightly with the vibration that he could not speak and tell his mother about the boys on the playing field.

Joshua watched the doll rock back and forth until his stomach felt bad and he was thankful for the increasing darkness. In the twilight the town was way behind them and only carlights swept across their faces from time to time. Then they were past where the cars were, and the night smell of the fields, grass and honeysuckle, was strong. He sat back in the seat and waited for the first glimpse of their house. In the corner of his mind he knew his father's hands were on the steering wheel, but he stared hard ahead, past where the carbeams illuminated the underbrush, and gradually forgot about the hands. In the violet night he did not want to tell his mother anything or to do anything but stare out the window past the streaming trees to see the dark roof of their house. When he saw it, he knew the time would be nothing until it was breakfast again because he would go to bed very soon.

Then the car went up the drive, and dreaming, he saw the wagon in the yard where he had left it and imagined himself playing with it tomorrow up under the dark windows of the house. His father would be away upstairs somewhere although he might come to the window for a moment. The silence after the car stopped awakened him, and he looked up to see the house, blue in the shadow like the trees themselves. The windows were dark and easy to look at with only a tiny red point from the setting sun in each one, small and disappearing to nothing.

William H. Guy

Actaeon

1

Bartholomew Matthiesson turned a porcelain handle and waited for the flow of water. First there was no sound, then a faint visceral gurgling. Then water tumbled. This was no modern sink, these fixtures fragments of forgotten worlds, turn-of-the-century handiwork. He bathed his hands and face. The road had been clotted, full of clods. He would need a night's rest to adjust, to calm himself.

He had not foreseen this journey. Teaching in summer boarding school had promised to detain him through July near Philadelphia, close to the sea, anchored by duties. The school spewed forth its charges every Friday for the weekend and left the masters to a deafening silence on the grounds. That silence had proved excessive, maddening in its fourth assault, had driven Bartholomew seaward, driven him to Cape May.

He could not have pretended to be happy or settled. Past age twenty-five; alienated from or uninterested in all his old friends, they married, freed of existential queries in flurries of domestic happiness; he found himself, as now, at unexpected and inconvenient intervals, the powerless victim of some unmoored energy inside himself, released in sudden ill-considered gestures like this doubtful journey. In some uncertain way, his presence here warned Bartholomew that Pamela was asserting herself within him, had seized on his innards, that this trip was merely a means of rolling with the forcible psychic blows her memory dealt out inside him. She still lived in him with all her wrangling wilfulness.

Emerging from the Lafayette Hotel to walk before dinner, he crossed Beach Avenue to the asphalt promenade running alongside the sand. In secret, summer was enacting its decline. Sunlight, burnished and sad, like some old sailor's relic, tilted. Raw wintry shadows stuck out from underneath old buildings. Late afternoon gusts provoked the sea's unmannered musketry. Autumn tinged the rim of evening.

She had served as the first, the only outlet for his streams of poetic extemporizing. She had listened. After a fashion she had loved what others had found only odd or laughable. Then when the first wave of self-revelation that had established their relationship subsided, left to build with little things what had gone neglected in the early torrential stages of love, each had proved impatient, accusatory, disaffected. Still anxious to exhibit her discovery, Pamela had tried to lure him into contact with others, to strengthen him (she said) with others' insights, to keep their love alive through the agency of others. Bartholomew had left her in self-defense, but in a way had not left her, had found himself still desperately answering her as if her barbed persuasive words had stuck in him.

Now baffled, left to himself, he had lost his medium of self-expression, the mind of another. Inwardly, he heard the strange concatenation of words his mind devised to mark the scene around him. But such *trouvailles* had long since ceased to amaze his own indifferent spirit. Air-starved and light-deprived, the strange words that rattled in his skull—O feel the interflux of seasons—were destined to perish like bees in a bottle.

2

Dinner was served. Dowagers swooped down upon the dining room almost with the first motion of the hostess to unhook the velvet cord stretching across the entrance. Their charge always caught the waitresses off guard, who should have been prepared by past encounters but to whom the scuffling chairs of early diners sounded as a summons or a last alarm. They rustled up to tables breathless, smiling of course, surprised. Their cheeks would blush as parasols are pink.

Bartholomew trailed this first brigade of diners and might have slipped unnoticed to a table, but, newly arrived, he was to wait until his hostess assigned him a place (in keeping with a usage understood and accepted by longtime guests of the hotel). His hostess approached him, smiling from some fruitless depth of feeling, gracious as ever, her face the same painful Punchinello face, appalling, a comic mask turned tragic, aging (what did she do in the winter months?). Bartholomew felt sick returning her smile, wondered if it showed.

An outstretched hand. "*Mister* Matthiesson. I heard you were back. It's been so long." She wandered on about his mother's visit here last summer, people Bartholomew should remember, dying. Dying herself. She wore too much perfume, as always. "Sharon will be your waitress. You may remember her sister from several years ago. Isn't it funny how families keep coming back here?" She scurried off to find Sharon.

Bartholomew wondered: would Sharon be beautiful? As a boy he had dreamt of finding love beside the sea. There would have been so much to show her: breakers on the rocks of Philadelphia Beach; the Admiral Hotel in the pale fire of a winter sunset; desolate salty rumors. He had dreamt of winning a waitress from the Lafayette. A man now, he had no casual, cunning words to win her. Besides, his family had always been served by unattractive waitresses, thanks to their charming hostess, this same woman now serving Bartholomew.

A ballet was beginning. The guests in place, the first uncertainty of entrances and exits overcome, along the carpeted central aisleway, among the arteries and avenues of tables, waitresses filtered outward from the kitchen like the sweet influence of summer flowers. They reinforced that miracle of all prodigious dancers: lifting trays, treading the ground, disdainful women, their stern strength could take flight, could shimmer.

Sunlight was swimming along Decatur Street. Bartholomew's chair faced backward, away from the sea in a port where all became like Ishmael, water-gazers. Twenty years before, with his family, in a cottage on New Jersey Avenue, across from the rotting Playhouse, he had sat each night at dinner, sawed-off sovereign of the wind and water, facing backward, imagining beyond marshes, beyond high-and-dry-lying hulks of old fishing boats, cornfields where night came on in a green pneumatic flush.

The sunlight he saw now had troubled him then: sigil of death; certainty of autumn; sender of high-walled schoolrooms, worn, varnished desks, half-hearted schoolboy singing, fervent meditations on a name—Mary Pointz, that girl across the aisle, essence of Cape May Point and ruined cornfields.

Sharon was serving him now, moving about his table with small bird-like gestures. Bartholomew hardly had presence of mind enough to speak or notice the meal she brought or notice that she too was unattractive, his mind flooded with brief, brilliant images of other times.

3

After dinner, walking on the boardwalk, Bartholomew saw children churning to escape from parents; old, comfortless widows, haggard mothers of six, seven, or eight innocents; merchants counting money; sailors leaning against railings, smoking or sizing up some girl; tall men, thin men, fat men, lonely men; adolescents of both sexes, tenants of new bodies, knowingly unknowing; Philadelphia housewives in white blouses, black slacks, white socks and pin-curlers, pushing baby carriages; niggers dressed to the nines; old salts, bristly and grey, men of the sea, of sparse gestures and nimble fingers; bulky Jews with fat, black cigars; parents, grandparents, grandchildren; a one-eyed man; spidery spinster schoolteachers in long silk dresses and cruel, crooked, strait-laced shoes.

Before the portrait painter ($1 for 3 minutes) Bartholomew paused. Somewhere in the garden of lost time he had misplaced his own boyhood portrait painted on this same spot by some nameless woman sprouting beside the sea that summer in smock and Garbo hat, feline, evasive, taciturn. Her spiritual descendent (or was she the same?) now painted a girl with soft, falling curls, delicate and wistful, stray silken strands.

Suddenly as he watched artist and subject, a flash of darker memory taunted Bartholomew with Pamela's baby picture, which she had shown to him one privileged afternoon: Pamela pink and round, giggling, soft and naked. Pain, true physical sensation, seized Bartholomew's heart; a cold damp feeling swept over his spine. He turned, met an old man face to face, winced, fought his way through the crowd, slumped to a bench at some distance from the painter's easel. She still lived inside him. Someday every stray experience would not call to her in him. But now he hurt. Now he remembered the tale of her antecedent lover, their lovemaking. He had never known her innocent.

Two hundred yards away, at Decatur Street, by the Lafayette, a girl, a woman crossed Beach Avenue, turned toward Convention Hall. The green of her garments set off a blush of sunburn, a torrent of golden hair.

Bartholomew seemed to discern the pattern love had mapped out inside him, the massive rationalizing mechanism, yet gave it free rein, resigned to a sort of helplessness. Each encounter with a woman offered a new innocence, if not the certainty at least the hope of purity, the purity he wanted, experience shackled with purity, undemanding female innocence to which no adjustment, for which no sympathy was necessary.

Looking up from his well of painful memories, he watched with severe detachment a woman in green approach. Her beauty was lush, abundant, like a rustling summer field. Warm radiance ran outward like waves from her body. He remembered dimly, he grasped at a distant boyhood afternoon when tears had flowed, when a female presence had soothed him, brushed away sadness. He felt once more on his forehead the kiss of a queen. The great gap in his spirit opened by memory closed of itself, healed by her influence.

4

Daily life in the Lafayette ended shortly after ten o'clock. Aged guests retired. The TV was extinguished. True, activity in the cocktail lounge was incipient, would reach some sort of summit three hours later, but that life bore little relation to hotel life other than the understood, obviously necessary one of swelling hotel coffers. The lounge was sealed off. Music from its combo filtered through inaudibly to the cavernous lobby whose wicker chairs, wicker lamps, and fading, flowered cushions smelled of decay and old, deflated harmonies.

Around ten, the night clerk began spooking around the premises. His duties began at eleven, but, with time on his hands, he came down to the lobby and got in the way as the afternoon shift tried to lock up for the night. He would have no responsibilities: the safe would be locked, only the petty cash box available for purchases of newspapers and tobacco. He waited to put out all but a few lights, douse gaiety, usher in bilious, bug-ridden silence.

Shortly after eleven, Bartholomew passed through the lobby, returning from the Beach Theatre where he had meant to induce sleep with a movie. He stopped at the counter to buy postcards. The night clerk shuffled forward. Bartholomew never forgot a face. He remembered the night clerk from years back, remembered his name was Charlie.

Four years before, staying at the Lafayette with his family, Bartholomew had gone out once with Sylvia, a girl from his college working that summer at the hotel, Sylvia with her brown eyes like buttons, her braided hair, her pedigreed toes, her impudent New York working girl accent. She and Bartholomew had spent an evening ironically undercutting the previous sentences of each other. At one o'clock they had ridden the blue rocking chairs on the hotel porch, wrapped in a cloud of mosquitoes. Sylvia had waxed eloquently irate on the conditions for the hotel waitresses: cramped in ungainly quarters, some back corridor of the hotel; a miniscule bathroom, one shower for twenty-three girls!

At two o'clock, the curfew hour for waitresses, Sylvia had gone in. She had knocked on the lobby door (locked at twelve) so that the night clerk, whose name and nastiness she had already catalogued for Bartholomew, might let her in. Charlie had pulled the door open and had peered out; had croaked, "All right, come on in, you've been out there long enough."

"Do you have any stamps?" Bartholomew asked Charlie in the present.
"Nope."
"Has there been some sort of change? I always used to get stamps at this time of night."
"No stamps."
"Can I get any postcards tonight?"

"Get'm in the morning."

Bartholomew climbed the stairs with feelings of mingled grief and rage until he felt doom, damp as a dishrag, settle near his spine, permeate all feeling. The lights in the lobby had suddenly become too sordid and sinister to bear, emblems of Charlie's life, great glaring bulbs, illuminations from the future foreshadowing Bartholomew's own life-to-be. He wondered how one paltry man had held out so long against life's little inanitions, countless defensive encounters at counters. He wondered if Charlie's life, a life rubbed raw, a life of naked light bulbs, was supportable, a life without shade or softening influence, a life without kindness.

5

The next morning, after a pleasant walk, Bartholomew returned to the hotel just after eight o'clock for breakfast. He planned to eat, take his books to the beach, rent a canvas chair before midday crowds filled in the seascape, and spend at least a morning on his lessons. The wash of weekend commuters, East Philadelphians, would arrive that afternoon, inundate the beaches, make work impossible.

Morning promised a hot day; the flower beds beside the Lafayette already smoldered faintly. Inside, the lobby bustled. Old folks were up and about, buying newspapers, mailing letters, managing another day. Just as Bartholomew felt cleansed and consecrated by the primal hour, so these older guests felt still useful rehearsing former gestures, as if mannerisms could bring back old responsibilities.

A different light flooded the dining room at breakfast. If evening light had suggested meadows muffled with swarming mosquitoes and great shadowy webs of green, morning light suggested the sea or something of the sparkle of winter sunlight on freshly fallen snow. Brightness had banished the lassitude of evening. A new day beckoned, untouched by experience, awaiting the imprint of action or desire.

The waitresses moved in strange, somnambulant rhythms at this hour. Some positive pursuit might have forced wakefulness upon them, but too often the tables they served lay empty (if the lobby bustled, the dining room remained curiously inert, as if older guests knew that beyond breakfast, which might be put off, lurked a truer wilderness, the yawning day). Subconscious motions brought to life avatars within them, little girls rubbing sand from their eyes.

Even inside, seated at his table, Bartholomew still savored something of the renewal his walk had inspired. His waitress seemed to share this feeling. "Where do you find such energy?" he asked her. "Your compatriots all seem to be asleep."

"Oh, I just feel like being up. It's such a gorgeous morning. I'm out till all hours every night, but I'd never miss this sunshine."

"You should be out riding bicycles, then."

"I told my roommate that. I told her one morning we're going to get up at quarter to six and ride bicycles, but she sort of vetoed that."

Embodiment of brightness, Sharon served him cereal, toast, eggs, and bacon, the right breakfast for a morning's work. Bartholomew had begun to relish this day. A morning spent bending over a poem, seeing in it what had never been seen, identifying all artful touches, that would be something. He needed to give himself to something.

Toward the front of the dining room, after stacking dirty dishes from the first meal she had served that morning, a waitress stooped to lift her tray, then turned toward the kitchen as Bartholomew rose to leave. He moved with minor enthusiasm at the thought of a morning's concentrated study. She moved with artful disdain, her hip thrown out to ward off the heaviness of her burden. Yet kindness shone in her face, kindness and the blush of fresh, clear morning. She and Bartholomew passed one another in the aisle, she failing to notice him, he recognizing the woman he had never expected to see again, the woman who had passed him on the boardwalk the night previous.

6

That afternoon on the beach, Bartholomew lay slumped in a chair at the edge of the multitude. Preferring solitude, he had, earlier in the day planted himself close to the jetty, hoping to avoid the concentration of bathers near the center of the beach. As the day wore on, however, and space became scarce, the crowd had overflowed in his direction.

He had brooded on his two confrontations with that nameless woman. She had called him back toward life from the hazy frontier between action and intellect where he was threatened neither by life's distant, muted reverberations nor by the rarefied semblance of existence he viewed in literature; she had broken through his ring of psychic defense, had troubled him with the suggestion, too preposterous to believe yet too promising to disallow, that she might offer redemption, that she might stand as a bridge back to life. He found himself loving her desperately, absurdly, with all the fierce intensity of one whose capacity for violent emotion has been pent-up, baffled, and which, when sensing an outlet for its stored-up energies, surges toward that breaking point with dangerous, unexpected force.

Or perhaps the whole torturous discipline of the mind dissolves, not just at one point, but everywhere. Bartholomew felt the riot of old hungers he had managed to beat down for months at a time. A company of Greeks lounged by the boulders underneath the promenade. One among them, a woman, probably near fifty, her once firm body devolving now but still blessed with fine olive-colored skin, lay stretched on her back. Those Greeks no doubt took lodgings back among the marshes where indifferent, weather-worn, year-round residents survived the sordid days. That woman: if she would take him with her now; the sun falling; heat, grime, and moisture at their worst; among those nameless frame buildings; if she would take him to her bed, take him to her body in maternal pity and sluttish derision; that would be good; that was what he longed for.

It was four o'clock. All was suspended. One suspected the hour was late, but the sun still sprawled high above the buildings of the town, and clumps of bathers swarmed along the beaches. Shadows told true time, between buildings, precursors of the stifling green of twilight. Bartholomew, in a sudden bolt of energy, had made his way toward the hotel; had passed along the walkway between hotel and motor inn; had skirted the side entrance to the cocktail lounge where, within, bartender and waitresses conversed in the cynical, low-key dialect appropriate to their sun-starved, air-conditioned ambience; had threaded his way through the bath house, superannuated now that guests could bathe from their rooms, a vestige of that mythological climate in which no gentleman moved through the hotel without jacket and tie, no lady moved without softly rustling silk dress; had climbed up the back stairs, the acceptable means of access for bathers (the lobby was still off limits), stairs under which bellboys jawed and bantered away the stagnant, mosquito-stricken afternoons.

Bartholomew climbed to the second floor of rooms (the hotel's third floor), turned right, walked a few steps, turned right again and faced the long stretch of hallway leading back to his room, that hallway ending in a large window opening toward town, meadows, and marshland beyond. The westering sun did not shine directly through this window but rather in at an angle, filling the opening with autumnal radiance, like crystals of light in a vase of goldenrod. As a boy, Bartholomew had tried to imagine Cape May in autumn. His mind had discerned mournful solace in thoughts of fallen beauty, decayed buildings, the crumbling year. The substance of such imagined scenes lay stretched before him now. But a moral aspect overrode the aesthetic pleasure his childhood imagination had fixed upon. Bartholomew envisioned the inhabitants of each room he passed: old couples, aged widows, spinster schoolteachers: alone, alone, alone. He felt the familiar sodden doom. He suffered torments of thirst, moved through the parching dust of autumn, over frayed carpet worn by shuffling, dead, despairing feet.

Then he heard a sound of water, from the deep heart of the hotel, across the hall from the door to his room. Curious, knowing of no bathroom at this end of the building (for, while each room had its own sink, toilets and bathtubs were housed in large bathrooms serving blocks of guests), he moved toward the sound, too full and gushing for a sink, which seemed to emerge from an unexplored corridor that broke off from the main hallway just across from his door. A green curtain hung across the passageway.

Bartholomew drew back the curtain. Disoriented momentarily, he soon realized what he had uncovered. The Lafayette was an E-shaped building without the middle bar of that letter, fronting on the sea with two wings projecting back toward town. Within the fold of that rearward projection stood a separate structure not quite entirely sundered from the main hotel. A two-storied connection ran between that auxiliary building and the hotel's Decatur Street wing (where Bartholomew's room was situated). This connecting structure, as much glass as wood, resembled those covered walkways thrown from luxury liners to their docks. Bartholomew was looking across that connecting walkway into the provisional building. Then Sylvia's words returned with all the force of revelation: one shower for twenty-three girls, somewhere back in the bowels of the old hotel. At the end of the tunnel through which Bartholomew peered stood a pink-walled room and from that room spilled the sound of water. A waitress was bathing within.

He felt suddenly sick and no longer master of himself. He succumbed to the anticipatory wash of pleasure that precedes sure sexual conquest. He felt terribly exposed and feared that someone might walk down the hallway, force him to forego the presence of whatever unknown object his fierce bodily energies had already fixed themselves upon. He looked about him, then felt strange guilt. Knowing that some previous lover had known Pamela's body before he had, he pictured himself in the same relationship to some subsequent lover of the unknown girl within the corridor. He glimpsed a brief, brilliant image of himself smearing mud on a swan. He wanted to walk away.

Unsettled, indecisive, Bartholomew cast a last glance down the mysterious passageway. Within, for a moment, he saw passing, like mottled notes of music through the spirit, the polished, naked body, the glistening presence of that same woman who, last night, this morning, had called to him before.

7

After a tasteless dinner, Bartholomew went to another movie, where he spent much of his time dreading the next day's trip back to school. The thought of a mere two-hour drive to Philadelphia was deceptive, because to get to school, an hour of wrangling traffic lay beyond that preliminary parkway journey. Perhaps driving in the early afternoon, he might avoid the weekend travelers and Sunday drivers converging in the smoggish sunset somewhere between six and nine o'clock. Only two weeks of summer school remained. Bartholomew suspected this weekend excursion had been a capital piece of folly. He might have held off two more weeks and vacationed less hectically.

He thought of August, that limitless bog of boredom, of the school year starting again. He thought of these less receptively now, less tolerant of the armour he had girded round himself, of prep school teaching, of disciplinary, social, and athletic responsibilities. Off and on he had toyed with the notion of returning to graduate school, of picking up where he had left off, twelve hours en route to a Ph.D. He might meet women, might move toward love again, sound for sympathy, divine by lover's instinct a vein of understanding. Such thoughts carried Bartholomew so far, then sickened him at the facile two-by-two coupling of humankind.

He squirmed at the thought of wasted afternoons. He still cared about time, still attached significance to individual moments. When, he wondered, would time no longer matter? When would the heaving slag of afternoons, the avalanche of aimless hours swallow him up completely? He had once projected a plan of reading, hoping to use time wisely. He had hoped to really know something, to teach with a clear conscience, to teach well, knowing his words took root in fundamental learning. Learning escaped him like the hours. For each book he lopped off his reading list, a hundred grew in its place. Knowledge only shows her monstrous qualities to those who try to master her.

The movie ended. A shabby, sallow brightness sprang up, flooded the theater. Leaving his seat, Bartholomew kicked over a box of half-eaten popcorn; stepping on stale kernels, he glued them to the floor. Nearly laughing, he thought that all his life heretofore had brought him to this moment, that being in this theater was all he had to show for twenty-five years of living.

He longed for freedom, fullness, no matter where, anywhere out of *this* world.

8

The Lafayette's third-floor hallway which had, that afternoon, called forth declivitous images of autumn was lit at night by a row of rancid light bulbs like those seen through kitchen windows on winter afternoons. Once in that hallway and considering how seldom he knew in his life any frenzy or form of elevated existence (as in reading poems or listening to music), Bartholomew justified to himself movement toward what he now knew to be the evening's destination. Or perhaps he felt no need to justify. He walked directly to the curtained corridor. He might have missed something had he waited. He was too eager. He thought of the pervert's loneliness, lost in the wilderness of cities.

He pulled back the green curtain but peering within, failed to recognize the scene before him. The rustling crimson colors of the bathroom, the gaudy supra-sensual pink of four o'clock had given way to a bilious shade of gloom. The muddled textures of the hallway, the same moral overtones of solitary afternoons and evenings, had impregnated the corridor. At intervals Bartholomew heard voices, shreds of conversation, rasping news from home or talk of school. He remembered a Saturday night in college, the woman's campus deserted, he late for his date, for the concert that all were attending. He had passed by a door, had seen two dateless coeds conversing, had wondered: does each think of the other *unwanted*?

He peered down the corridor again, then snapped his head back suddenly. A waitress at the other end was looking back toward him. He had gazed through the smallest possible separation between wall and curtain. Perhaps she had not seen him. Perhaps she would go away. He looked again. It was Sharon, his waitress, anchored, it seemed, in that aperture, with firmness and moral vigor. She pointed a menacing finger. "We've called the office. Now you get out of here!"

Bartholomew whirled, crossed the hall, burst into his room, shoved the door shut behind him. He tried to blot out his agitation. His aspirations had been wrenched and manipulated, channeled by contingencies back into this boxlike, airless, suffocating room. His experience that afternoon had surpassed all satisfactions of ordinary love. Since then he had moved in spirals of multi-colored sound, had glimpsed full-blown (as blossoms explode in brilliance), again and again, encased in dappled gold-on-green, the sculptured posture of a moment, the form of that same mysterious woman frozen, caught forever; had suspected somewhere, everywhere around him, an attainable sun-filled room furnished in plush green velvet, where happiness was possible.

Once, on a similar brink of revelation, Bartholomew had watched a woman in a crowd. A stranger, an ugly clown, alien to himself, winking and vulgar, had slid up beside him, cracked some crude jest about the woman they had both been watching. Bartholomew had not been about to define his attraction that day, his elevation approaching ecstasy. Similarly, he had not pondered his reasons for returning to the corridor. Others, like Sharon, like the ugly jester, were willing to stigmatize his actions.

Bartholomew felt sudden thirst, decided to soothe it in a boardwalk shop. He stepped back out into the hallway. Charlie, the night clerk, was fidgeting in front of the corridor, wearing the well-worn carpet. "You been walkin' in the halls?" Charlie asked, but Bartholomew failed to link the question to his own actions. So Charlie muttered, "That your room?"

Bartholomew stammered, "What do you mean? Certainly that's my room."

"Then make sure you stay in it."

"Really, I don't know what you're talking about."

Charlie, in flinty tones, said, "You know what I'm talkin' about. Either in your room or out of it. No wanderin' in the halls."

9

Night was now fitful. Swollen clouds and gusts of wind had rolled in off the Atlantic. Rough, ragged waves muzzled among boulders, even humped up onto the asphalt promenade in their indignation. Shops were closed or closing. Last customers bolted food, fingered last items of displayed costume jewelry. Adolescents, out as late as they dared, scuttled homeward. Bartholomew gulped root beer under the sign of Taylor Pork Roll. The manager had doused all lights save one greasy bulb that smeared darkness with indifferent illumination.

"Summer's good as done for," he said.

"It's only July," Bartholomew suggested.

"Been rainin' off and on since I got here. Haven't had one week without three or four days o' rain. People goin' home disgusted. Weekend customers not comin'. If it don't pick up by the middle of August, I'm goin' to Miami, see my brother down there. Haven't had a vacation in twenty-three years. I'm sick of it."

Bartholomew moved toward Philadelphia Beach, but once past the line of protecting shops found the wind too biting for such a long walk. He sat on a bench. Clouds dribbled rain. This weekend excursion now loomed as a monstrous tactical error. He saw his actions not only of the last school year, his season underground, but toward Pamela as wholly self-centered, and recognized his need to shuffle off selfhood, to serve something.

To his left he heard a woman laughing. Toward Philadelphia Beach, in the weird lamplight, a man and a woman, locked in each other's arms, lurched laughing in his direction. The man was a sailor. The woman wore a sailor suit, had lissome hips. Bartholomew no longer questioned the destiny that brought this woman before him for the fourth time. He hated her now for betraying the myth that had sanctified them both that afternoon. Had she washed herself for this? Bartholomew wished he could wash her of all experience, whiten her for his impress.

Stray cars swept by, rubber tires splashing over the rainy pavement. The lovers passed. Bartholomew wrenched his neck in a spasm of regret. In the distance, like a blue-burnt ember in the fog, light from Henri's, symbol of love, haunt of Cape May's lost generation, flowed. He remembered his deliberate self-removal in college from all such collegiate dives. He had felt older, wiser than those within. But what more desirable existence had his wisdom offered him?

The lovers were nearly out of sight. Bartholomew rose, shivered, glanced about, and followed them.

William H. Guy

Living at home

Plum Borough is a long ride from Point Breeze
To teach in a public high school. The car
My father bought me helps of course. It frees
Me for a job unquestionably too far
Away from home without it. That much
Is solved, the ride remains. The ungodly
Hour I get up each morning is not such
A joy either, six o'clock, to set my hair and see
Beyond our fence Penn Avenue the same
As when I went to bed, dark and not well-
Lit, dawn still distant, cars taking aim
Already in that fog outside. I can smell
Their engines cooking. Things did seem worse
When I first started teaching last September.
I was so nervous. I kept fumbling in my purse
For pencils. I couldn't remember
Anything for three or four days. I forgot
The French word for *desk* and had to stand
There shaking. I kept thinking this was not
Possible, this was not the life I'd planned,
There had to be some way out of all this pain,
It was not meant for me. No sooner was
I home each afternoon but I began
Thinking of the next morning, how the buzz-
Saw sound of my alarm would cut through the quilt
I had pulled over my head in sleep, so soft,
So feathery. Time seemed to shrink, to wilt
Like an undernourished flower in a loft,
Whenever I wanted it to last longest.
There was no relief from the way my life
Was going. The world was a sink where strongest
Bacteria survived. In that strife

Of small excrescences, I was another
Germ, no more. That was a painful lesson
After my pampered childhood. Mother
Was proud of my new job. Pulling my dress on
For me one morning, fussing with my hair,
She said all the women at the club thought
It was marvelous how much French *grammaire*
(That was their little joke) I knew. I caught
My dress on a corner of the bed and ripped
It as I ran out into the hall, fighting back
Tears till I reached the bathroom. Then I tripped
On a rug there and bruised my shin (it turned black
The next day for my students to see). I lost
Track of why I was crying, whether
For the throbbing in my leg, for the cost
Of getting my dress fixed, or for the leather
I had found serving me where a heart served
Other people. Imagine someone treating
Her own mother like a servant who deserved
Hanging. What could be more self-defeating,
More self-destructive? I am no longer
At home in my own house. I sensed that soon
After my parents and my two younger
Sisters brought me back from graduation last June.
I had changed during my four years at college.
I felt almost ashamed of returning
To the same street with my new knowledge
Of myself and of the world, my new learning,
As if I had not been quite clever enough
To escape completely, as if at the last
Moment some sentinel had snatched the scruff
Of my neck and lugged me like a rabbit past
All the scornful, I-told-you-so faces
Of the neighbors. Oh, I could stand in the yard
And exchange little inane commonplaces
With Mr. and Mrs. So and So, hard
Put to carry it off like a well-accomplished
Hausfrau, nodding and smiling when I'd finished
As I'd seen my mother do.

                              But it was all
A trap. I recognized and worked against
Their cunning. Whatever boost to their morale
My presence gave I personally felt fenced
In and desperate, but not enough to say
'Life ends here for me, this is where I stop
Struggling.' I did not intend to stay
In the same house forever. I did not prop
All hopes in a corner of the cellar
With my odds and ends from school. I am not shrill
And spidery yet. My friend Claudia Keller,
That irrepressible gay whippoorwill
Companion of my youth is gone, married
To a doctor. Tim Beckman, that fat funny
Boy whom five of us girls one day carried
Up the street like a sack and dumped in a runny
Garden after it had rained, our war
Prisoner, has joined the Marines. He is handsome
And well-muscled now, and may die before
The year is out. Have I learned anything from
Living at home if I still expect to find
The same people playing in the same back yards
And alleys, as I still see them in my mind,
Wrapped in scarves and sweaters if it's cold, guards
Posted to keep our enemies from snooping,
Or, when warm weather comes, switching to sports,
Letting girls play in the outfield, grouping
And re-grouping, scraping legs clad in shorts
Sliding into third base on the concrete
Diamond? Hasn't this year's experience
Been tending toward one truth, that retreat
Into the past is not possible in this instance?
What good are all the places where you knew joy—
The streets and swings and sandboxes, the doll
Houses left standing, the steps where a boy
First kissed you, the swaying fortress in a tall
Tree—if something inside you has altered,
If, with imperceptible decay, some
Sustaining vision of your world has faltered?

213

The chaos which ensues when old truths become
Obsolete, are discarded, can filter down
To a solitary life, can leave that life
Swirling blindly in a dark lake, likely to drown.
I once pictured an ordered progress: daughter to wife
To mother to some final secure bliss
Of Indian summer where contentment reigned.
That was the good life I could expect. This
Is what I face instead: Alert, well-trained
Enemies on every side, in the classroom,
On the Parkway which I travel each day,
In my own house; a taste (like brass) of doom
Filling my mouth almost before the grey
Light of morning unshutters my eyelids or
That clock I mentioned does its dreadful office;
My sisters banging on my closed door
At night, my sole (in their case) benefice
Seeming to be a willing ear, a willing
Mind, both of which, when the time seems right to them,
They will sluice open and submerge, filling
Me in on their new romances, each gem
Of each boy's conversation in the lunch
Line or between classes by their lockers,
Asking me if they should play this or that hunch
On Sadie Hawkins Day despite what mockers
Might say in the weeks following their ploy
About girls being too forward, girls sinking
Teeth into the man they want, gobbling up some boy.
Their talk preserves me from that gadfly, thinking.

What is it I want? Certainly not to hive
Up in some single room like a hermit.
I don't hate my family, but to thrive
In a family atmosphere, to submit
Myself once more to a system I was sent
To college to outstrip, to grow beyond,
Seems to me not only an argument
Against having *been* to college, having spawned
A new self (because I thought, 'Soon I must

Face the world'), having 'commenced,' but also
An abdication in its own right, a thrust
Against living. It is cold tonight. Snow
Is predicted. From my window I can see
Lights twinkling on the hills above Homewood.
One stray car whisks by like a refugee
From darkness. Fear cringes in the neighborhood
Of Park Place School. Trains rumble in the distance.
Through the upper hallway of our house a thread
Of light probes. I find my way to my parents'
Room. I kiss them both goodnight. My inbred
Skittery fears propel me to my own bed.
I do not sleep. Between the acting of a dread
Thing and its outcome, another day is dead.

James Applewhite

A cycle of family poems

My grandfather's funeral

I knew the dignity of the words:
"As for man, his days are as grass,
As a flower of the field so he flourisheth;
For the wind passeth, and he is gone"—
But I was not prepared for the beauty
Of the old people coming from the church,
Nor for the suddenness with which our slow
Procession came again in sight of the awakening
Land, as passing white houses, Negroes
In clothes the colors of the earth they plowed,
We turned to see bushes and rusting roofs
Flicker past one way, the stretch of fields
Plowed gray or green with rye flow constant
On the other, away to unchanging pines
Hovering over parallel boles like
Dreams of clouds.

                At the cemetery the people
Surprised me again, walking across
The wave of winter-bleached grass and stones
Toward his grave; grotesques, yet perfect
In their pattern: Wainwright's round head,
His bad shoulder hunched and turning
That hand inward, Luby Paschal's scrubbed
Square face, lips ready to whistle to
A puppy, his wife's delicate ankles
Angling a foot out, Norwood Whitley
Unconsciously rubbing his blue jaw,
Locking his knees as if wearing boots—
The women's dark blue and brocaded black,
Brown stockings on decent legs supporting

Their infirm frames carefully over
The wintry grass that called them down,
Nell Overman moving against the horizon
With round hat and drawn-back shoulders—
Daring to come and show themselves
Above the land, to face the death
Of William Henry Applewhite,
Whose name was on the central store
He owned no more, who was venerated,
Generous, a tyrant to his family
With his ally, the God of Moses and lightning
(With threat of thunderclouds rising in summer
White and ominous over level fields);
Who kept bright jars of mineral water
On his screened, appled backporch, who prayed
With white hair wispy in the moving air,
Who kept the old way in changing times,
Who killed himself plowing in his garden.
I seemed to see him there, above
The bleached grass in the new spring light,
Bowed to his handplow, bent-kneed, impassive,
Toiling in the sacrament of seasons.

My grandmother's life

A window opens an edge-steamed pane
Past the scent of water. A pot is boiling
On the cast iron range, thin lid falling
Tink, tink, after the steam-breaths. My grandmother
Is peeling peaches into an enamelled pan,
Slicing the sweeter, bruise-dark flesh onto
Spots chipped black like knotholes. I know
All this but see only through the window,
Which is part of myself. I look down on and enclose
The brick-squared garden, herbs and a few roses
        straying and delicate
In the shade of a great pecan overawing the house,
Which rocks that ground like a floor of water

When wind rises in it. I see sage and thyme,
    crinkled parsley.
And within those balanced markings, bricks in
Soil strewed white from our sandpiles,
Flecked with the pecan's thin bark; in possessing
That yard infused with the purest of vapor,
Struck into unburning flame by the sunshine,
I possess my life.

    My grandfather's strength stands
In chunks of wood by the range, pine bark
Still on some like frosting on cake.
A five gallon carboy is breathing of the mineraled
    water of Seven Springs.
Seventeen miles away it starts by the river
That the creek of our town curls into, creek
That's sliding like polished wood though ripply
Four blocks away from my window. That space
Is filled with the knowledge of clouds, with the balloon-head
Womanly thoughts of trees, with the call
Of a mourning dove lonely in time, seeking
To draw all back beyond birth with the timbre
    of its cry.
Odor of the carboy clasps as with a skin
Those sprays of leaves, rose bush twined
Backward into time with rheumatic knottings.
Sweet mineral breath from the heavy glass jar
Is the breath of her presence, which change
In my weight or height or knowledge of others
Changed not at all. Breath of the kitchen
Is her invisible presence behind me, charging
The air of seeing with that moist, enabling light
Which is love.

    So down the lane out of view
Past the wood shed furred with splinters,
Ranked with lilies, where grasshoppers roosted
    chewing tobacco
To be caught by their cellophane wings, to the slab
Of granite shaded always cool in the past

Beneath the scion pecan of my uncle's planting,
Is an easy trip. There with my cousin I'm hidden
From the self who remains in the kitchen, self
Who is the water and air of unchanging
Repose, clear first flesh of existence.

On the stone seat cool in its summer-long shadow,
I am a child with the child in her velvet dress,
A boy with the tomboy climbing the tree;
I change with her, feel the pain of another
Love layered on the love which alone is like sight
And breath and water.

      And though I roam from the yard
Tossed like the pecan in a stormy wind,
The base of my feelings shapes itself
With a pliant air about leaves of roses
Enclosed by four sides of brick.

My grandparents have lain together
In their graves for years, their tall white house
Is rented to strangers.
Yet I know the yard, the stove, the bruise-sweet peaches,
The thick-glassed jug of water, live fresh in me now
As in the moments they sank into sight.
And one last thing
Came only as I lay half-dozing, restless
With a childhood fever I'd caught from my son.

In the strictness of thirst I sipped at water
From the old carboy of my grandfather's;
I'd found it at my parents' months before,
Had washed it and set off driving, to feel my way
      back through the sandy farms
To the source of a water I remembered.

Along low fields lying within breath
And presence of the river, I passed gardens
Of flowers, prismatic facets flaring heavenward
The colors of sunlight. I stopped at the river's park
For my sons to breathe, as I had,
The pine needles steaming on clay.

The Neuse slid still in its bends with a rippled sheen.
Willows in strong sunlight beside held an air
Of infinite patience, and above and far over the forest heads
Was a hazed atmosphere indifferent to time.
I turned away, that space
Permeating inward like the mourning dove's
Desolate call. I drove away beckoned by wisps
Of that vapor, the highway in sight cracked open
By wedges of the spanish moss I'd seen.

As I lay tormented with heat and thirst, I dreamed
Of embracing my wife's round thighs, of pillowing
My head on her belly, to be soothed by her breathing
Like a sea-surge. And I was again in memory
        searching for the spring.

Late afternoon now, thunderheads piled in giant indifference
On their one-way mirror of air, reflecting one another
In brilliant marble. Road openings winked out of thickets
Of pine or tangle-starred sweet gum
In wrong-way seduction, inviting with honeysuckle
And the fragrance of leaves. My wife stood beside me;
Her thighs were smooth as stretches of beach sand
        embracing a bay,
Burning as sun-fire breaking on water. A road's mouth
Gaped between wooden fence posts, curved gently
Up a hill, I saw the old spa's wooden hotel,
Another curve and the deep-sanded road broke open
Upon the springhouse rich with water.
I dreamed I touched the mouth of her womb.
I roused to a light through shrub-tangled dark
Past my window, some lonely bulb or a star. A dream shone
Bright in mind from the month of my grandmother's death.

We are wading in a warm, shallow bay.
Yellow sand stretches in a shape of arms,
Or of a pear, a flower's bell, a lily.
I have a sense of retracing steps.
As she leads me by the hand, her figure, always
Slight, slender as a girl's, is again a girl's.

In straits between distant sand-slips
Where bay and sky arc together,
My new baptism awaits in a shimmer of light.

Stopping for gas

Entering the small town (Sims or Baily,
a crossroads) we see, smell
lumber stacked airily, sawed lengths
from the hearts of trees
the color of sunlight; and I think,
as always, of something black
in the expression of an Esso station
with its cave of a grease house going into shadows;
but there is no soul-dark
painted on the pillars smudged from tires
with swipes of grease. And I remember:
the Esso red in bands around pumps,
in borders under windows, shook
like night-road beyond lights to my wounded eyes.

Nine or ten years ago. It was here
where I could drive no longer. I pulled to the pumps,
stood out eaten by my acid thoughts. Bought
a bottled orange drink to suck like sawdust
in the dry water-shimmer of heat.

Nine or ten years ago that day I walked
wobble-kneed to the john, poured my arid
stream with a rattle like dried peas
into the basin;—that day I was leaving Durham
and my wife for good I thought if a sick
numb thing in your head and body like an iron
truck tire wedge is a thought.

So now on these trips to visit my parents
sometimes I stop here for gas.
I buy us orange drinks sweet

as if really from trees, while the big
country kid in coveralls works the pump
I see and smell fresh lumber the color of my wife's
hair, take my youngest son to the Men's Room where
we cross our streams like a magic charm.

Dream of ascent

Through a blue-buoyant lake of air wavers
The wrinkled vastness of the mountain valley.
Filaments radiate from our fingertips, web us
To the sun's magnetic beams. My son
Is behind me, the arrowy aim of his breastbone
Is aligned with mine. We have passed over
The cities of men, I know soon the dream will change,
But now for a moment we soar, tasting
With our breasts and our limbs
The billows of pure ascent.

Wires crisscross the skyline and flight
Is the motion of a car. We slide along streets of a new city
We've lived in before, where the whiteness of houses seems sight.
We are known and awaited; it only remains
For me to recognize from the incredibly
Quick blur of scenes from my past which rush by
Unseen by the others, like a secret locomotive
Rushing inside facades of the roadside,
The look which will signal our turning.

Then the one face has flashed and I turn, follow
A narrow alley until the car is motionless
On a sloped earth yard where the fall leaves blow
And are heaped against fenders. I can see
From inside myself the rooms which are contained
In the house beside us. White and old.
Grooved boards. The stairway rises, the worn carpet
Has in its pattern the richness of skeined smoke,
Of birds of paradise quick within vines.

The top door opens into a room
With white-made bed smooth as the snow over hummocks.
The walls are blue, phase into the dimension
That deep sky shows through the individual
Squares of glass. Over the bed hangs
A portrait smoked by time.
I turn to catch my son;
His arms are about my waist.
I don't wish him to see it yet
I am not ready (unworthy and afraid) to be for him
That countenance deep as space between boles of a winter
Forest in its gilt frame, through the darkened glass.

Reynolds Price

The knowledge of my mother's coming death

Saturday

Our meetings now are allegorical. Each week I haul my soiled clothes
thirty miles—my house to hers. Each week she brings them clean—her
house to mine. This afternoon in May we meet at mine. She sits before
my window in my new chair—its saddle-brown obscured by her blue dress,
her gray hair streaked by green light off my trees. I face her from the sofa,
near enough—she sees me best at three yards distance now. We talk of
daily things—her car, my leaking roof—as one man's hands might speak
to one another, thirty-two years of mutual life between them or like cooled
lovers, joined but satisfied. I even roam her face, discovering beauty—the
dark gold eyes, the open smiling mouth (spread wings but resting)—all as
familiar as if I had made it. I partly have. All but the neat scar railing
down her forehead, one inch behind which beat two aneurysms, bared
two years ago but covered at once, untouched and lethal. Her time-bomb,
she calls it—who knows the time? But not today. Not now it seems. We
are spared again. The sun is in the window now, behind her. She is
bright. She turns from me an instant. The line of her features transmits
warm light. Her face has assumed the translucence of age—youth and
age—and I think inside my own sound head, "I have loved you all your
life," then remember she lived twenty-seven years before starting
me. Still I do not feel I have lied or blubbed. She says "Four-thirty" and
faces me. She must start home before the evening rush so I end on
money, as I mostly do—but offering not asking. Proud as a camel (her bank
account under twenty dollars) she smiles, "Not now. Save till I'm
needy."—"But you'll let me know?"—"I'll let you know. When I need
anything I'll call on you." We walk to her car. She says, "I'll see you when
your clothes are dirty." I offer again what I've offered before—to take the
clothes to a laundry here, spare her the chore. I intend both kindness and
separation. She recognizes both, accepts the first, laughs, "And put a fat
blind sixty-year-old widow out of work?"—"No," I say. She says, "You hate
this. I know you do." I look up rebuked but she means her car—its color,
milk-green. I do, I forgot. "I forgive it," I say.—"Thank you," she says,

smiles, we kiss, she starts. Her car snaps smartly down my drive. She does not look back. I watch her dust as she reaches the road, is consumed by leaves, think, "The best woman driver in history," then suddenly know, not coldly nor in fear but know for the first time without the least doubt—"That is the last sight I have of her."

Sunday

I know it is day but I still lie dreaming, the frail quick thread that races morning—scraps of rhyme, clever retorts, problems dispatched. Then I calm, fall awhile; fall slower, slower till in stillness I endure this knowledge: my mother and I move in her car (whose color I no longer hate) through the heart of a city. She drives as always effortlessly, the visible sign of her inner grace. I sit on her right in a passenger's daze. She stops for a light and another car stops on her side, close beside her. The passenger in that car is a girl aged twenty. She could easily touch my mother's face, its left profile, but instead she stares and I watch her stare. It slowly becomes a crouch, a frown, then a silent scream. The light goes green. My mother shifts gear, moves forward first, proceeds through the junction, continues her way. Yet terror is stuck in my chest, a stob. I study what half of her face I can see—the right profile, unchanged, at work. I know what waits on the left side though—the girl's frown has only confirmed my knowledge. I say "Mother" calmly—"Look here at me." Half-smiling she looks full-face a moment—the time she can spare from the road—and I see my oldest fear enacted. The artery beneath her left profile presses forward—a tree. A bare purple tree, rocks forward, peels downward silently. I think, "She is dying. I must take the wheel." But she faces the road, still efficient though dead, bearing me forward—her urgent task.

I wake, the stifling weight of dread. At breakfast I down the impulse to phone her, but by noon when I still have not thrown the dream, I drive ten miles to visit a friend, then do not tell him, sit gray and quiet in his room a bombsite, he whole at its center laughing on. At last he says, "What has ruined your day?" I say, "I have dreamt my mother's death." He takes an unseen world for granted (battles it daily), says "That would ruin it."

Monday

That friend is with me at my house now. He sits in the new chair and I sit opposite. The doors are open to the loud spring night. We laugh against it, then are suddenly silent—a natural pause. But the night has paused with us, entirely still, and in that silence (two seconds at most) a tide turns against us, against the house. The night lunges brute at every opening, every dark pane. We two seem under crushing assault, hopeless, surrendered. I look to him, look first to his hands—broad knob-knuckles, they are gripped to the sides of the chair, blood gone. His face looks to me from the pitch of a shudder. He is bearing the brunt. Then the surge subsides; first from me, more slowly from him. We sit a moment exhausted, grateful. Then I half-laugh, say toward him "What happened?"—"Nothing," he says. I have not guessed but I know he lies. And now I cannot accept a lie. I say, "But it did—and to you. What happened." He does not—cannot? will not?—face me. "Not *happened*," he says. "It has not happened yet."

Not yet but will. I am sure now of waiting.

Tuesday

I have eaten my supper, stacked the three dishes. In an hour I must drive ten miles, a meeting. The trip takes less than twenty minutes, but I start to go now, pulled out of the house by my ancient fear of missing things—trains, friends, the smallest chance. I wrench on a tie, rush into my coat, take a single step from closet to door. The phone rings. Now. Do I know? Have I learned? No. The instant of fright, leap of response are my constant reactions to telephone bells—that all news is bad. I stop its ring, pause before Hello, embracing the silence. A strange woman's voice, "Is this Mr. Price?"—"Yes," I say. She does not name herself—"I am here at your mother's . . ."

I have not learned from the three past days but now I know. I silently recite in unison with her—"Something has happened to your mother."—"I know."—"You know? It only just happened."—"I mean that I know what has happened," I say. "Where is she now?"—"The ambulance has just left for Wake Hospital."—"Thank you," I say, "I will go straight there." I lower the phone, hear her speak against extinction, raise it again, take the explanation this stranger must give. She inhales deeply—"Reynolds" (awards me my first-name, consolation), "she was talking on the telephone, sitting in this chair where I am now. I was across from her, saw it all. She stopped herself in the midst of a sentence, put her right hand to her forehead slowly, looked at me and said, 'I have a terrible pain in my head.' Then she dropped the phone and looked at her lap and began to pick at the nap on her skirt as if it was stain. Then she slumped on herself so I went to her. You don't know me but I . . ." I thank her, say I am on my way. Then in cold efficiency (a gift from my dream) I call the hospital emergency room. A woman answers. I give my name, say, "My mother is on her way to you now.

She cannot talk, will be unconscious and I want to warn you what to expect. She has had two cerebral aneurysms for some years now. They are on either side of the optic chiasma. One was ligatured two years ago with a Crutchfield clamp. The other has burst."—"All right," she says, "we'll be looking for her." I say, "I am coming there now myself." "All right," she says—then, "Are you a doctor?"—"No," I say.—"You sound like a doctor."—"No," I say.—"You know so much I thought you must be." She intends it as compliment, has time to talk on—"How do you know so much?" she says. I tell her, "I keep my eyes very clean," then am seized in a scalding strangling shudder, set the phone in its cradle, say aloud to the room, "What do I know, what will anyone know who cannot, will not read plain warnings; who if I could read, could still not save my love from death?—save her skull slowly filling itself, a bowl of blood?"

Kathryn Vale

A grain, perhaps of wheat

After lunch Maylene had washed and dried all the dishes, working
with her slow warm laziness like the lemony sunlight that poured through
the window over the sink and spilled in round pools on the scuffed linoleum
floor. Now she was wiping the red-speckled table top, pulling the dish cloth
toward her into the streak of sunlight that made the hairs on her arm glint
gold, feeling the spindling metal legs of the table shift this way as she
pulled, and then as she pushed the cloth back across feeling the table shift
back that way, and watching the sunlight catch in the drops of water left in
the tracks of the dish cloth, sunlight drying them slowly to a dusty film
over the glinting red specks.

"You still moonin' around in here?" The floor creaked under her father's
heavy footsteps. He stopped by the door and set the bag of grapes he was
carrying down on the stove. "Get in yonder and help your mother."

The creaking radiated out through the house and into the bedroom
where her mother was ironing. Their voices drifted back to where Maylene
stood, low at first, like the rolling of summer heat thunder, and then his
voice sharp and dry and crackling like lightning.

"... be no-'count all her life. I brought them grapes you wanted."

"I'll look after the grapes directly. You watch how you talk about your
own child, Durane Nobles. She might have been like Pat Rackley, and then
where'd you be?"

"Hnh. Out in the bushes gettin' her with a belt, I reckon."

And then the voices quieted back down. Maylene had been standing
so still that it felt as if all the weight had left her body except for her hands
that were heavy and tingling. She might leave her body altogether if she
didn't quickly touch something with her hands. She rested them for a mo-
ment on the table top until the weightless feeling went away and then she
turned and went quickly and quietly out the back door, out onto the wide tilt-
ing porch, past the old tire split open and filled with geraniums and past the
washing machine and the box of dirty clothes and quietly down the back
steps before they could hear her.

The back yard was bare, packed and dusty, with low places that the dog had hollowed out by the steps and in the cool damp dirt by the spigot. The trees were tall, bare except at the very top where a few leaves scraped together. Their roots erupted out of the hard-packed earth like the ringed scaly three-toed feet of the chickens that pecked around in the yard.

She hurried past the trees down the rutted road, past the sheds with the machinery out front, some rusty and crusted with dirt, some new and bright yellow, past the grape vines, even past the shed where the mule was standing, lazily shuddering the flies off his back. She cut through the corn field down the rows of corn that almost closed far over her head, whispering and scraping once in a while. When she was in deep enough not to be seen from the road, she gathered her dress under her and sat down on the dry rocky dirt. There was a plant by her feet that grew out flat and lacy like the white doilies in the living room. She wiggled her toes in the brown heavy shoes and then slowly unlaced the shoes and pulled them off.

The sun baked and shimmered off the dry dirt. She wished for the cool of the living room, dark shiny furniture and white curtains blowing faintly and her mirror that made everything all right. It was an oval mirror, hanging on the wall straight across from the front door, and the door stood open all summer, so she could go and look in the mirror and see all the view through the door out across the field reflected and clear but somehow even more at a distance than if she had just looked out the door. She could see the still green grass with dark misty ribbons of shade and beyond the highway a field covered with tall unmoving green oats and the shadow of a cloud moving over it and at the far edge of the field a fence and behind the fence the deep misty woods and one section broken out of the fence so you could see the clean matted brown path that led down deep into the woods and never ended, never would end, so long as you didn't go there and only looked at it through the mirror. And at the never-endingness of it a cool peacefulness would settle around her.

But things were usually the way they had been this afternoon. She didn't dare look because somebody would catch her there and if it was her brother Earl he would tease her about looking at herself in the mirror and her father would tell her to quit mooning around wasting time and her mother would look sad but at least keep quiet about it. And all of that frightened Maylene because if her mirror should be taken away, if anything should happen to that never-endingness, she didn't know where she would go to find it again.

She sighed and wriggled away from the rocks that were sticking her. The morning glories that twisted around the corn were closed up in tight folds. It made her think of what her mother called "private parts," it looked like a naked little girl baby when you were giving it a bath, with the flower petals all folded in and hidden even between its legs. She thought how her own body was like that.

She heard the truck rattle by, caught a glimpse of it bumping down the road. That would be her father driving back down to the fields. She stood up and brushed off the back of her dress and picked her way across the rows of corn. It didn't matter which way she went, every path she knew on either side of the weeds led to the creek. And sometimes, where the creek formed a pool, it was still, like a mirror.

At the edge of the corn field she had to step over a shallow ditch. After that, in among the trees, the ground got smoother with pine needles matted slick and prickling under her feet and an occasional patch of dark cool springy grass. She passed in and out of the strips of light and shadow that lay over the path, listening to the thudding rhythm of her feet on the earth and hearing, even softer than the sounds of her feet, the gurgle of the creek, hidden from her sight by a tangled bank of briers. Then at last the briers ended and she saw a wide circle of pine trees, tall around the clearing that sloped down to where the creek slowed into a deep, still pool. Maylene slipped under the low pine branch that reached out like the bar on the door of a secret room.

Then she saw them. Two white bodies bright on the pine-straw with the sun full and bright on them moving and silent except for the slipping moving of the leaves and grass under them, and she thought they must be fighting except that they moved together swiftly and violently and stiffly locked to each other even by the way they moved. She must have moved or made some sound because suddenly their heads jerked up and their faces turned to her with their mouths gaping and dark like fish gulping water and she saw that it was Earl and Pat Rackley.

"Turn your back, Maylene," Earl said and the words were hollow and dry in the long silence after he spoke and she turned away.

The air was vibrating with small bright shocks of soundlessness, as if the stillness of the woods had been a mirror that had just shattered into a thousand pieces.

Then she heard the rustling sounds and Earl's footsteps coming toward her. He had his pants back on and he raked his brown hand through his dark tumbled hair and stood in front of her with his chest heaving and pinestraw in his hair and a trickle of sweat drizzling down over the blue vein in the side of his brown neck.

"Don't you tell anybody what you seen." His words still sounded hollow and loud.

She heard Pat's voice from behind her. "She's old enough to know, Earl. You better make her not to tell."

He looked beyond Maylene at Pat. "Yeah, but she ain't bright enough."

Maylene turned and Pat had put on her blouse and shorts and was sitting on the ground combing her long blonde hair with her fingers. She looked at Maylene hard as knives.

"I'll tell Mama about that picture you stole if you tell," Earl said.

She thought about the postcard she had slipped out of the family album, a picture of a still cool lake.

"Swear you won't tell."

She nodded her head dumbly.

"She won't tell. She's secret-like anyway." He turned back to Maylene. "Go on home."

That night her mother made them all gather in the living room before they went to bed while she read the Bible. When her mother went limping and thumping over to the dark table where the Bible lay open on a pink and green crocheted doily, her father immediately stood up and turned off the television and clumped into the kitchen.

"Got to go look about the mule," he muttered. They could tell by the noise he made in the kitchen that he was getting his jacket off the peg behind the door and clumping out onto the back porch to smoke his pipe in the cool soft summer night. His leaving was as much a ritual as the soft sad glance of her mother's face caught in a haze of light as she leaned over the table lamp and turned it on, as the creak of the black rocker as she sat down in it and rocked back and forth and back and forth, flipping through the thin red-edged pages, as the familiar nasal complaining voice that rose and fell with the squeak-squaw-squeak-squaw of the rocker and the bumbling buzz of moths on the window screens.

Earl was sitting sprawled over on the couch, one leg up on it, his head flopped down, his dark hair falling in his face, picking restlessly at the bumpy red roses in the upholstery of the couch. Maylene was sitting still in the plain straight-backed chair, watching her mother's face. It was a plump, sagging face, lit to a yellow glow by the lamplight, wisps of grey hair blowing across her forehead with an occasional breeze from the window.

"Be not deceived," she read, "Evil companions corrupt good morals." Earl did not look up. "Awake to soberness and sin not."

Maylene knew what she had seen Earl doing must have been a sin, and that he felt ashamed because of that, and she thought how her stealing a postcard was a sin too, but it didn't make her feel bad the way she thought she probably ought to. It didn't seem to matter only because of the Bible.

"... for some have no knowledge of God" squeak-squaw, "I speak this to move you to shame" squeak-squaw.

Then Maylene knew suddenly that the wrongness in it was what it had done to the stillness, the never-endingness of the woods, and she knew that Earl would never understand *that*, he would think maybe it was wrong by the Bible but he wouldn't see this other thing, and neither would her mother, so how could she tell them? It would be like trying to tell them why she looked into the mirror.

"But some one will say, How are the dead raised? and with what manner of body do they come? Thou foolish one, that which thou thyself sowest is not quickened except it die: and that which thou sowest, thou sowest not the body that shall be, but bare grain, it may chance of wheat, or of some other kind; but God giveth it a body even as it pleased him; and to each seed a body of its own."

Seeing that Earl was determined not to listen, her mother sighed and gently shut the book and bowed her head for a prayer. The picture of the white bodies in the sunlight swam in front of Maylene's eyes again and she felt herself reach out to them to touch them, but she couldn't. She felt as if she would cry that they were beyond her reach, that she could not touch her mother sitting there in the lamplight or her father out on the dark porch, the spark glowing in his pipe. They had always been beyond her. Their ways were not her ways. She could not touch them no matter how hard she tried.

The next day she had to finish the ironing. She stood in the bedroom, her face turned toward the blue flowered wallpaper, passing the iron back and forth over the heavy starched shirts, letting things pass in and out of her mind.

She had been in Miss Futrelle's sixth grade last year; she would have to repeat next year. She had repeated her grades so much that she liked it now, going back to the same classroom with its smells of sour milk and crackers and sweat and chalk dust and oily board floors. She would sit in the back corner and watch the soft bright boys and girls come in, the ones from town that she never even tried to talk to because she had learned long ago there wasn't any use to try.

But last year she had had a friend. She was almost like Maylene, with thin brown arms and faded dresses and dull hair and the hateful hard brown shoes that laced up. She liked Corette because Corette was like her. They would go out at afternoon recess and sit on the gnarled roots of the big trees that grew on the side of the schoolyard and talk.

One day Corette, who had lips that were always a little cracked and dry-scaly, had said, "Do you like me, Maylene?" her eyes wide and earnest.

"Yes, do you like me?" And when Corette had said yes they went back into the classroom holding hands. Maylene noticed that Corette's hand was damp and sticky but she still liked to hold hands with Corette because then she would have a friend, someone that she could at least reach out and touch. But she never told Corette about the mirror.

One day they had been sitting out under the tree when a girl walked by pushing a baby in a stroller. Most of the other children were playing baseball out in the big field that was bordered by the trees. The girl came over to where they were sitting. It was a warm day and the shouts went spinning off the playground and through the still warm air. Then there would be a hard crack as the ball hit the bat.

"Y'all see my baby?" Her hair straggled in front of her strange wide staring eyes. Her mouth hung open slightly and her joints seemed big and bony and she talked fast and mumbly.

"I used to go to school here too but I stopped and had my baby."

Corette leaned over and whispered to Maylene. "My daddy says she's crazy."

Then Corette turned back to the girl. "Where's your husband?" she asked, squinting her eyes to inspect the girl.

"He's in the army. He stays gone all the time. He won't here when the baby came. I went to the hospital," the girl left the baby and sat down under the tree with them. She grinned and tossed back her hair, her eyes shining and eager, "and they gave me a shot with a needle ten inches long." Maylene gasped and the girl nodded. "That's the truth. They put a needle in my veins and tied me down on a table and cut me with a knife, and afterwards I couldn't make no water for three days. I laid there three days and three nights until they thought I was going to bust."

Just then Miss Futrelle had come stepping rapidly over the dusty playground in her thick-heeled shoes, calling them to come in, so they had to leave the girl sitting there disappointed under the tree.

"Don't you ever talk to her again if she comes around here." Miss Futrelle was shaking her finger in their faces and they nodded dumbly.

After that Maylene had thought about it a lot, had wondered if those things would happen to her like they must happen to other people, but now, thinking about it, standing pressing the iron over the shirts, she knew that wasn't the way it would be. Her friend had been passed on to the next grade and now she would be deprived of even the touch of Corette's damp hand.

She set her hands palm down on the ironing board, feeling it solid beneath the rough cloth of the shirt, feeling that this was all she could touch.

Her mother was standing in the doorway holding a full paper bag. "Maylene, I want you to go down to the store and take these grapes to Mr. Rackley. I told Mrs. Rackley I'd send them before now, so I guess you'd better not dawdle on the way like you usually do."

She turned off the iron and took the bag, cool and wet where it had been in the refrigerator. She left the house and walked down the hot dusty road to the store. The sun baked down, hot and still, burning even through the thick soles of her shoes. The corn stretched tall on her right and left, hardly rustling at all in the still heat. She stopped once to pick some morning glories from the side of the ditch; they were tight closed in the heat, and then she remembered what her mother had said about hurrying, so she shifted the weight of the sack and held the flowers in her other hand and walked on down the road again.

Rackley's store had a low, sloping roof out in front with pumps for gasoline like posts that held up the porch roof on a house. The packed dirt under the roof was stained with oil and grease, and a yellow dog was curled up beside the wobbly cinder block steps. When Maylene opened the screen door the flies buzzed off it and around, in spite of the balls of cotton stuck in the screen to keep them away. It was a little cooler in the dim shade of the store.

Mr. Rackley was sitting by himself tilted back in a straight cane chair, his feet propped up on the grate of the black stove. He was thin and old and his back was bent over with arthritis. Maylene knew that was why he couldn't work the farm and why he needed her father for a tenant farmer. All Mr. Rackley could do any more was keep his store, handing you change out of the cash register with his knotted swollen fingers. He was drinking a Nehi and eating a candy bar when Maylene came in and he greeted her in his funny way.

"Heyo, Maylene." Her mother had said he talked funny because he had been raised across the river.

"I brought you some grapes." She held out the sweaty cool bag. As he laboriously got to his feet to take it from her, she set the morning glories down on the black top of the stove so she could hand him the bag more easily with both hands.

"I thank you." He shuffled over to the counter and set the bag down. "Why don't you sit awhile since it's so hot?" There was only one chair because Mr. Rackley didn't like the niggers to be hanging around inside the store much.

"I can't stay," Maylene said. She looked at the glass cases full of candy and cookies and the dusty boxes on the dark shelves and the long red humming box where the drinks were.

"Well, you're getting too old to sit on my lap, I reckon." Mr. Rackley had gone around behind the counter. His clear blue eyes were friendly and teasing and made her think of when she was a little girl sometimes sitting on his lap in the store. She had always liked him.

He came around the counter and handed her a candy bar. "You eat that on the way back."

He crossed over to the stove and lifted one of the round lids on its low black top, unconsciously brushing the morning glories in with the rest of the paper and trash.

"Thank you," Maylene said, "Good-bye."

She trudged back down the burning dusty road, thinking how for a minute she could almost have reached out and touched Mr. Rackley, but for some reason it had become impossible and he was as far away as any of the others.

The sun burned on her back and she felt little trickles of sweat running down. Her feet were dusty from the road. Suddenly she cut down across the cornfield, down the path that led back up to the creek.

The woods were no different. They were cool, still, misty, unbothered by anything that had ever broken their stillness. She approached the clearing from the other side, kneeling down to take off her shoes. She buried her feet in the cool grass, standing in the still pool of sunlight that cut down from above the pine trees. Cool dampness rose from the still waters of the creek and hung in a still mantle of mist over the trees and grass and pinestraw and even suspended in the air like drops from a fountain caught still in one frozen moment forever. The stillness never ended.

She walked down the tiny sloping bank over damp roots that caught the clay to make steps. She put her feet in the cool still water and then lay down so that her head rested on the bank and the cool water held her and touched her. She felt the light and shadow flicker on her, only the shadows of leaves touching her. She opened her hands slowly into the water and closed her eyes, growing her roots to the water and opening her petals to the sky.

Fred Chappell

February

Wouldn't drive and wouldn't be held;
So they tied cotton line around the neck and it
    backed,
Clipped steps, as the rope stretched and throbbed;
Whereat;
They shot it clean through the shrieking brain.
And it dropped in a lump.

    —The child, dismayed
With delight, watches the hog-killing; feels
Sharply alive in its tangle. And recoils,
Attempting to hold it sensible; and fails;
All the meaning in a brutal hour.

They bring the sledge down, and difficult
With the horse plunging white-eyed, hoofs
Askitter in the slick steep bank; the blood-smell's
Frightful and he snorts; head clatters back.
The pig's still gently quivering,
    he's got a blue and human eye.
Lug it over and tumble it on, and the horse
Goes straining. The men swear
And grin, their teeth show hard in the piercing air.

    Frost gauzy on leaf and stone,
    The sky but faintly blue, wiped white.

... And into the yard. The fire popping and licking,
They roll the big black cauldron to it. Saturday,
The neighbor women and men and kids, the faces
Broad with excitement. Wow wow across the gravel,
The cast iron pot; settles on the flame,
Big egg in its scarlet nest. Dark speech of the men,
Women waiting silent, hands beneath the blue aprons.

Long spike rammed through the heels
And up he goes against the huge-armed oak
And dipped down in, dipped again, so
His hair falls off. (Swims in the filmed water
Like giant eye-lashes.) Like a pomegranate
His belly shines and bulges. He's opened
And his steam goes up white,
The ghost of hog in the glassy morning.
They catch his guts.

    —The child, so elated he's drunk
With the horror, as they undo joint
And joint, stands with the men; watches
Their arms. They yank and slash, stammer
Of blood on the denim, eyelets of blood
On arm and fabric. They laugh like scythes,
Setting the head aside to see the dismantling
With its own blue eyes—still smiles
A thin smug smile . . .

    And they cleave him
And cleave him, loins: ham:
    shoulder: feet: chops:
Even the tail's an obscure prize.
He goes into buckets, the child hauls
From hand the hand the pail all dripping.
Top of the heap, tremulous as water, lies
The big maroon liver.
    And the women receive him.

Gravely, with high courtesy.

The kitchen is glossy with heat, surcharged
With the smell of hog, and every surface
Is raddled with the fat. He slides
His finger on the jamb, it feels like flesh.
The whole lower house is filled with hog,
A bit of him in every cranny. Where
Does it all come from? —A most unlikely prodigious
    pig.

And now the women, busy, talk
Within the great clouds of oil and steam, bared
Elbows, heads nodding like breezy jonquils.
Clash of kettles, spoons
Yammering in the bowls, the windows opaque gray
That the early sun cannot pierce.

      Outside it's warmed. They're gleaning
The last of him and the slippery whisky jar
Goes handily among them. Wipe their mouths
With greasy wrists. And the smug head
Is burst and its offerings distributed: brain:
    ears: and the tail handed off with a clap
      of laughter.
They lick the white whisky and laugh.
And his bladder and his stomach sack! Puffed
Up and tied off and flung to the kids,
Game balls, they bat them about,
Running full tilt head down across the scattered
    yard.
And then on a startled breeze
The bladder's hoist, goes high and gleams in the
    sunlight,
Reflecting on its shiny globe
The sky a white square
And the figures beneath, earnest figures
Gazing straight up

Fred Chappell

Darkened light

When, at three o'clock in the morning, the great dim ghost rose standing by my bed and said, "Come, go with me," I didn't hesitate. I clasped the cool smoky hand and departed. Whether it was my physical body that journeyed or some sort of immaterial envelope I neither knew nor cared. I didn't even glance back into the sheets to see if I lay there.

We went a long way, and though my head was stuffed to bursting with every kind of question, I kept silent. The world beneath was no longer dark; it shone with various colors, pleasantly, like a child's crayon drawing. Presently we began to go faster and faster—or perhaps the globe itself began to revolve faster—and the colors melted all together and the globe diminished in size until it was no larger than a washed jewel and fell away beneath us, shrinking to a candescent blue point and then vanishing entirely. After that it was total darkness and a great awesome silence for a long while; and then the blackness was punctuated with streaks and points of brilliant white light and there came a rushing sound, as of swift wind, though nothing touched my body.

From the moment I had gone forth I felt that I was on the verge of some queer revelation, that I was about to witness something of great importance. This feeling persisted through the whole adventure, and even now when I remember there seems to be something—an event, an image—of moment just out of my line of sight, just beyond earshot. There was, is, about it all a feeling of *impendingness.*

Now there came a sensation of slowing, though the smears of light, which I took to be star-shapes stretched and tormented by the speed of our flight, began to appear more quickly and more frequently until the whole firmament was surfeited with blinding light. Here we paused awhile and I gazed into the heart of that light which moiled and leapt and reached out arms of lacy fire. If there was heat or other radiation I was insensible to it, receiving only the spectacle of the light in its joyful agony, quaking and pulsing as it strove to manifest its own being in the same instant that it strove to negate that being. It was not mindless; if singing and dancing are not mindless, but instead the appreciable workings of personality, then this drama of light was intelligently assertive in the same way.

We stayed no longer but passed through the center of that fire as through a film about as tangible as a cobweb. Again came the absolute darkness, but there was an impression of a less terrific speed in our flight. And the space in which we journeyed seemed no longer boundless but enclosing. We traveled rather as if we struggled against it. The dimensions of whatever sort of body I had taken seemed not strictly palpable but not quite immaterial either. There was a half-smothering quality in this new area about us. At last we burst through this odd place. It had seemed a shoddy unfinished kind of space and when we reentered the pure customary space with the stars ranked before us like a fireman's buttons I felt pleased and refreshed.

In a while a destination became evident. We passed a blue-white sun and three inner planets and began to settle ourselves, tentatively and waftingly as butterflies, in a fourth world which rose below us like an immense red, yellow, and black carpet lifting itself. We skimmed along the atmosphere and came to rest at last in a city. I thought the city sleeping or dead. We walked, in quite ordinary fashion, through streets and plazas. Each object, every building, was cyclopean, some of the structures towering perhaps a mile above the ground. The geometry was uncanny; the angles were acute or obtuse, no right angles, and many of the buildings looked somehow to fold back in upon themselves, so that their surfaces were both outside and inside at the same time. Every prospect was dizzying and looked granular to the sight, as if even the minute particles which composed the building materials had been turned askew to one another. The breadth of the spaces did not quite correspond to the immense heights of the city; the streets and lanes were not quite so spacious as I would have expected. Yet there was no feeling of constriction nor even of narrowness about us.

Most strikingly there was about it a feeling of—how shall I say?—of the primal. The city looked not only the result of sophisticated engineering, of accumulated technological knowledge; it retained evidences of the first-ness of things. It was as if this city could be read as a kind of history book, in which the beginnings of whatever race built it were as evident as the present moment, to which this city was monument. When I inspected closely the wall of a building I discovered that every centimeter of it was hewn, had been chopped out manually from some kind of material I could not recognize.

We walked on and on.

I felt an urgent desire to glimpse one of the inhabitants of this world;

I felt that I dearly needed to know if in encountering one of the creatures which lived here I would experience the same outlandish kinship I already felt in looking about the city.

But for a long time there was no indication that the place was inhabited. An easy silence hung over every plane and corner as I followed the obscure spirit who guided me about. Then there began what at first I took to be a tremor of the earth, a gentle regular quivering that grew gradually in intensity as we went forward. But it was not a movement of the earth; it was a deep dark music. As soon as I had recognized it for what it was it seized my mind as wholly as a gently falling snow. It was in no way harmonic, but instead a single slow bass line of almost unrepeating microtones: resonant, elating. I could not determine its source.

The city was huge and widely varied in terms of space and structure. I thought that perhaps it was centerless, but as the music continually increased in intensity (though not in volume) it occurred to me that if we came to the source of the music we would find the midpoint of the city.

Under the brilliant blue-white sun colors burned with a hard vividness. Indeed, these colors, primaries with others which I could not name, looked not really to be properties of the surfaces from which they emanated. They seemed to stand a slight bit away, so that I felt that if I touched any wall or corner I would have pushed my finger through the color, and through a film of oil. But in attempting this, I found that my body was touchless. A curious phenomenon, considering that my body and that of my ghostly companion, cast shadows, and not single shadows, but multiple shadows, faint, all tinted with the various strong colors that flamed about us.

At last we drew into a large park-like area and I saw at once the source of the deep music we must have been following. All about, in shapes as irregular as cloud formations, stood huge clumps of spongy fungoid-looking vegetation of varying pastel colors. Wide sinuous paths cut through this growth to arrive at a large paved circle of gray stone or metal. In the center of this circle stood what I must describe as a fountain. It rose, tier upon unyielding tier, high into the bright air. It jetted without let or surcease from the top of a shining onyx-black substance, but so steady and continous was the impulse of the fountain that I could not tell whether this substance was watery or oil. Actually, it looked like cold black stone as it dropped from tier to tier in strait unwavering streams. And then I thought perhaps it was some fantastically complex sculpture of two materials: the veined leaf-green stone of the fountain, the sheeny black stone in descending arabesque. And it was from here the music issued; it was still no more loud than before, but it was more heavily resonant and it permeated sharply my whole figure. When I happened to glance at my shadows I saw them throbbing and dancing like blown candleflames in helpless obeisance to the music of the fountain.

I was able finally to turn my attention (but not entirely) from the fountain and I saw beyond the paved area a scarlet ramp, glowing scarlet, broad and with the irregular angles. The ramp led to another of the gigantic structures, a sort of double pyramid with the upper section inverted so that it looked like a strange hourglass. The building was dull orange in color and as I looked at it the thought came to me that if I was going to see one of the makers of this alien city, it would come forth from that building. No sooner had I thought this than the wall peeled away at the ramp juncture and the creature appeared. It looked like nothing so much as a huge coarse dense tangle of rope. It came down the ramp with a kind of monumental slowness. I could see no means by which it propelled itself, nor could I discover the center of its intelligence nor any organs of perception. But though there were no external indications I was certain that the creature was feminine in gender, and there arose in me a vehement wave of tenderness and awe. My heart went out to it entirely and if the body which I then possessed had been capable of worship I might have fallen to my knees.

And then I seemed to tip over backwards, the landscape surging up from behind me and washing over my sight in a confused blur. When I regained my equilibrium I found that we were traveling once again; once again my hand was joined to the hand of my dim companion. The stars and the planets and the broad silence of space welled up about us and quickly disappeared. We seemed to be traveling even faster than before, in mere moments traversing vast tracts of the universe. And just as suddenly we halted. Floating before me in the void, surrounded by emptiness and a sparse starlight, was a yellowish object not larger than a thumbnail. I drew closer to inspect it and found that it was a fly, a delicate fly, made painfully of gold and worked finely to the last impossible detail. There it floated, absolutely apart from everything else that existed. I stared at it, thinking that if I could understand its existence I would perhaps understand the most important thing there was to know.

Then we were traveling again, returning to earth. We did not return by the same way we went out, and soon I found myself lying once more in my own familiar bed. My companion stood for a few seconds at my bedside and then, without a sign of farewell, dissolved away, leaving me alone. I scrambled upright and sat on the edge of the bed, clutching my knees.

It seemed to me that things, that everything I knew, was more nearly comprehensible to me now than formerly. Although I could not articulate what I understood, I felt that I did understand. But of course there was no way of proving this.

Contributors

James W. Applewhite, Phi Beta Kappa, 1958, editor of the *Archive*, won Second Prize in the *Virginia Quarterly Review* Contest in 1966. Several of his poems are in *The Young American Poets*, ed. Paul Carroll. In 1970 a poem for which he won five hundred dollars appeared in *The American Literary Anthology*, vol. 3, ed. George Plimpton and Peter Ardery. His collected verse, *Steps From the Stream*, is ready for publication. Duke recently awarded him a Ph.D. He and his family live in Greensboro, where he is an assistant professor of English at the University of North Carolina.

Michael Brondoli, 1970, won the Anne Flexner Memorial Award in Creative Writing and a Book-of-the-Month Club Writing Fellowship in his senior year. He is now in Italy writing a novel, which he first worked on under the direction of Reynolds Price.

Fred Chappell, 1961, editor of the *Archive*, was given twenty-five hundred dollars by the National Institute of Arts and Letters for his "contribution to literature," that is, for *It is Time, Lord* (1963), *The Inkling* (1965), and *Dagon* (1968). His fourth novel, *The Gaudy Place*, is expected soon. The Louisiana State University Press is to bring out a volume of his poetry. In 1967–1968 Chappell and his family lived in Italy and Greece on a Rockefeller Grant. He is an associate professor of English at the University of North Carolina, Greensboro.

Angela Davis, Phi Beta Kappa, 1963, wrote "Mr. Rudishill" in the summer after graduating from Duke. She and her husband, Richard Kollath, live in Greensboro.

Burke Davis III, ex- 1971, lives in Williamsburg.

Sean Devereux, 1969, twice won the Anne Flexner Award.

William H. Guy, 1968, lives with his wife in Princeton, working on a Ph.D. in English. In college he won an award sponsored by the American Academy of Poets.

Josephine Humphreys, *summa cum laude*, 1967, and her husband, Tom Hutcheson, live on Johns Island in South Carolina. She is completing work *in absentia* on her doctorate at the University of Texas, Austin.

Katherine Humphreys, *summa cum laude*, 1968, and Wayne Guckenberger, her husband, live in Cincinnati.

Mac Hyman (1923–1963), 1947. His "The Hundredth Centennial" was run in the *Paris Review* and was collected in *Best American Short Stories* (1955) and in *Best Stories from the "Paris Review"* (1959). His novels are *No Time for Sergeants* (1954) and the posthumous *Take Now Thy Son* (1965). The Louisiana State University Press, Baton Rouge, brought out *Love, Boy* (1969), letters selected by William Blackburn, with an introduction by Max Steele.

Wallace Kaufman, *magna cum laude*, 1961, editor of the *Archive*, has published two textbooks, half a dozen short stories, and poems numerous enough for a volume. He is an assistant professor of English at the University of North Carolina, Chapel Hill, and lives with his family on a farm. Recently on a semester's leave, he participated in a program sponsored by the National Endowment for the Humanities.

Clifford Johnson, 1966, a Ph.D. from the University of Virginia, lives with his family in Pittsburgh. He is an assistant professor of English at the University of Pittsburgh.

Caroline Krause, ex-1964, won fifty dollars for "Dinesen" in a *Story Magazine* college contest just before that periodical folded up. She and her husband, Clay Hollister, live in New York.

Gail McMurray, 1970, is a graduate student in English and her husband, McNeil Gibson, a medical student at the University of North Carolina, Chapel Hill.

Reynolds Price, *summa cum laude*, 1955, editor of the *Archive*, won the Faulkner Award for a distinguished first novel written by an American in 1962, *A Long and Happy Life*. Then followed *The Names and Faces of Heroes* (short stories) in 1963, *A Generous Man* in 1966, *Love and Work in*

1968, and *Permanent Errors* (short stories) in 1970. Some of Price's short stories have been widely anthologized—e.g., translations into Russian and into Arabic. All told, his books have been translated into a dozen languages. He received a Guggenheim Fellowship in 1965 and a grant from the National Endowment for the Arts in 1966. He is an associate professor of English at Duke.

Nancy Rottenberg, 1968, and her husband, Philip Crump, are graduate students at the University of New Mexico, Albuquerque.

Ann Saalbach, 1970, won the Anne Flexner Award in her freshman year and second prize in this same contest in her senior year.

Wendy L. Salinger, Phi Beta Kappa, 1969, wrote all but the first of her poems in this book in a class taught by George Starbuck at the University of Iowa, where she is now a teaching fellow.

Joan Swift, *née* Angevine, Phi Beta Kappa, 1948, editor of the *Archive*, studied poetry-writing with the late Newman Ivey White at Duke and at the University of Washington with the late Theodore Roethke. A volume of her verse, *This Element*, came out in 1965; another is ready for the press. She and her husband, Wayne Swift, and family have moved recently from Seattle to Oakland.

Katherine B. Taylor, ex-1970, wrote the sestina "In the Home" in Tom Kirby-Smith's class at the University of North Carolina, Greensboro. *Intro 2* (1969), a Bantam anthology, includes one of her poems.

Anne Tyler, Phi Beta Kappa, 1961, won the Anne Flexner Award twice. Her first novel, *If Morning Ever Comes* (1964), grew out of a story she wrote in college for Reynolds Price. Knopf also brought out *The Tin Can Tree* in 1965 and *A Slipping Down Life* in 1970. She is the author of more than a dozen published short stories. She and her Iranian husband, Dr. Taghi Modaressi, a psychiatrist, and their two daughters live in Baltimore.

Kathryn Vale, *magna cum laude*, 1965, editor of the *Archive*, lives in Hanover, New Hampshire, where her husband, Gordon Livermore, is an assistant professor of Russian at Dartmouth. She has recently earned a Master of Philosophy degree at Yale.

Susan Walker, 1968, is a graduate student at the University of North Carolina, Chapel Hill.

Jane McFall Wiseman, 1968, lives with her husband, Michael Brown, in St. Louis. She has recently been awarded an M.A. degree in English at the University of Illinois. Her story in this book comes from *Growing Up in America*, ed. R. A. Rosenbaum, New York, 1969.

George R. Wood, 1971, after serving with the Marines in Vietnam, returned to Duke as a sophomore. In 1969–1970 he edited both the *Archive* and his own privately printed *Above Ground Review*.

David Young, 1969, teaches English in the schools at Katonah, New York.

George Young, Phi Beta Kappa, 1963, is an assistant professor of Russian at Dartmouth. He rewrote for this volume "Corn Knee High," which first came out in the *Archive*.